SO-ADF-236

Theological Union
LIBRARY
Chicago, Ill.

WITHDRAWN

Religion, Man and Destiny

In this challenging book, Julian Huxley, distinguished biologist, philosopher and humanist, proposes a faith based on man's ability to reason, to seek the truth, to realize his highest and most creative powers.

He views man as a self-contained, self-sufficient entity. He suggests that to know what has been, to contemplate with awe what man might yet make of his own destiny, is to be reverent and, in turn, religious.

Drawing upon history, anthropology and psychology, Huxley enlivens his argument with wit and scholarship. His credo transcends skepticism in affirming a faith which is intellectually credible, morally responsible and emotionally satisfying.

"One who wishes a deep insight into a most considerable movement in religious thinking would do well to read Professor Huxley's book."
—*Harry Emerson Fosdick*

THIS IS A REPRINT OF THE ORIGINAL HARDCOVER
EDITION PUBLISHED BY HARPER & BROTHERS

The Catholic
Theological U
LIBRARY
Chicago, Ill

Other MENTOR Books of Interest

Evolution in Action *by Julian Huxley*

A world-famous biologist describes vividly and clearly the process of evolution. (#MP491—60¢)

Man in the Modern World *by Julian Huxley*

Stimulating essays on vital issues from Huxley's "Man Stands Alone" and "On Living in a Revolution." (#MD148—50¢)

Varieties of Religious Experience *by William James*
Introduction by Jacques Barzun

A new edition of James' classic work on the psychology of religion and the religious impulse. (#MT320—75¢)

Religion and the Rise of Capitalism *by R. H. Tawney*

The influences of religious thought on the social and economic structures of the world. (#MT507—75¢)

JULIAN HUXLEY

The Catholic
Theological Union
LIBRARY
Chicago, Ill.

Religion without Revelation

EX LIBRIS PROVINCIAE
PRO STUDIO THEOL.
S.S. CORDIS JESU.

201
H986r

A MENTOR BOOK

Published by THE NEW AMERICAN LIBRARY

30,611

COPYRIGHT © 1957 BY JULIAN HUXLEY

New and revised edition.
All rights in this book are reserved.
No part may be reproduced
without permission. For information
address Harper & Row, Publishers, Inc.,
49 East 33rd Street, New York, New York 10016.

Published as a MENTOR BOOK
by arrangement with Harper & Row, Publishers, Inc.,
who have authorized this softcover edition.

FIRST PRINTING, NOVEMBER, 1958
SECOND PRINTING, MAY, 1961
THIRD PRINTING, FEBRUARY, 1964

MENTOR TRADEMARK REG. U.S. PAT. OFF. AND FOREIGN COUNTRIES
REGISTERED TRADEMARK—MARCA REGISTRADA
HECHO EN CHICAGO, U.S.A.

MENTOR BOOKS are published by
The New American Library of World Literature, Inc.
501 Madison Avenue, New York, New York 10022

PRINTED IN THE UNITED STATES OF AMERICA

Contents

How is religion still possible? This question is posed by so able a thinker as Dr Merz as the question of paramount importance, and he can find only a paradoxical answer.

It is a question which seems to be taken seriously by many otherwise intelligent persons, who are thereby stranded in the end on all sorts of hidden sandbanks. They do not ask: How is walking still possible? They do not ask: How is hunger still possible? Yet it is really the same kind of question.

It is always marvellous to find how people worry themselves over unnecessary problems, and spin the most fantastic webs of abstruse speculation around even the simplest things. Religion, if it is anything at all, must be a natural organic function, like walking, like eating, better still, like loving. For the closest analogy and, indeed, real relationship, of religion, is with the function of reproduction and the emotions of sex. The functions of eating and walking are more or less necessary to life in their rhythmic recurrences, and it is legitimate in their absence to endeavour to stimulate them into action. But the function of religion, like that of love, is not necessary to life, nor may it with any certainty be stimulated into activity. Need it? These functions are either working within you or they are not. If not, then it is clear that your organism is in no need of them at the present moment, and perhaps is born without the aptitude to experience them. And if so, there are those who will tell you that you represent a superior type of humanity. Therefore, whether if not so, or whether so, why worry?

I do not indeed myself think that the inaptitude for the function of religion—ancient as the religious emotions are—represents a higher stage of development. But I am sure that either the function is there or it is not there, and that no intellectual speculations will take its place or hasten its manifestations.

Religion, like love, develops and harmonises our rarest and most extravagant emotions. It exalts us above the commonplace routine of our daily life, and it makes us supreme over the world. But, like love also, it is a little ridiculous to those who are unable to experience it. And since they can survive quite well without experiencing it, let them be thankful, as we also are thankful.—HAVELOCK ELLIS (in *The Forum*, 1924).

Preface

This book first appeared twenty-eight years ago. After it had gone out of print, a much abridged version was published by Watts in their *Thinkers' Library* in 1941, but this too is no longer available. Numerous enquiries, both from this country and America, made it clear that it was still in demand: and I am accordingly republishing it. The new edition has undergone considerable revision and alteration, notably by the substitution of wholly new chapters in place of the original Chapters 3 and 8.

The new Chapter 3 consists of a previously unpublished essay on Science and God, originally used as the basis for an address given under the auspices of the Ethical Union during the Bristol Meeting of the British Association in 1956, while the new concluding chapter incorporates material from the third of my Dyason Lectures, on 'Evolutionary Humanism', published by the Australian Institute of International Affairs in 1954.

I gratefully acknowledge the help I received from Mr. H. J. Blackham, who kindly (and very efficiently) undertook the thankless job of revision during my absence in North America; and I also wish to thank my publishers, Max Parrish, for their willingness to undertake the book's re-issue, and their care and interest during the process.

*

A great deal of water (and, alas, a good deal of blood) has flowed under many bridges since the book was first published. I shall not attempt to discuss the relevance to my subject of the changes during that period, but shall confine myself to three points which have forced themselves on me personally.

The first is the importance in human history of over-all idea-systems (which I take to involve beliefs, attitudes and

general assumptions as well as intellectual ideas, and to include religions and loosely formulated 'ways of life' as well
as rigid ideologies). Idea-systems in this sense play the same
sort of rôle in cultural evolution as do skeletons in biological
evolution: they provide the framework for the life that
animates and clothes them, and in large measure determine
the way it shall be lived.

This brings up my second point—the need for ideological
unification. The Cold War is a war between idea-systems,
both of them vulnerable. Our Western idea-systems are
vulnerable because they are insufficiently unified to possess
any powerful intrinsic driving force (their strength is in their
freedom and their resistance to brute totalitarianism). But so
long as their dualistic splits persist—between natural and
supernatural, between God and the world, between matter
and spirit—so long will our Western civilisation be schizo-
phrenic in the original sense of that term, so long will our
idea-systems fail to provide much of a dynamic for truly
purposeful action.

My third point is the need to increase knowledge and make
our comprehension ever more comprehensive. New knowledge has been the basis for all new and more satisfying ways
of life, from the discovery of fire and metal-working to that
of intra-atomic and intra-psychic energies. And idea-systems
must aim at making man's increasing knowledge comprehensible and effective. The Communist idea-system of Marxist
ideology has had plenty of driving force: it is now proving
itself vulnerable because its over-rigid unification on the
basis of a premature and inadequate synthesis has made it
incapable of keeping up with our knowledge of the facts of
nature (including human nature) and social development.

Keeping up with the facts is an essential for any enduring
idea-system: only by incorporating new facts and new modes
of organising knowledge can idea-systems remain effective
organs of man in society. For do not let us forget that, in the
long run, all that deserves to be called *progress* in man's
history depends either directly or indirectly on new comprehension—new facts or new interpretations, new knowledge or
new organisations of knowledge. This applies as much to the
abandonment of magic as to that of alchemy, to the rise of
monotheism as to the spread of agriculture and civilised life.

There are those who maintain that because a religious
experience differs from a scientific experience, therefore religion can never legitimately be the subject of scientific analy-

sis. This is wholly erroneous. Any set of phenomena can be treated by the method of science. A striking feature of the history of science is the steady extension of scientific method into ever new fields, from the physico-chemical to the biological and on to the historical, the social and the psychological. Religion is one of the latest fields to which the method of science has been extended. The resultant sciences of comparative religion and religious psychology are already yielding deeply interesting results, which will certainly be of value in leading humanity out of the religious impasse in which it now finds itself.

One of the major results has been the realisation that God is one among several hypotheses to account for the phenomena of human destiny, and that it is now proving to be an inadequate hypothesis. To a great many people, including myself, this realisation is a great relief, both intellectually and morally. It frees us to explore the real phenomena for which the God hypothesis seeks to account, to define them more accurately, and to work for a more satisfying set of concepts and symbols to represent them in our mental organisation.

What the world needs is an essentially religious idea-system, unitary instead of dualistically split, and charged with the total dynamic of knowledge old and new, objective and subjective, of experience scientific and spiritual. This is not merely desirable but urgent—urgent for individual men and women, urgent for the separate nations of the world, urgent for mankind as a whole. It is against that background that I present this revised version of my book.

Christmas, 1956.

Religion
without
Revelation

Science . . . makes impossible any religion but the highest.
—Canon B. H. STREETER, *Reality* (1927).

To mistake the world, or the nature of one's soul, is a dangerous error. He that thinks the Heavens and the Earth not his, can hardly use them. . . . Whatever we misapprehend we cannot use, nor well enjoy what we cannot use.—THOMAS TRAHERNE, *Centuries of Meditations.*

A system of dogmas may be the ark within which the Church floats safely down the flood-tide of history. But the Church will perish unless it opens its window and lets out the dove to search for an olive branch. Sometimes even it will do well to disembark on Mount Ararat and build a new altar to the divine Spirit—an altar neither in Mount Gerizim nor at Jerusalem.— A. N. WHITEHEAD, *Religion in the Making* (1927).

If we are to assume that anybody has designedly set this wonderful universe going, it is perfectly clear to me that he is no more entirely benevolent and just in any intelligible sense of the words, than that he is malevolent and unjust.—T. H. HUXLEY, *Life and Letters.*

I am not so lost in lexicography as to forget that *words are the daughters of earth, and that things are the sons of heaven.*—SAMUEL JOHNSON, Preface to his *Dictionary.*

Vox dei revelatur in rebus.—FRANCIS BACON.

Truth can never be opposed to Truth.—Canon BUCKLAND, *Bridgewater Treatises,* vol. i. (1837).

> You say there is no substance here,
>   One great reality above:
> Back from that void I shrink in fear,
>   And child-like hide myself in love:
> Show me what angels feel. Till then
> I cling, a mere weak man, to men
>   —WILLIAM CORY, *Mimnermus in Church.*

Every new mind is a classification. . . . But in all unbalanced minds the classification is idolised, passes for the end and not for a speedily exhaustible means, so that the walls of their system blend to their eye in the remote horizon within the walls of the universe. They cannot imagine how you aliens have any right to see—how you can see!—R. W. EMERSON, *Essays.*

The fact that a believer is happier than a sceptic is no more to the point than the fact that a drunken man is happier than a sober one. The happiness of credulity is a cheap and dangerous quality.
—G. BERNARD SHAW.

1

A Preliminary Statement

I have called this book *Religion without Revelation* in order
to express at the outset my conviction that religion of the
highest and fullest character can co-exist with a complete
absence of belief in revelation in any straightforward sense
of the word, and of belief in that kernel of revealed religion,
a personal god.

This will probably be a new conception to most people.
Accordingly I shall have to spend a good deal of my limited
space in justifying my case with the aid of evidence and argument. But evidence and argument are too frequently tedious.
The average man prefers statements to arguments, conclusions to evidence. There is something in this attitude. We can
often make up our minds more readily about a man after we
have heard him proclaim his case briefly than we could if
we had listened to him make a complete step-by-step logical
justification of it.

At the risk of repetition, therefore, I propose at the outset
to state my beliefs briefly in their main outlines, without the
attempt at full justification by reasoned argument. This will
give my readers a preliminary view; if they do not like it,
there is after all no need for them to go on with the book.
Later, after a personal digression, I shall come to impersonal
exposition and argument; and finally shall present what seem
to me the right conclusions.

What then do I believe? I believe, in the first instance, that
it is necessary to believe something. Complete scepticism does
not work. On the other hand, I believe equally strongly that
it is always undesirable and often harmful to believe without
proper evidence. Everything which we believe, except the
logical necessities of mathematics and formal logic, is believed
on external evidence of one sort or another, although the
evidence may have been assimilated so long ago, or so com-

pletely, or so intuitively, that we are not conscious of it. To take a simple and trivial example: when we say that a ball which we see in the distance is spherical we are basing this statement on the frequently repeated evidence of our past experience that objects which appear to the eye of a particular shape and with a particular kind of pattern of light and shade are, when explored by touch, found to possess a particular shape we call spherical; and we had to learn all this very thoroughly (although we have by now forgotten all about the learning process) when we were babies. But even when there is not this necessary interpretation of the evidence of one sense in terms of the experience derived from another, but a direct utilisation of the materials provided by one sense only, we are still believing on evidence. When I feel a marble with my fingers, my eyes being blindfolded, I can judge directly by touch that it is a single spherical object. But everybody knows (or, if he does not, let him immediately try the very simple but fundamental experiment) that if I cross two adjacent fingers and feel the marble between their crossed tips, it will be obstinately judged to be double, in spite of all knowledge to the contrary. Thus even the simple judgments of sense may be illusions, and when I say that I believe something because I saw or heard it, I am backing the view that I did not happen to be deluded. When we come to more complicated beliefs, such as a belief that so-and-so is really angry with us although he is doing his best to appear friendly, or that someone else is an honest man and will never take an unfair advantage, it is still more clear that we are all the time weighing evidence and arriving at a conclusion (however intuitively) on the balance. And we are often wrong. How frequently it turns out that A's apparent anger was only dyspepsia, or that we were sadly mistaken as to B's honesty!

Apart from intellectual mistakes or sensory delusions, however, there is a still more potent source of error in emotional distortion. Even serious investigators have not always escaped having their conclusions coloured by their desires, seeing what they want to see, and even more, not seeing what they would prefer to overlook. An angry man is a notoriously bad witness; and the judgments of first love about the beloved object are quite generally discounted, and that not only by cynics.

There is thus a certain practical difficulty. We must believe something, for otherwise we should never act. On the other hand, we must not believe everything, or believe too readily, or we shall act wrongly. Most people would say that they are completely justified in the certain belief that the sun will rise next morning; on the other hand, there is for this no inherent necessity of the same nature as the inherent necessity for two and two to make four; something might perfectly well happen to prevent its rising; and we might believe in the existence of this something. As a matter of fact, a great many people at one time or another have believed that the world would end on a particular date, and therefore that the sun would not rise one fine morning; and this belief (although always, so far, it has proved erroneous) has often very radically affected their lives. The closing months of the year A.D. 999 were accompanied by the most improbable scenes of orgy, terror, and prayer, owing to the belief that the world would end at the millennium; and even in our time the members of an American sect sold all their possessions very cheap and went to await the end of the world and a translation to heaven on a convenient hill-top.

Experience has quite definitely shown (if only humanity could be persuaded to profit by her!) that some reasons for holding a belief are much more likely to be justified by the event than others. It might be naturally supposed, for instance, that the best of all reasons for belief was a strong conviction of certainty accompanying the belief. Experience, however, shows that this is not so, and that, as a matter of fact, conviction by itself is more likely to mislead than it is to guarantee truth. On the other hand, lack of assurance and persistent hesitation to come to any belief whatever are equally poor guarantees that the few beliefs which are arrived at are sound. Experience also shows that assertion, however long continued, although it is unfortunately with many people an effective enough means of inducing belief, is not in any way a ground for holding it.

Neither is a claim to be the recipient of a revelation the least guarantee that belief in the subject of the revelation is justified; for both madmen and false prophets have made the claim.

The method which has proved effective, as matter of actual fact, in providing a firm foundation for belief wherever it has been capable of application is what is usually called the scientific method. I believe firmly that the scientific method, although slow and never claiming to lead to complete truth, is the only method which in the long run will give satisfactory foundations for beliefs. The scientific method is the method which, in the intellectual sphere, is the counterpart of that method recommended by the apostle in the moral sphere—test all things; hold fast to that which is good. It consists in demanding facts as the only basis for conclusions; and of consistently and continuously testing any conclusions which may have been reached by new facts and, wherever possible, by the crucial test of experiment. It consists also (and this is not sufficiently recognised by the generality of people) in full publication of the evidence on which conclusions are based, so that others workers may have the advantage of the facts, to assist them in new researches, or, as frequently occurs, to make it possible for them to put a quite different interpretation on the facts.

There are, however, all sorts of occasions on which the scientific method is not applicable. That method involves slow testing, frequent suspension of judgment, restricted conclusions. The exigencies of everyday life, on the other hand, often make it necessary to act on a hasty balancing of admittedly incomplete evidence, to take immediate action, and to draw conclusions in advance of the evidence. It is also true that such action will always be necessary, and necessary in respect of ever larger issues; and this in spite of the fact that one of the most important trends of civilisation is to remove sphere after sphere of life out of the domain of such intuitive judgment into the domain of rigid calculation based on science. It is here that belief plays its most important rôle. When we cannot be certain, we must proceed in part by faith —faith not only in the validity of our own capacity of making judgments, but also in the existence of certain factual realities, pre-eminently moral and spiritual realities. It has been said that faith consists in acting always on the nobler hypothesis; and though this definition is a trifle rhetorical, it embodies a seed of real truth.

Finally, however (and this is a truth which has been often wholly unrecognised, and never popular), there are other occasions on which belief is not only not demanded, but is, in the phraseology of medicine, contra-indicated. When there exists no evidence or next to no evidence, and when the conclusion to which we may come can have no influence on the facts, then it is our duty to suspend judgment and hold no belief, just as definitely as it is our duty, when practical issues hang on our decision, not to suspend judgment, but to take our courage in both hands and act on the best belief at which we can arrive. This duty of refraining from belief is often imposed upon men of science in their work, in order that they may in the long run arrive at greater certitude; it is also imposed upon them in other cases in order that they may not encourage false hopes of certitude. When applied to whole problems, this attitude of mind generally goes by the name (first coined by Thomas Huxley) of agnosticism. I hold it to be an important duty to know when to be agnostic. I believe that one should be agnostic when belief one way or the other is mere idle speculation, incapable of verification; when belief is held merely to gratify desires, however deep-seated, and not because it is forced on us by evidence; and when belief may be taken by others to be more firmly grounded than it really is, and so come to encourage false hopes or wrong attitudes of mind.

That is a long exordium, I fear. It must be justified by the fact that our beliefs about Belief are among the most important that we may possess, and this all the more since we rarely stop to give their existence a thought.

I hold, then, that all our life long we are oscillating between conviction and caution, faith and agnosticism, belief and suspension of belief. That neither faith nor agnosticism is in itself the better way, but that each has its right occasions. That beliefs which are well enough for individual occasions of practical necessity may be wholly unjustified and unjustifiable when made general or when taken to dispense from further enquiry. In fact, I hold that beliefs are essential tools of the human mind—no more than tools, but no less than essential. That there is therefore no more sense in using the same sort of belief to help in solving both problems of ultimate and universal values and the practical problems of daily necessity than there would be in using a kitchen scales to determine atomic weights, or, vice versa, a string galvanometer for the purposes of the job electrician. And that there is no more justification for wasting time and energy and hope in drawing conclusions about subjects on which inadequate evidence exists than in founding a Department of State for the breeding of hippogriffs, or inventing a method for crossing bridges before one comes to them.

*

Now that all this has been said, the ground is clear for more definite statements. In the first place, I believe, not that there *is* nothing, for that I do not know, but that we quite assuredly at present *know* nothing beyond this world and natural experience. A personal God, be he Jehovah, or Allah, or Apollo, or Amen-Ra, or without name but simply God, I *know* nothing of. What is more, I am not merely agnostic on the subject. It seems to me quite clear that the idea of personality in God or in any supernatural being or beings has been put there by man, put into and round a perfectly real conception which we might continue to call God if the word had not acquired by long association the implication of a personal being; and therefore I disbelieve in a personal God [1] in any sense in which that phrase is ordinarily used.

For similar reasons, I disbelieve in the existence of Heaven or Hell in any conventional Christian sense. As for any pretended knowledge about the Last Judgment, or the conditions of existence in Purgatory, it could be disregarded as what it is, mythology from racial childhood, and left to die a natural death, if it did not require to be attacked as the too frequent cause of unfortunate practical effects, such as causing believers to pay money to priests for the supposed benefit of souls in the other world.

As to the existence of another world or another life at all, there I am simply agnostic: I do not know. I find extreme difficulties, in the light of physiological and psychological knowledge, in understanding how a soul could exist apart from a body; but difficulties are never disproof. It also seems clear enough that many ideas about a future life owe their origin to the most primitive kinds of speculation and superstition among barbaric or savage races, and have survived largely owing to man's enormous conservatism in regard to tampering with what has come to be regarded as sacred. Further, that many other such ideas are merely the expression of man's deep desire and longing for a continuation of life after death for himself and for those he loves. The desire is real enough, the longing deep enough, but, alas, desire and longing, as we all know in regard to earthly happiness, are not sufficient reasons for the existence of what is desired or longed for: and the existence of a future life can no more be proved by the arguments from human need or the incompleteness of this life, than can the most passionate love, or the most tragic incompleteness of a solitary existence, ensure that a woman

[1] Under the term *personal* God I include all ideas of a so-called super-personal God of the same spirit and mental nature as a personality but on a higher level, or indeed of any supernatural spiritual being.

should marry the man of her choice or indeed achieve marriage at all.

Finally, there is the so-called evidence from spiritualism. I have seen some of this, and read a good deal on the subject; there seems to be a good *prima facie* case for the existence of such 'super-normal' phenomena as clairvoyance and telepathy, as well as plenty of undoubted automatic writing, hypnotic phenomena, etc., but these have nothing to do with spiritualism in the sense of communicating with the spirits of the departed. The evidence for spiritualism itself is for the most part so trivial that it is really necessary to take part in a few séances to be able to appreciate what childish and dubious phenomena are uncritically accepted as evidence by believers in spiritualism. The truth seems to be that such people both wish and are ready to believe, and accordingly come to a decision on what is perhaps the most important and most difficult matter about which we could form a judgment, on evidence far slighter than what is necessary to send a case to a jury, much less to convict a man of a criminal offence.

But when all this discounting has been done, there remains the fact that we do not know; and so I am agnostic on this question. There are others who also say they do not know, but would like to be on the safe side. That is, of course, a common if not always a pleasant human weakness. But personally, I believe, and believe strongly, that if the standards of good and evil by which we ought to live this life are different from the standards by which we may hope to achieve satisfaction or blessedness in a life to come, then so much the worse for the universe and its governance; but I refuse on that account to modify my standards of conduct in this world, for that appears to me an outrage, and a surrender of the highest part of our nature.

Others believe that their standard of conduct need not be changed, but that they can ensure salvation in another world by special or additional observances or beliefs or offerings. This again I believe not only to involve a false antithesis but to be a denial of the highest religion. More than two thousand years ago the psalmist said that salvation required no propitiatory rites based on crude and anthropomorphic ideas of God; for the acceptable sacrifice is a broken and a contrite heart. The Christian world is supposed to believe this; but it, or the great bulk of it, still prefers to stick to what is essentially a magical view of the miraculous efficacy of formulæ, or of relics, or the invocation of saints, or of self-deprivation, or of prayer, or rites such as absolution by a priest.

I can hear many of my readers asking themselves what then is left for me to believe in of anything which can possibly be called religious. That such a question can be asked is due to a misapprehension—common enough, I admit, but none the less a misapprehension—as to the real nature and essence of religion. It is frequently taken for granted that religion is essentially a belief in a god or gods. Let me quote but two or three examples. The great pioneer anthropologist Tylor proposed 'a belief in spiritual beings' as what he called a minimum definition of religion; and Sir James Frazer understood by religion the propitiation of powers, conscious and personal in nature, believed to control the course of nature and of human life. Even Thouless, in his admirable approach to the psychology of the religious life, defines religion as 'a felt practical relationship with what is believed in as a superhuman being or beings.'

And yet such writers, however distinguished in their special spheres, should have remembered that one of the great religions of the world, namely Buddhism, in its original and purest form does not profess belief in any supernatural being; as Renan said, 'Buddhism is Catholicism without God' (and, by the way, added, 'this atheist religion has been eminently moral and active in good works'). They should have remembered that, as numerous workers on primitive religion testify, feelings essentially and obviously religious may be evoked in reference to an undefined sense of spiritual power or sanctity inhering in objects such as fetishes or events such as death, without linking them up with belief in any spiritual being.[2]

What, then, is religion? It is a way of life. It is a way of life which follows necessarily from a man's holding certain things in reverence, from his feeling and believing them to be sacred. And those things which are held sacred by religion primarily concern human destiny and the forces with which it comes into contact.

On the other hand, all sorts of objects and ideas not in themselves calculated to arouse the religious emotion do, as a matter of fact, come to be held sacred by this or that religion, as cows by the Hindu. The beliefs of that religion in contact with which we have grown up are apt to usurp the idea of sacredness; but I wish to emphasise at the outset that I am

[2] See, for instance, Marett, *The Threshold of Religion;* or Crawley, *The Tree of Life.*

speaking in the most general terms, and that this specifically religious emotion of sacredness may be felt in relation to any object or thought, within or without the bounds of what we may be accustomed to think of as religion, within or without the bounds of any organised religious system.

The idea of supernatural beings is one of the commonest among the objects, events, or ideas which are thus believed in as objects of reverence; but belief in supernatural beings is not an essential or integral part of the religious way of life, nor, conversely, are the objects of religious feeling necessarily supernatural beings.

I believe, then, that religion arose as a feeling of the sacred. The capacity for experiencing this feeling in relation to various objects and events seems to be a fundamental capacity of man, something given in and by the construction of the normal human mind, just as definitely as is the capacity for experiencing anger or admiration, sympathy or terror. What is more, we experience each of these feelings or sentiments in relation to certain general kinds of situations. There is no specific connection between any given object and a particular feeling, but there does exist one type of situation in which men tend to feel anger, another in which they tend to feel admiration, another in which they tend to feel reverence. But (and a very important *but*) in every case, the type of situation which tends to arouse any particular feeling is always found to alter with experience and education. Many of the situations which arouse fear in a child cease to arouse fear when he has grown up; many situations which arouse fear in a young savage would not do so in a civilised child of the same age; and vice versa.

So it is with the religious feeling, the sentiment of sacredness. No one expects a child of four to have the same kind of religious life as a boy of sixteen, or either of them as a man of thirty. Nor should any one expect a savage to have arrived at the same religious attitude as a civilised man with different cultural background and with centuries of developing tradition at his back. The situations which arouse the religious feeling cannot be expected to be the same in the various cases. This elementary truth has, however, not been grasped by many missionaries and missionary societies; and the failure to grasp it has often led to disastrous results.

The history of religion is the history of the gradual change in the situations which, with increase of experience and changed conditions of life, are felt as sacred. It is in the main (like the history of humanity as a whole, or the history of science as a whole) a history of progress—not unaccompanied by set-backs, by side-lines which take a downward direction, by friction, and conflict, but, both as regards its highest level and its net sum, definitely progress. Regarded as progress, the history of religion is a history of the purging of the religious emotion itself from baser elements such as fear, and of the substitution of ever larger, nobler, and more rational objects and situations on and in which the religious sentiment may spend itself.

This change is effected in a number of ways. In the first place, man reasons about his religious feelings and thoughts, or at least attempts to find reasons by which they may be justified. By this means, in relation to a mainly emotional, non-rational ground or raw material of religion, an intellectual scheme is brought into being, a definite set of beliefs, a primitive theology. The beliefs and their objects are intimately associated with the original pervading sense of sacredness, and so themselves come to be felt as sacred. The precise details of the process, in so far as it can be pieced together from history and from the study of comparative religion, are complex; I shall try to explore them a little more fully in a later chapter. The main and most essential steps appear to have been, first, the personification of the powers revered and religiously feared as brooding over human destiny; then the progressive unification of these powers, resulting in the substitution of few gods for innumerable spirits; and finally the fading or fusing of the several gods into one God.

Meanwhile an analogous process had been taking place on the moral side. With increase of physical control and intellectual comprehension, human destiny was seen to be more and more a matter of morality; the acquisition of the sense of personal holiness, less a matter of ritual or propitiation, more a matter of righteousness. Inevitably, in such circumstances, the governance of the world came to appear more concerned with morality, less a mere affair of arbitrary power. And since the idea of supernatural beings was by this time firmly enthroned as part and parcel of religion, moral qualities were increasingly ascribed to spirits and to gods. First of all, this moral ascription was fitful and incomplete, just as the intellectual unification was slow and also for a long time incomplete. The moral character of the great majority of gods is strangely mixed. It has been said that a people gets the government which it deserves: it can with at least equal truth be asserted that a people worships the gods which it deserves. The mixed moral character of gods reflects the mixed moral motives and incompletely unified morality of most men and most societies.

But, just as the logical intellect and the thirst for ever more ultimate causes pushed on the unification of the separate personal gods, and demonstrated them, against the inertia of tradition and so-called common sense, to be but different aspects of a single more ultimate divinity, so the logic of the moral sense and the craving to make out of a disconnected series of acts, moral in different ways and degrees, an organised moral life with all its parts related, led to unification in the moral sphere as well. Moral contradictions were gradually eliminated from the character of god, and different aspects of that character came to be more highly exalted—love, for instance, being elevated into the supreme place, above power and above justice.

Once more, since in all these changes morality was brought into ever closer and more constant association with the specifically religious sense of sanctity, it too became regarded as in itself sacred, of its proper nature religious.

A very similar process runs its course in the growing mind of every individual human being who does not merely put on a reach-me-down religion, but with intellectual and moral effort, often with pain and grief, achieves his own religious development. His ideas are at first little more than states of feeling, experienced perhaps deeply but with vagueness and without comprehension. His reason develops, and he cannot help but try to use it to make sense of the sacred chaos. His moral sense grows, he becomes the prey of moral conflicts: if he is to attain to peace of mind and stable maturity, he must adjust the warring interests, and see that order and unity are masters in his moral house. He must, too, bring his moral and his intellectual schemes into some reasonable relation with each other, and both into relation with his feeling of what is worthy to be held sacred.

The essential of all this, to my mind, is that religion is an activity of man which suffers change like all other human activities; that it may change for the better or for the worse; that if it stand still and refuse to change when other human activities are changing, then the standing still is itself a change for the worse; that as it grows, it cannot avoid coming into contact both with intellectual and with moral or ethical problems; and that with the development and broadening of human experience and tradition, religion becomes inevitably preoccupied with the intellectual comprehension of man's relation to the universe, and with the attainment of a coherent and unified moral life as well as with its more original quest for emotional satisfaction in the sphere of the holy. This emotional quest also shows a characteristic development. If at the outset it concerns itself mainly with putting man right with objects or beings regarded as endued with sacred power, and with the release of his perplexed spirit from the heavy burden of sacred awe, in later stages its most urgent desire is to gain the quality of holiness for the man himself, and to arrive by one road or another at an assurance of personal salvation. Finally, in its most developed and highest manifestations, this emotional side of the religious life aspires to a sense of communion with the divine, and to the peace and security which spring from the surrender of the individual will to what is usually described as the will of God.

It remains now, very briefly, for me to make some preliminary statement as to how I would interpret the religious view of God, since this, and all its corollaries, seems to me to be the one essential point of difference outstanding between 'religion' and 'science' to-day—religion in the sense not only of Christian orthodoxy but of all theism, and science not only in the sense of physics, chemistry, or biology, but of organised knowledge and thought based upon a naturalistic outlook.

Once adjust this difficulty, and there remains no conflict of principle. All the vital facts of religious life remain: they but want re-defining in new terms. The living reality will need to change its clothes—that is all.

But meanwhile the difficulty is there; and it is a formidable one. Humanity in general, and religious humanity in particular, has for so long been habituated to thinking mainly in terms of an external, personal, supernatural, spiritual being, that it will indubitably be extremely difficult to abandon this view and see God, under one aspect as a number of vital but separate facts, some material and some spiritual, but, regarded as a unity, as a creation of the human soul (albeit a logical and fruitful one), compounded of the hard facts of soulless nature and the spiritual and intellectual aspirations of the nature of man, the two organised into a single whole by the organising power of the human mind.

This same organising power operates in other spheres, in the same way, and equally fruitfully—it can blend the hard facts of nature's chaos with its own spiritual aspiration for order, into the glorious achievement of a so-called Law of Nature; it can equally blend the hard facts of nature, including the humdrum and the tragic, with its own thoughts and its own aspirations for beauty, into that organised expression of experience which we call a work of art. In an almost more intimate way it can blend the hard facts of life and the aspirations of the human mind for happiness and virtue into the single organised whole which we call character.

In all these cases the processes at work are in their general nature the same. In all, they involve the fusion, in human experience, of outer fact and inner capacity; in all cases they involve—in so far as well and truly carried out—the utilisation of one kind or combination of capacities to the utmost possible extent or in the highest way. Let it, however, be pointed out at once that this fusion of inner and outer is what goes on in all experience, however humble. Even a simple sensation, as of the red colour of a rose, is the product of the external 'hard fact' of light-waves of a particular range of wave-length, together with the human capacity for subjective awareness, brought about through the structure of the retina and the nervous system and the mind's powers, the inner and the outer being inextricably fused in the actual sensation, *red*.

Such elementary considerations as these take the sting from the cynic's definition of life as consisting in moving matter from one place to another—granted that that is one aspect, and often a regrettably large aspect of life. But life also, and on a higher level, consists in bringing matter into relation with mind, and so generating experience. What is more, one of the mind's capacities is the capacity for organising experience into forms of increasing richness of content, increasing beauty, increasing truth. Through this organising capacity, the mind creates new and higher values, or, if you prefer, new forms of experience which possess higher value.

Finally, the reconciliation between the two apparently conflicting definitions of life is found in what may be regarded as the highest activity of all, namely the moulding of mere matter in conformity with mental experience—making matter express the vision of beauty, forcing the body to follow the physical or moral laws which the mind has perceived, utilising the pure intellectual experience of the physicist and mathematician to control and harness natural forces in ways which neither nature herself nor human ignorance could do, making the material subserve the ideal. These achievements are represented by works of art, by moral and rational action, by machines like the dynamo or inventions like the aeroplane, by civilisation in so far as it deserves its proud name.

Nor let it be forgotten that one of the most potent ways of achieving this moulding of matter by and under mental experience is the influencing of other minds so that they shall share in the experience, which is in the first instance always individual. The man who succeeds in organising experience in a new way, whether to perceive *new* spiritual truth like Luther or St Francis, Jesus or Buddha; or to discover *new* natural law, like Archimedes or Faraday, Mendel or Darwin; or *new* forms of beauty, like Beethoven or Wren, Wordsworth or van Gogh: his experience dies with him, unfruitful save to himself, if he does not attempt and in some measure succeed in so controlling matter and the material means of communication between men that others can realise in their degree what the experience was. The mute Milton is both inglorious and unfruitful; he has hidden his talent in a napkin.

On this view man's idea of the divine, and his expression of it, is on a par with his discovery and formulation of intellectual truth, his apprehension and expression of beauty, his perception and his practice of moral laws. There is no revelation concerned in it more than the revelation concerned in scientific discovery, no different kind of inspiration in the Bible from that in Shelley's poetry. That is to say that there is no literal revelation, no literal inspiration; and it is mere prevarication to shift, as is often done, from one sense of these words to the other, from the wholly literal, implying revelation or inspiration by supernatural beings, to the descriptive-metaphorical, implying only the flashing into consciousness of something new, independent of the will, and carrying with it a quality of essential rightness.

In all spiritual activities we should expect steady change and improvement as man accumulates experience and perfects his mental tools. In art it is a triumph if a Beethoven or a Titian finds new ways of building beauty; in science it is acclaimed a triumph if an old universally accepted theory is dethroned to make way for one more comprehensive, as when Newton's mechanics gave place to Einstein's, or the assumed indivisibility of the atom was exploded in favour of the compound atom, organised out of subatomic particles; but in the religious sphere, owing largely to this pernicious view that religion is the result of supernatural revelation and embodies god-given and therefore complete or absolute truth, the reverse is the case, and change, even progressive change, is by the

great body of religiously-minded people looked upon as a
defeat; whereas once it is realised that religious truth is the
product of human mind and therefore as incomplete as scientific truth, as partial as artistic expression, the proof or even
the suggestion of inadequacy would be welcomed as a means
to arriving at a fuller truth and an expression more complete.

But even if it should be admitted, as in point of fact it is
admitted by an enlightened minority, that religious truth is
never absolute, and must never be bound by the shackles of a
pretended literal revelation, but is progressively discovered
and built up, that would not bridge the gulf of which I have
spoken. For it might be held (as it is by most of the enlightened minority in question) that it was a progressive discovery
of the attributes and activities of a supernatural being.

What grounds are there for denying that this is so? They
are numerous and complex, and can only be fully appreciated
after some study of comparative religion and religious psychology. In this chapter I can do no more than state them baldly
as I see them. In the first place comes the undoubted fact that
man at most levels of culture has a strong penchant for personification. Primitive peoples personify all sorts of natural
objects, and the same process continues into quite late stages
of culture. There must be very few Europeans who to-day
would not admit that river-gods, nymphs, and fauns were
mere projections of personality into non-personal objects, that
the sun is not a living being, that the lightning is not produced
by the volition of Jupiter or any other deity. The same is
undoubtedly true of tutelary spirits and gods. Early Christian
Fathers like Tertullian indulged in ironical mirth over the
innumerable domestic and other minor deities of the Romans;
it certainly seems difficult for us to conceive of worshipping
or propitiating separate spiritual beings who looked after (*inter
alia*) the household, the door, the threshold, the farm, the
child's bed, its learning to walk, and the growth of its bones!
And precisely the same difficulty is experienced when we try
to imagine separate personal beings presiding over different
aspects of life, like Venus, Bacchus, or Mars.

Together with the undoubted fact of wholesale personification in the earliest stages of human culture, there is the equally
undoubted fact of the gradual limitation during historical
time of the personifying tendency and its results. This occurs
in three ways. On the one hand, as man perceives more clearly
the connection between things and events, and comes to see
more of the unity underlying the apparently disjointed chaos

of phenomena, the number of separate personifications is reduced, but their scale or scope is correspondingly magnified. In the second place, their relation to material happenings is put more in the background: the personified sun, for instance, becomes a supernatural being who controls the sun, the sea envisaged as a god becomes the sea controlled by a god of the sea. And thirdly, their sphere of activity becomes curtailed. If the rainbow is generated by the refraction of the sun's rays on falling rain, it is not set in the sky as a sign by God. If the plague is inevitably generated by the *Bacillus pestis* and spread by rat-fleas, an outbreak of plague can no longer be looked on as a sign of divine wrath. If animals and plants have slowly evolved through hundreds of millions of years, there is no room for a creator of animals and plants, except in a meta-phorical sense totally different from that in which the word was originally and is normally used. If hysteria and insanity are the natural results of disordered minds, there is no place remaining in them for possession by devils. In short, if events are due to natural causes, they are not due to supernatural causes. Their ascription to supernatural beings is merely due to man's ignorance combined with his passion for some sort of 'explanation': they are myths—in other words, sacred versions of Just So Stories. For both these reasons we must at least be prepared to discount any statements made as to the existence of super-human persons.

There exists also a psychological reason to the same effect. Personality is the category most easily understood by man, since he himself has personality. The readiness with which he indulges in personification is seen to-day exemplified in various facts of psychology. Many cases of automatic writing and automatic speaking, of visions and auditions, have been recorded and investigated. In almost every case in which the possessor of these gifts has not been an educated and criti-cally-minded person, it is found that he or she tends to think of them as the products of a separate and external personality, although there may be no question but that this is pure illu-sion. The most remarkable and developed examples of such personification of subconscious, repressed, or partly disso-ciated portions of the mind are seen in the so-called 'controls' or 'guides' of mediums. Without doubt in some cases the 'guide' is deliberately invented and impersonated by the nor-mal consciousness, because it is considered *de rigueur* for a professional medium to be under control by a spirit guide. But, equally without doubt, in some other cases the phenomenon is perfectly genuine, often occurring only in hypnotic trance, and consisting in a spontaneous personification of certain detached parts of the mental system. For such reasons also it behooves us to be very cautious in accepting assertions as to the existence of other personalities besides our own—simply because the error is so easily fallen into and so obstinately believed in.

And there is, finally, the merely negative but still real difficulty of conceiving personality even remotely like our own, which is not in association with a material brain.

To those who approach the matter without any prepossessions as to the existence or non-existence of superhuman personal beings, and have taken the trouble to look into something of the history of religions and the workings of the human mind, it certainly seems as if this one basic tendency towards personification had been at work throughout the whole gamut of gods, and that there is in this respect only a difference of degree between the simplest animism and the highest monotheism. Between one and the other there has been a great consolidation and unification, much rationalising and much purifying: but underlying both is the same broad and unwarranted assumption, namely, that the forces which affect human destiny and are felt to be sacred are, at shorter or longer remove, the result of the activities of supernatural beings of a nature similar to that of our own personality.

If we were prepared to admit that the ascription of personality or external spiritual nature to gods were an illusion or an error, our comparison of religion with science or with art would then be complete. Each then would be a fusion of external fact with inner capacity into vital experience (or, looked at from a slightly different angle, each is an expression of that vital experience). There does exist an outer ground and object of religion as much as an outer object of science. The fact, however, that this outer object is by most religions considered to be an external divine being is, philosophically speaking, an accident; it remains real whether so considered or not, just as the outer objects of science remain real whether we consider that laws of nature inhere in them or in the human mind. Not only so, but the ascription of personal being to religion's external object is best thought of as in origin a natural and inevitable error of primitive thinking, now surviving in highly modified form, a mistaken projection of personality into the non-personal. It is thus an error of judgment comparable (though on a larger scale) to the alchemist's error in superposing on the facts of chemistry, as then known, his belief in transmutation and the philosopher's stone, or the error of early biology in superposing on the facts of putrefaction a belief in spontaneous generation.

If, however, this superposed belief and its corollaries be removed, what remains of the reality? The answer is 'a great deal.' That reality includes permanent facts of human existence—birth, marriage, reproduction, and death; suffering, mutual aid, comradeship, physical and moral growth. It includes also other facts which we may call the facts of the spiritual life, such as the conviction of sin, the desire for righteousness, the sense of absolution, the peace of communion; and those other facts, the existence and potency of human ideals, which, like truth and virtue and beauty, always transcend the concrete and always reveal further goals to the actual. It also includes facts and forces of nature outside and apart from man—the existence of matter and of myriads of other living beings, the position of man on a little planet of one of a million suns, the facts and laws of motion, matter, and energy and all their manifestations, the history of life. I say that it includes these; it would be more correct to say that it includes certain aspects of all these and many other facts. It includes them in their aspects of relatedness to human destiny; and it includes them as held together, against the cosmic background, by a spirit of awe or reverence. If you wish more precision, it includes them in their sacred aspect, or at least in association with an outlook which is reverent or finds holiness in reality.

Finally, it includes them not merely disjointedly, as so many separate items: it includes them in a more or less unified whole, as an organised scheme of thought; and as a matter of fact this scheme tends in its higher manifestations to be organised somewhat after the pattern in which a human personality is organised. It is this, among the other causes that have been mentioned, which helps to give this organised scheme of thought the illusion of possessing personality.

I may quote from an earlier essay: 'By organising our knowledge of outer reality after the pattern of a personality, we make it possible for it to interpenetrate our private personality. If, therefore, we have in any true sense of the phrase, "found religion," it means that we shall have so organised our minds that, for flashes at least, we attain to a sense of interpenetration with the reality around us—that reality which includes not only the celestial bodies and the rocks and waters, not only evolving life, but also other human beings, also ideas, also ideals. This, to my mind, is what actually occurs when men speak of communion with God. It is an organising of our experiences of the universe in relation with the driving forces of our soul or mental being, so that the two are united and harmonised' (*Essays of a Biologist*, p. 284).

The organisation of this scheme of thought may be pursued with greater or less degrees of thoroughness, just as the poorly organised mental life which is all that any infant possesses may in the adult be organised into a personality of greater or less degree of unity and richness.

The organisation of the external raw material into what is usually spoken of as God resembles closely the organisation of external raw material by other human capacities into what are usually called Laws of Nature. Both are products of the human mind, but both have their external ground. However, the external ground of the idea of God differs from the external ground considered, for instance, by physico-chemical science, in being partly spiritual. In so far as it includes among the forces affecting human destiny the general ideals of humanity, even so far as it includes one's individual ideals (since those reach out far beyond the limits of personality), it includes spiritual realities.

This, be it noted, is a very different thing from saying that the ground of religious experience is wholly spiritual; or from asserting, with some philosophers, that the ground of all reality and existence is wholly spiritual, which hypothetical ground, then christened Absolute, is inserted from above through the philosophical trap-door as a substitute for the God built up by religion or by quite other methods and out of quite other aspects of reality. I feel strongly that this *deus ex machina* of certain philosophers is a dummy God, no more like the rich, vivid and compelling experience of divinity which is enjoyed by many religious persons than is shadow like substance, or than is a chemical formula like the reality which it partially represents.

Europe has for so long been obsessed with the notion of personality in God that it is difficult to begin thinking along other lines. It is an interesting commentary on this fact, that opponents of the orthodox idea have usually taken one or two courses. Either they have so reacted against the current idea of God that they have thrown the baby out with the bathwater, rejected the whole ground of divinity and not merely

the ascription of personality to it, and so been forced into a
negativist attitude, compelled to satisfy their natural and
normal religious needs in other ways and other spheres. Or
else they have continued one aspect of the process of refining
the idea of God which is to be seen operative during religious
history, but continued it in a wrong direction, to a *cul-de-sac*:
they have accepted the idea of an external God with an essentially or wholly spiritual nature, but have pushed to their
logical conclusions the two processes which we have already
discussed—the removal of God further and further behind
phenomenal fact and event; and the purging of human limitations from the idea of the divine nature. These two tendencies
together have led to a God almost as watered-down as the
philosopher's Absolute, a God who has not only been stripped
of the limitations of human form and human frailty, and been
put above the limitations of space and time, but for whom the
type of organisation we call personality is also apprehended
as altogether a limitation, and who has been gradually meta-
morphosed from a divine person into a super-person, and
from this into mere spirit, vague and remote, which in some
imperfectly comprehended way pervades or supports the
universe.

To me, the first of these two attitudes is like the attitude of
a man who should refuse to employ the waters of a river to
irrigate a desert because it was currently believed that the
river flowed by means of some mysterious indwelling vital
power, and he disagreed with this interpretation; while the
second attitude is like that of one who had a theoretical objection to all limitations, and would therefore prefer to break
down the river's banks and spread its waters out thin as a
flood, instead of still further organising its flow by means of
irrigation works.

For my own part, the sense of spiritual relief which comes
from rejecting the idea of God as a supernatural being is
enormous. I see no other way of bridging the gap between the
religious and the scientific approach to reality. But if this rejection is once accomplished, the abyss has disappeared in the
twinkling of an eye, and yet all the vital realities of both sides
are preserved. The mental life of humanity is no longer a civil
war but a corporate civilisation. Within it there will be conflicts, frictions, adjustments; but these are inevitable, and
probably necessary for full vitality, and if they take place
within a whole which is organised for unity and production
instead of duality and strife, there will be advance.

If religion be a way of life founded upon the apprehension of sacredness in existence; if, as is the case, the human consciousness be not satisfied with the mere experiencing of sacredness and mystery, but attempts to link this up with its faculty of reason and its desire for right action, trying on the one hand to comprehend the mystery and to explain the reality which it still feels sacred, and on the other to sanctify morality and make right action itself a sacrament; if this linking up of rational faculty and morality with the specifically religious experience of holiness has resulted in organising the external ground of religion as what is usually called God; and if, finally, there be no reason for ascribing personality or pure spirituality to this God, but every reason against it: then religion becomes a natural and vital part of human existence, not a thing apart; a false dualism is overthrown; and the pursuit of the religious life is seen to resemble the pursuit of scientific truth or artistic expression, as one of the highest of human activities, success in which comes partly from native gifts, partly from early training and surroundings, partly from sheer chance, and partly from personal effort.

The insufferable arrogance of those who claim to be in sole possession of religious truth would happily disappear, together with the consequences which arise when such people are in a position to enforce their views—consequences such as bigotry, religious war, religious persecution, the horrors of the Inquisition, attempts to suppress knowledge and learning, hostility to social or moral change. The appeal to absolute authority (a product of the race's intellectual childhood) could no longer be admitted, whether an appeal to a sacred book, a divine founder, a revealed code, or a sacred church. All such appeals would continue to carry some weight, but could not be considered a court of absolute appeal, beyond the bar of reason or change. No longer could the legitimate affairs of this world be neglected on the pretext of attending to those of the next, nor unscrupulous medicine-men, priests, or religious organisations feather their nests out of the pretended supernatural power which they wield. No longer would the hideous terror of everlasting hell torment innocent children or distort the lives of men and women, nor the true comfort of religious worship and contemplation be turned out of its course, as the result of fear of a personal, omnipotent, and exacting God, and forced into the channel of propitiatory sacrifice, the meaningless mumbo-jumbo of certain types of ritual, and what I can only describe as the 'begging-letter' type of prayer.

Men will cease to be able to regard religion as a patent medicine of the spirit, but will be forced to see it for what it is, an art to be learnt. It is an art of spiritual health. They will be able to acknowledge the obvious fact that sanctity properly pertains to certain ideas and to certain basic human relations, and that it may come to lodge, through the accident of association, in particular places and events and things, without being thereby called upon to admit that a God exists in or behind the thing or idea, or has given supernatural sanction to the human relation.

To take an example: human love and marriage can possess this sanctity, can be a sacrament, just as well to two complete atheists as to two devout Christians, just as fully if regarded as a human development from animal mating relationships as if supposed to be divinely ordained. Unfortunately, the upholders of the sanctity of marriage too often apply the term sanctity somewhat in the way of the primitive savage. They prefer to think of the institution as surrounded with a divine sanctity which forbids man to touch or even to discuss it, a negative taboo, instead of leaving the sanctity where it belongs, namely, in the possible beauty of the relationship itself, and therefore welcoming all attempts to adapt the institution to human needs and aspirations. It is really very remarkable to reflect, when one is confronted with certain aspects of Christian morality, that the founder of Christianity himself, nineteen hundred years ago, proclaimed that the sabbath was made for man, not man for the sabbath.

Once it is realised that the sanctity that inheres in places or buildings, in ritual or ceremonial, is imparted to them by the human beings who have felt them as sacred, then no-one of religious inclinations will be debarred by credal difficulties or what he regards as dogmatic absurdities from participating in worship. For worship itself will be seen to be not a bowing down before a spiritual idol with supernatural powers, nor a placation of a jealous God, nor organised celebrations and praise in honour of a beloved ruler. It is an opportunity for a communal proclaiming of belief in certain spiritual values; for refreshment of the spirit, through that meditation guided by pure desires which alone deserves the name of prayer, and through the sense of contact with spiritual mysteries which disappear or are not thought of in the rush of practical life; for expressing in music or liturgy various natural religious emotions of praise, contrition, awe, aspiration, which otherwise should remain without adequate outlet. Creeds are necessary if one is to have an organised church at all; but far too much stress has been laid by religious bodies on confessions of intellectual faith. With the acceptance of the view here maintained, creeds would automatically have to be adjusted to the new outlook. The test of formal membership of a particular religious organisation would still reside in the acceptance of particular beliefs and ideas; but these different schemes of thought would be all particular aspects of a more general scheme, and matters would be so arranged that intellectual barriers, in the form of creeds and dogma, should not prevent a religiously minded man from worship in a church not of his own sect, just as a lover of art is not compelled to make a profession of belief in impressionism or cubism or pre-Raphaelitism before being allowed to enjoy an exhibition of paintings.

I have sketched some of my ideas so far as I can see them run. Do not let it be supposed, however, that I have any illusions about their range or completeness. They represent to me merely a single step.

We do not know what the future will bring forth. The visions of to-day may be the facts of to-morrow; much of the scientific truth of a century ago is historical lumber to-day; the 'self-evident' truths of morality and of social science, such as the sovereign independence of nations, or the unassailability of private property, or the radical indecency of the female leg, are replaced by other equally 'self-evident' but quite contradictory truths. The only moral to be drawn is that each generation must do its best, content that its conclusions should be scrapped later, provided only they have helped humanity's advance.

The same is true of religion. A complete monotheism is impossible to the primitive mind: even where it has been nominally accepted, the worship of subsidiary sacred beings has always crept in. The early Jews who pinned their faith to the success of the Jewish people, and were not concerned about a personal future life, could not have foreseen that from their midst would spring Christianity. One can make but a few steps at a time. I have no doubt that the advance of thought and discovery will reveal to us wholly undreamt-of facts concerning the nature of matter and its relation to mind or spirit; when that happens, a new orientation of religious thought will be needed. Meanwhile the one main step that can be taken now, in the light of the present development of thought and knowledge, I have already laboured: it is the reform of theology on the three-fold basis of agnosticism, of evolutionary natural science, and of psychology.

There is little comfort in the assurance that science has been reconciled with religion unless the religion it has been reconciled with is a good religion.—L. P. JACKS.

By the continual living activity of its non-rational elements a religion is guarded from passing into 'rationalism.' By being steeped in and saturated with rational elements it is guarded from sinking into fanaticism or mere mysticality, or at least from persisting in these, and is qualified to become a religion for all civilised humanity.—R. OTTO, *The Idea of the Holy.*

All problems of religion, ultimately, go back to this one:—the experience I have of God within myself differs from the knowledge concerning Him which I derive from the world. In the world He appears to me as the mysterious and marvellous creative Force; within me He reveals Himself as ethical Will. In the world He is impersonal Force; within me He reveals Himself as Personality.—ALBERT SCHWEITZER, *Christianity and the Religions of the World* (1923).

The monotheist is apt to overprize the mere unity in his Ideal, forgetful that unity, if it grow too great, is tyrannous. . . . Indeed, more than once in history a divine unity and concord has been attained at a cost of human colour and the rich play of interest and feeling. . . . The Ideal is not merely a unity; it is quite as much a wealth and a diversity. So that Triune monotheism might be looked upon, perhaps, as a measure of religious self-protection. It is an anchor cast to windward, lest the drift toward unity wreck the very conception of the Ideal.
          —G. M. STRATTON, *Psychology of the Religious Life.*

He alone is the true atheist to whom the predicates of the Divine Being, for instance, love, wisdom, justice, are nothing.—FEUERBACH, *The Essence of Christianity.*

When their tabernacles are broken down, and the sun in his strength quells at last the unclean fumes of their censers and sacrifices, their eyes are blinded with that splendour, and they cry out that the world is darkened.—Sir FREDERICK POLLOCK.

There are Christians that place and desire all their happiness in another life, and there is another sort of Christians that desire happiness in this. . . . Not the vain happiness of this world, falsely called happiness, truly vain: but the real joy and glory of the blessed, which consisteth in the enjoyment of the whole world in communion with God; not this only, but the invisible and eternal, which they earnestly covet to enjoy immediately; for which reason they daily pray, Thy Kingdom come, and travail towards it by learning wisdom as fast as they can.
Whether the first sort be Christians indeed, look you to that. They have much to say for themselves. Yet certainly they that put off felicity with long delays are much to be suspected.—THOMAS TRAHERNE, *Centuries of Meditations.*

In this opposition between the essentially finalistic microcosm and the purely mechanical macrocosm lies the ultimate foundation of the age-long struggle between science and religion, the first constrained by reason founded on facts to deny finality [purpose] to the universe, the second urged irresistibly to affirm it by the imperious demands of feeling.—E. RIGNANO, in *Psyche* (1926).

2

A Preliminary Interpretation

If what I have said in the preceding chapter is in principle correct, then current theology requires re-interpretation. It is also evident that many differences of detail would be possible in the interpretation, according both to the church or sect chosen and to the individual temperament of the interpreter. That elasticity of framework which has made it possible for Christianity to appeal to men of all grades of culture and to societies in all stages of development is one of the most notable facts about it. God the Father, for instance, must wear very different aspects to a Catholic mystic and a Hell-fire revivalist preacher.

But the broad outlines of the picture were drawn alike for all by the Council of Nicæa, when it laid down the doctrine of the Trinity with its three co-equal persons. That doctrine, in spite of occasional intellectual revolts from its incomprehensibility, has appealed to the European mind for so many centuries that even the most bigoted opponent of Christianity would have to admit that the doctrine satisfies certain human needs and corresponds in some way with reality.

As I see it broadly, 'God the Father' is a personification of the forces of non-human nature; 'God the Holy Ghost' represents all ideals; and 'God the Son' personifies human nature at its highest, as actually incarnate in bodies and organised in minds, bridging the gulf between the other two, and between each of them and everyday human life. And the unity of the three persons as 'One God' represents the fact that all these aspects of reality are inextricably interconnected.

The First Person of the Trinity, on this view, would be the theological name for the outer force and law which surround man whether he like it or not. There may be mind and spirit *behind* these powers, but there is none *in* them. The powers thus symbolised are strange, often seeming definitely alien, or even hostile to man and his desires. They go their ways inevitably, without regard for human emotions or wishes. They constitute the *mysterium tremendum* of religion. On the other hand, they are not always hostile or alien. The spring follows the winter; nature may bring the storm and the flood, but she also blesses with abundance; the powers of nature kill and terrify, but they also bring the sun to shine, the breeze to blow, and the birds to sing; they are powers of generation as well as of death.

In general, the forces and powers personified as the First Person are those which affect human life not only with their inevitability, but also with their quality of being entirely outside man. They may influence and subdue man, or man may influence and control them; they and man's mind may be fused in experience; but in themselves they are not only given, but external.

The realities symbolised in the Third Person of the Trinity, however, if my reading of theology is at all correct, are those which are equally given, but, from the point of view of humanity as a whole, internal. From the point of view of the individual man, on the other hand, they have the peculiar quality of being felt as partly internal, immanent, belonging to the self; partly external, transcendent, and far greater than the personal self. They are ideals of value, and are inevitable to an organism which like man has reached the level of conceptual thought.

Once general ideas are possible, they come to include abstract ideas or ideals. If I can make use of conceptual thought at all, I can have the general idea of *truth* in the same way as I can have the general ideas of *circularity* or *hardness*. But the general idea of circularity embraces not only the individual circular objects I have known, but includes them all in and refers them all to an abstract idea of perfect circularity, to which only approximations can ever in actual fact be made. So, with even more force, as regards hardness; and so with truth. Truth includes not only all the true propositions I know and their individual if partial trueness, but also the ideal of complete and absolute truth by which every proposition must be judged as to its individual truth. And the same is the case with the moral virtues like mercy or courage or justice, with the ethical virtues of righteousness, with the æsthetic virtue of beauty. As soon as we begin to think at all, we perceive there is an ideal beyond every actual; and the more we think, the higher and the more extensive does that ideal become.

As we advance in experience, we find that our own dis-

coveries, however intense, are but a limited and minute fraction of those that are possible; our knowledge of the actual
and our conception of the ideal both enlarge enormously as
the result of discovering the discoveries of others. With this
the ideal becomes less merely personal, and is discovered as
coextensive with humanity, and thus, while losing nothing of
its height, acquires new vastness of extension.

The rôle of different ideals within that sphere of reality
which has been personified as the Holy Spirit has differed enormously in different ages and in different individuals and sects.
It differs according to the scale of values which is adopted.

To take a few extreme cases, partly from other fields, there
have been artists to whom æsthetic truth, artistic rightness
of perception and expression, have been infinitely more important, more valuable to them, than intellectual truth or any
moral qualities. Their contemporaries have generally repro-
bated them, but posterity has been blessed in their achievements. In precisely the same way the man of science may live
mainly and chiefly for the discovery of new truth, and put
that at the top of his pyramid of values, neglecting beauty
and the more human and domestic virtues. Or, finally, there
have been many religious men and women who have found
the assurance of salvation, the sense of righteousness, or the
delights of religious contemplation, so far more valuable than
anything else that they have 'made themselves eunuchs for
the kingdom of heaven's sake' or in other ways expressed
their asceticism and their contempt for so-called earthly
values; or have given themselves up so completely to the
mystic life, neglecting good works and ordinary religious
observance as well as secular values, that they have become
objects of scandal even to the faithful.

In general, however, the ideals enshrined in the conception
of the Holy Ghost include in the highest rank those of
Righteousness with special reference to purity, and of Truth
with special reference to the sense of illumination, though
they, of course, include many others as well. But it should not
be supposed that the reality behind the Third Person of the
Trinity consists solely of ideals. It includes also all those
'winds of the spirit' which appear to come from some extra-
personal region to fill the sails of the mind. We all know well
enough that we may perceive an ideal, understand that it
should be followed, and yet draw on no interior force which
enables us to live by it or through it; and equally that we may
be seized and possessed by spiritual forces which we do not
recognise as having previously been part of our personality,

uprushing we know not whence to drive us onwards in the service of some ideal. This, in some form or another, appears to be the almost universal experience of those who in obedience to their temperament and gifts have devoted themselves to pure art, pure science, pure philosophy, or pure religion: they seem when most successful in their work to be least personal. The same in its degree is true of all of us in our everyday life. General Booth once said that religion was something that came to us from outside: this is a singularly unsatisfactory definition, since it would apply equally well to a dozen other activities of the mind—we have only to recollect what we experienced when we first fell in love, or when we performed some action in obedience to a sense of inward compulsion, but against all the feelings of our everyday personality.

The reality behind all these cases of irruptive spiritual force is constituted by those parts of the inborn capacities of mind and soul which have not been utilised in the building-up of personality. These inborn capacities of men, theirs through no merit or fault of their own, are given to them once and for all by heredity and early environment. The utmost that we, as individuals and persons, can do is to utilise fully the capacities which are thus presented for our use; we often do not even use them, but leave them to rust.

The contemplation of our own selves and human nature, the miracle of its existence as a product of natural evolution, the amazing fact that a man is a mere portion of the common and universal substance of the world, but so organised as to be able to know truth, will the control of nature, aspire to goodness, and experience unutterable beauty—that is perhaps the fullest way in which the givenness of our capacities comes home to us. But it is not everyone who is prone to contemplation. To most people the two chief ways in which this reality (which I have asumed to be one basis for the doctrine of the Holy Spirit) becomes realised are in the irruption into conscious life of mental powers not at all or not fully utilised in the building up of personality, and in the swallowing up of self or personality in the consciousness of something larger and more embracing. The building up of personality consists in adjusting the wholly or partially disconnected instincts and tendencies with which we are born into a connected whole in which the parts are in organic relation with each other; to this we are forced by experience, by the outer and inner conflicts which naturally occur but must be adjusted if we are to lead a life worth living, and by the light of reason which confronts the actual with the possible and the ideal.

This organised mutual relation of mental capacities and tendencies, each adjusted in some measure to the rest, and each thus becoming not merely one in a sum of properties, but an essential part of an organic unity, is what we call the personal self. But it is by no means necessary that all our capacities should be early or indeed ever thus organised in mutual relation; and in so far as they are not thus organised, they remain outside the self, outside the personality. On the other hand, it is always possible for some experience to bring any such disconnected portion of our mental and spiritual outfit into connection with the organised part, and for this connection to be not merely a transitory one, but to remain, and to involve the permanent addition of something new to the personal organism. Whether the connection be permanent or merely temporary, it is often experienced as the irruption of something outside the self into the self; it is also often experienced as a recognition of mental forces within the self which had previously been unrecognised—a bewildering sense of powers which seem at the same time immanent and transcendent in regard to the self. Both these ways of experience will be realised to be perfectly natural if the principle which I have outlined of the upbuilding of personality is accepted. There must always be a fringe of faculty only in part and dimly connected with the strongly personal central core where organisation has proceeded furthest. There may also be wholly untapped regions, or, more frequently, minor systems which are definitely kept apart from the majority by the psychological forces of repression. The more apart or the more unrealised the faculty has been, the more its recognition will come as a sense of an external gift: the more it has been in subconscious connection with the rest, the more will it appear as immanent. But in most cases at least the experience will combine the two at first sight incompatible notions of invasion of the self from outside, and the discovery of powers that are permanently and inevitably immanent within the self.

The other aspect of this problem to which I referred consists in the process, in a sense opposite to that we have just been considering, in which the personality, instead of adding to itself, has the sensation of being swallowed up in something larger than personality. This, however, will occur naturally whenever the pursuit of some ideal comes to dominate strongly over the immediate interests of the self. Any ideal, by its very nature, is beyond the limitations of the individual, beyond the particulars of place or time: and yet, of course, the ideal in any actual case is grasped and acted upon by an individual personality. Here again, therefore, there comes in the double sense of internal and external, immanence and transcendence in combination. Complete absorption in a mathematical problem, complete disregard of danger in the wish to save a child from a burning house, complete neglect of all the ordinary business of life by the man or woman in love, complete oblivion of the outer world in mystical contemplation, whether religious or æsthetic—in all such occasions self is forgotten, the ordinary interests of the personality are swallowed up and dominated by a supra-personal interest which yet is organically connected with the personality.

In all cases, in our attempt to translate the terms of Christian theology into terms of our own, we may say that what has been described as the Holy Spirit is that part of human nature which impresses by its givenness, by its transcendence of the personal self regarded as a self-centered mental organisation, and by its compulsive power of driving human nature on towards an ideal.

Finally there remains the second person, the Logos, the Son. In order not to be misinterpreted, let me remind my readers at the outset that orthodox theology, in regard to the Second Person of the Trinity, presents us with a doctrine far from simple, the result of a long process of development. The original idea of a temporal Messiah, destined in his lifetime to lead the chosen people to success, soon gave place to that of a Messiah shortly to come again in glory and bring the end of the world and the justification of the elect. As time went slowly by and the Second Coming tarried, this idea too faded, and the messianic idea was transferred more and more to the kingdom that is within, to the problem of personal salvation. Here it made intimate contact with various of the existing mystery religions, which, long before the birth of Jesus, were built upon the idea of worshippers obtaining holiness through some form of mystical communion with the god, and upon the possibility of transferring sacredness from god to man; Christianity both borrowed from and lent to these, on the whole receiving more than it gave. In the first few centuries of its existence it also made intimate contact with the Judaised Greek philosophy of which Philo is the most celebrated representative. Here it encountered the idea of the Logos and eventually incorporated it, in a way peculiarly its own, with the messianic idea, both of course being linked up with the historical figure of Jesus. But even so, the doctrine of the Second Person was by no means established. As everyone who has an elementary acquaintance with Church history is aware, the full divinity of the Son—Messiah-Logos-Jesus—was long in dispute. For a large and important body, Christ was definitely less than divine, subordinate to God; and it was only after three centuries of theological dispute and development that the Council of Nicæa gave Christianity the doctrine of Christ as co-equal with God the Father, which it has retained with little or no modification to the present day.

When I speak of the Second Person of the Trinity, therefore, I am not referring to the historical Jesus, nor to the idea of Jesus which was present to the minds of the twelve apostles or the early church, but to this complex idea, as presented in the Nicene creed and subsequent theology, deriving from Jewish and pagan religious sources, from Greek philosophy, and from patristic theology, as well as from the man Jesus, the facts of his life and death, and the legends associated with him.

And this, I make bold to say, embodies the fundamental reality that only through human nature, through personalities with all their limitations, is the infinite of the ideal made finite and actual, is the potential which we have recognised behind the term Holy Spirit realised in the world, is the apparently complete discontinuity between matter and spirit bridged over. Modern science is able in one not unimportant particular to amplify the original doctrine. Through our knowledge of evolutionary biology, we can see that human nature is not, as a matter of fact, alone in this; but that human nature merely does more efficiently, more completely, consciously, and on a definitely higher plane, what other life had been doing gropingly, unconsciously, and partially for æons before man ever was. We can therefore say that the nature which finds its highest expression in human nature constitutes this bridge; since, however, it is, so far as we know, only human nature which mediates fully, or indeed at all in certain domains, between ideal and actual, between spiritual and material, it is only human nature which need be fully considered, although the evolutionary background lends a richness and a solidity of foundation to all the conceptions involved.

This same conception, of human nature being in its highest aspects divine, is found in many places. It animates the myth of Prometheus who stole divine fire from heaven for man. It underlies the frequent deification, usually after death, of heroes and great men. Even in our own days there has been a definite cult of Lenin in Russia, his picture taking precisely the same place in some households which the sacred ikons do in others; and Mussolini was known as 'the Myth' by the more enthusiastic of his followers. It is at the root of Blake's allegorical mysticism, and Wordsworth's famous Ode. It made possible the existence and power of such ideas as the divine right of kings or the infallibility and supreme power of the popes, as well as the actual deification and worship of the Roman Emperors during their lifetime.

To me it is simply the obverse of the ideas which have already been considered in relation to the Christian doctrine of the Holy Ghost. It is a matter of plain fact that all the faculties of human nature which seem most obviously immanent, yet possess in some degree the property of transcendence, in the same way in which the reverse was also found true. And this, as I have already tried to indicate, follows inevitably from the human faculty of conceptual thought, the concept always, by its mere nature, transcending every particular in the general, and automatically providing an ideal goal for every direction and every striving.

Orthodox theology, naturally moving within the bounds of the theistic conception, prefers to interpret these facts by saying that God was incarnated in human nature in the person of Jesus; and, when both liberal and logical, by admitting also that God is partially incarnated in all human beings.

I prefer to say that the spiritual elements which are usually styled divine are part and parcel of human nature. Thus the reality personified as the Second Person of the Trinity becomes to our re-interpretation the mediating faculty of human persons between the infinity of the ideal and the finite actuality of existence.

Finally, there remains the relation between the three persons of the Trinity, regarded as personifications of three aspects of reality. It has been in one sense the great triumph of Christianity to have built up this elastic and vital doctrine of the Trinity, in spite of its apparent incomprehensibility. This doctrine, for instance, made it clear that the object of worship was not merely external power which must be feared or loved as the case may be, but also internal power, immanent in or at least entering into human nature, and operating through and by means of human nature. In thus combining external and internal, it has been at a considerable advantage over completely monotheist religions like Islam, which inevitably lay too much stress upon external power, and also over non-theistic religions like pure Buddhism, which inevitably lay too much stress upon the inner life and divorce it as far as possible from outer realities. It also, through having the three persons combined into an indivisible whole, has been at an advantage over all polytheistic religions, in

which various aspects of reality are inevitably given too great
sharpness and independence of each other.

In our task of re-interpretation, we must ask what is the
reality which is symbolised by the union of the three persons
in one God. It is in this aspect of theology that I think the
facts of science may be seen to have the greatest value. Science
has gone a very long way towards proving the essential unity
of all phenomena. It has at least provided a strong basis for
a reasonable belief in their unity and continuity, which, in the
way in which it formulates itself to me personally, I will do
my best to summarise here.

I personally believe in the uniformity of nature, in other
words, that Nature is seen to be orderly once we take the
trouble to find out the way of her orderliness, and that there
are not two realms of reality, one natural, the other supernatural and from time to time invading and altering the course
of events in the natural.

I believe also in the unity of nature. Scientific discovery has
tended without ceasing to reduce the number of ultimate substances with which we have to deal. There exist a million
different species of animals and plants, each chemically different from the rest; each species contains thousands or millions of chemically different individuals; there exist an almost
equally unlimited number of separate and different substances
of non-living matter. Yet all these, alive or not, work with the
same energy, are built up out of the same matter, resolvable
into the same few score elements, and these very elements in
their turn (so the physicists tell us) are merely so many different quantitative arrangements of two kinds of units, of
positive and negative electricity. If the trend of discovery
continue, we shall eventually be enabled to see these positive
and negative electricities as two modifications of the same
basic unitary substance.

I believe in unity by continuity. Matter does not appear or
disappear, nor do living things arise except from previously
existing things essentially like themselves. The more complex
matter that is alive must at some time have originated from
matter that was not alive, but again by a gradual continuity, so
that only by comparing the last stage with the first could one
see how considerable had been the achievement. I believe in
this continuity of all matter, living or non-living; and I believe
also in the continuity of mind. If, as is the case, mind and
matter coexist in the higher animals and man; and if, as
is now certain, the higher animals and man are descended
from lower animals, and these in their turn from lifeless mat-

ter, then there seems no escape from the belief that all reality has both a material and a mental side, however rudimentary and below the level of anything like our consciousness that mental side may be.

In any case, I believe in the unity of mind and matter in the one ultimate world-substance, as two of its aspects. Such a view makes it unnecessary and indeed impossible to ask the question whether matter can have a direct effect on mind or mind on matter. I believe that whenever a thought passes in the mind, it is accompanied by a definite physical change in the brain. That particular physical change could no more happen without the passage of that particular thought than vice versa. When we say that a drug affects the mind, we mean that the drug affects the physical brain-process, and therefore the thought. When we say that the will affects the body, we mean that the body could only be affected in that particular way by a mental process called willing together with its necessary physical accompaniment. Mental and material are thus, to my belief, but two aspects of one reality, two abstractions made by us from the concrete ground of experience; they cannot really be separated, and it is false philosophy to try to think them apart.

This does not, of course, imply that the mental side of one process of reality may not be negligible, while in some other process it overshadows the material; any more than that it is impossible for one aspect of the material side—say the mechanical—to preponderate in one process, another—say the chemical—in another.

All reality then consists, as Whitehead put it, of events. The events are all events in the history of a single substance. The events looked at from outside are matter; experienced from inside, they are mind.

These assurances of unity, uniformity, and continuity, derived from the discoveries of physico-chemical science and evolutionary biology, were not available to the intellectual enquirers of earlier ages, who could thus only guess in the dark. The speculations of the Greek philosophers, for instance, as to the ultimate elements out of which the world is built and as to the evolution of life are in no way comparable to the view of science to-day. The one can rightly be described as a set of philosophic myths, while the other reposes upon tested and organised experience.

Utilising these assurances as part of our background, we can then proceed to envisage the relation between the three aspects of the unity of nature symbolised as the three persons of the Trinity somewhat as follows. The first person represents the power and externality of matter and material law, given and inexplicable. The third person represents the illumination and compulsive power of thought, feeling, will—the faculties of mind in its highest ranges and at the level when it deals with universals; these also are inexplicable, but must be accepted as given. The second person is the link between the other two; it is life, in concrete actuality, mediating between ideal and practice, incarnating (in perfectly literal phrase) more and more of spirit in matter. This progressive incarnation may be unconscious, as appears to be the case with organic evolution, or conscious, as in the deliberate attempt by man to realise his visions.

And all non-living nature is one matter; all life is constructed of and sprung from this same matter. Further, all thought and emotion, even the highest, spring from natural mind, whose slow development can be traced in life's evolution, so that life in general and man in particular are those parts of the world substance in which the latent mental properties are revealed to their fullest extent. Thus the three aspects of reality, so separate at first glance, are in point of fact genetically related in a single unity.

On the moral side too this unity underlying apparent diversity can also be traced. It may not solve the problem of evil, which is probably insoluble in the form in which it is usually stated, but it does contribute to the idea of a moral unity when movements and actions which at first sight seem neutral or evil are found on analysis to be inextricably part and parcel of a larger movement towards good. This is quite definitely so in regard to biological progress, and is also a commonplace of the human moralist.

*

I have in this chapter made some brief and extremely incomplete attempts at explaining the lines of thought that are in my mind, and at showing how certain ideas of current theology might be translated or interpreted in terms of this way of thinking. This must not be supposed to mean that I regard those doctrines of Christian theology, even when thus interpreted, as necessarily the best way of presenting the realities behind theology. The remaining part of the book will be largely taken up with justifying the line of approach which I have adopted, and in discussing other possible ways of expressing religious realities.

Though dogmas have their measure of truth, which is unalterable, in their precise forms they are narrow, limitative, and alterable: in effect untrue, when carried over beyond the proper scope of their utility. . . . In Christian history, the charge of idolatry has been bandied to and fro among rival theologians. Probably, if taken in its wide sense, it rests with equal truth on all the main churches, Protestant and Catholic. Idolatry is the necessary product of static dogmas.—A. N. WHITEHEAD, *Religion in the Making*.

We men of science, at any rate, hold ourselves morally bound to 'try all things and hold fast to that which is good'; and among public bene-factors, we reckon him who explodes old error, as next in rank to him who discovers new truth.—T. H. HUXLEY, *Life and Letters*.

Your astonishment at the life of fallacies, permit me to say, is shockingly unphysiological. They, like other low organisms, are inde-pendent of brains, and only wriggle the more, the more they are smitten on the place where the brains ought to be.—*Ibid*.

A practical man is a man who practises the errors of his forefathers. —BENJAMIN DISRAELI.

'The undevout astronomer is mad,' said eighteenth-century deism; to-day we are more apt to think that the uncritical astronomer is dense. There is a sort of colossal stupidity about the stars in their courses that overpowers and disquiets us. . . . Consciousness itself is essentially greater than the very vastness which appals us, seeing that it embraces and envelops it.—WILLIAM ARCHER, *God and Mr. Wells* (1917).

One begins to wonder whether the material advantages of keeping business and religion in different compartments are sufficient to balance the moral disadvantages. The Protestant and Puritan could separate them comfortably because the first activity pertained to earth and the second to heaven, which was elsewhere. The believer in Progress could separate them comfortably because he regarded the first as the means to the establishment of heaven upon earth hereafter. But there is a third state of mind; . . . if heaven is not elsewhere and not hereafter, it must be here and now or not at all.—J. M. KEYNES, in *The Nation and Athenæum* (1925).

EX LIBRIS PROVINCIAE
PRO STUDIO THEOL.
S.S. CORDIS JESU.

3

Science and God:
The Naturalistic Approach

Gods are among the empirical facts of cultural history. Like other empirical facts, they can be investigated by the method of science—dispassionate observation and analysis, leading to the formulation of hypotheses which can then be tested by further observation and analysis, followed by synthesis and the framing of broad interpretative concepts.

Thanks to the labours of social anthropologists, historians, archæologists, and students of comparative religion, the facts about gods are now so abundant that their comparative and evolutionary study can readily be pursued, while the progress of the natural and social sciences and in particular of psychology has made it possible to attempt a radical analysis of their nature, functions and effects. Theology was once called the Queen of the Sciences; but that was in an age when the word *science* was equated (as it still is on the continent of Europe) with the whole of organised learning. In the restricted modern English sense of the term, theology has been, as my grandfather T. H. Huxley said, only a pseudo-science. But if the scientific method were applied to its subject-matter, it could become a true science. As sub-sciences of such a truly scientific theology, we might envisage Comparative Theomorphology, Divine in addition to Animal and Plant Physiology, Psychodivinity, and Evolutionary Theobiology.

There are, it seems to me, three possible ways of envisaging and defining the nature of gods. In briefest terms, the first is that gods have real independent existence as personal but supernatural beings able to control or influence the natural world. The second is that gods are personalised representations, created by human minds, of the forces affecting human destiny. And the third, which is in a sense a compromise

between the other two, is that they are more or less adequate
attempts by man to describe or denote a single eternal supra-
personal and supernatural Being with a real existence behind
or above nature.

Before going further, I had better amplify these statements
a little. By *personal beings,* I mean beings endowed with the
higher attributes of human personalities—knowing, feeling,
and willing—integrated in an organised and enduring unity
of consciousness: by *suprapersonal,* I intend a being with a
nature akin to human personality, but beyond our limited
human understanding: and by *personalised representation* I
mean an attempt to describe or interpret natural phenomena
with an objective existence, in terms of action by hypothetical personal beings in or behind phenomena—in psychological
terms, the projection of the idea of supernatural personality
into our experience of nature and our ideas about destiny.

There are of course other types of attempted definition of
gods. For the consistent materialist and the fanatical rationalist, gods are pure fictions, not only without any real existence,
but without any basis or background in fact, invented by
priests and rulers to keep ordinary people in intellectual and
moral subjection. This is, to me, itself a fiction as gross as the
one it pretends to demolish, an error as childish as the seman-
tic error of taking the existence of the word God as evidence
of His real existence.

Then there are the attempts of theologians to evade the
dilemmas in which they are landed by the acceptance of an
all-wise, all-good and all-powerful God as ruler of a world in
which chaos and ignorance, suffering, strife and evil are such
regrettably prominent features. Some take refuge in the thesis
that God is beyond human comprehension, and that we must
therefore accept the apparent contradiction resignedly without attempting to understand. This is a counsel of despair and
an abrogation of man's intelligence and mental powers. If the
universe is ruled by a god, it must be our business to try to
understand his policy: if there is a divine design for the
world, a prime task of religion must be to discover and interpret it. If such understanding and discovery are intrinsically
impossible, then belief in god is a poor basis for religion or
for conduct.

Then there are the attempts to redefine god so as to fit in
with historical and scientific knowledge. We are told that god
is the Absolute, whatever that may mean; or 'a power, not
ourselves, that makes for righteousness'; without specifying
the nature of that power; or a general spiritual force behind

phenomena; or the everlasting ground of being; etcetera. However, to assert, like some idealist philosophers, that the ground of all reality is wholly spiritual, and then, after christening this hypothetical ground the Absolute, to pretend that it is a new and better version of the god built up by religion out of quite other aspects of reality, is intellectually unjustified. Such a god is only a dummy divinity, a theatrical *deus ex machina* dropped on to the religious stage through the trapdoor of metaphysics.

And for theologians to claim that god is 'in reality' some abstract entity or depersonalised spiritual principle, while in practice their churches inculcate belief in a personal divinity who rules and judges, who demands worship and submission, who is capable of anger and forgiveness—that is plain intellectual dishonesty.

*

Let me return to the three possible ways of envisaging the nature of gods. In the light of our present knowledge I maintain that only the second is tenable—that gods are creations of man, personalised representations of the forces of destiny, with their unity projected into them by human thought and imagination.

In parentheses I should say that I do *not* mean only our present knowledge in the field of natural science, but also our knowledge in the fields of history, prehistory, and cultural anthropology, of human psychology and of comparative religion.

This general statement on the nature of gods can be profitably reformulated and spelled out somewhat as follows. History shows an increasingly successful extension of the naturalistic approach to more and more fields of experience, coupled with a progressive failure and restriction of supernaturalist interpretation. The time has now come for a naturalistic approach to theology. In the light of this approach, gods appear as interpretative concepts or hypotheses. They are hypotheses aiming at fuller comprehension of the facts of human destiny, in the same way that scientific hypotheses aim at fuller comprehension of the facts of nature.[1] They are

---

[1] For an interesting philosophical discussion of the problem see Professor John Wisdom's essay on Gods in his *Philosophy and Psychoanalysis*. He rightly points out that statements about God are often statements about real phenomena, in the shape of experiences, but he does not come to grips with the view that the term *God* itself involves a hypothesis or assumption.

theoretical constructions of the human mind, in the same way as are scientific theories and concepts: and, like scientific theories and laws, they are based on experience and observable facts.

God hypotheses are part of a more general theory, the daimonic theory as it is usefully called, according to which supernatural spiritual beings, good, bad, or indifferent, and of very different degrees of importance, play a part in the affairs of the cosmos.[2]

The analogy between theology and natural science deserves a little further exploration. In the history of natural science the absolutist approach, involving *a priori*, dogmatic or purely rationalistic methods, has been gradually given up in favour of scientific naturalism—the progressive method of observation and hypothesis, followed by the checking of hypothesis by fresh observation.

As every schoolboy knows, many hypotheses and theories and so-called laws of nature have been abandoned or superseded in the light of new factual knowledge. Thus for centuries astronomical theory was subordinated to the *a priori* principle that perfection reigned in celestial affairs and that accordingly, since the circle was the perfect form, the heavenly bodies must move in circles. This led to the impossible complications of Ptolemaic astronomy, which fell like a house of cards when Kepler showed that elliptical orbits provided a simpler and more adequate explanation of the observed facts.

Again, the classical theory (which might better be described as a scientific myth) of the Four Elements—Earth, Air, Fire and Water—held the field for centuries, and it was possible by ingenious manipulation to fit a great many facts into its theoretical framework. But eventually this became impossible —the framework proved to be not merely inadequate but downright wrong; and the atomic theory, which is still in process of development, took its place. Similarly in biology, Darwin's work necessitated the immediate abandonment of the theory of creation in favour of evolution; and the Lamarckian theory of evolution by the inheritance of acquired characters has been dropped because it no longer fits the facts.

Gods, like scientific hypotheses, are attempts to understand the cosmos and explain or at least interpret the facts of experi-

[2] See Professor Ralph Turner's discussion of 'the Daimonic Universe' in his *The Great Cultural Traditions,* vols. 1 and 2 (McGraw-Hill, New York, 1941).

ence. But they differ from modern scientific hypotheses in various ways. For one thing, they are still largely dogmatic or *a priori*, deriving from authority or feeling or intuition instead of from constant checking and rechecking against fact. As a consequence, they no longer fit the facts; but in so far as they are formulated in absolutist terms, they cannot afford to die and be reborn in new guise. Authoritarian dogmas and revelations resemble the Struldbrugs of *Gulliver's Travels* in being condemned to an uncomfortable survival long after their original vigour and significance have been exhausted. Luckily, however, they differ from Struldbrugs in not being immortal. They *can* die—though usually their death is belated, so that they have kept their youthful competitors in the world of ideas out of their rightful place for far too long.

Gods differ even more radically from the hypotheses of science in being created by primitive and prescientific methods of thinking. They are thus unscientific in essence, and in the long run anti-scientific in their effects. Gods are among the products of what Ernst Cassirer in his notable three-volume study, *The Philosophy of Symbolic Forms*,[3] calls mythical thought, which is basically non-rational: it fails to exclude feeling and fantasy from its judgments, and does not operate according to the laws of logic or by utilising scientific method.

Mythical thought in Cassirer's sense includes three rather different modes of thinking and of framing its ideas and symbols. The most primitive, and the one which appears to operate inevitably in the earliest stages of individual life, I would call the magic mode. For magic thinking, the world is basically a reservoir of magic power. It works as a system of interacting magic influences, some diffused, some concentrated in particular external objects or processes, some intrinsic in man and operating through verbal symbols and ritual actions. Magic thinking apparently grows out of the infantile phase that Freud has characterised as that of the omnipotence of thought. The early infantile world is a world of feeling and emotion, of the satisfaction and frustration of desires. The infant speedily discovers that he can often obtain satisfactions by expressing his emotions; such expression is of necessity to some extent symbolic, an external symbol to others of the internal reality. That reality is a reality of emotion, intense and without compromise. Emotional thinking operates by the

[3] Yale University Press, New Haven.

primitive all-or-nothing methods of animal instinct: the personality is wholly possessed by one emotion—and then of a sudden it is not possessed at all. The expression of his emotions is the infant's only method of communication with the world outside himself. Only after learning to speak does he acquire the capacity for rational thought and the communication of non-emotional experience.

It seems clear that the idea of magic influence originates from this pre-rational phase of individual mental life, but is later enlarged by primitive society to cover the workings of nature as a whole.

Whatever its actual origin, it is clear that the magic mode of thinking operates by extending the idea of immanent power, emotionally and morally charged, from man's primal experience of it within himself to the universe around him. Magic is an interpretation of destiny in terms of pervading spiritual—or rather, non-material—influences or forces, making for enjoyment or misery, good or evil, fruition or frustration, and capable of being humanly controlled by appropriate methods.

Magic thought is a coherent and self-consistent system. It is also delightfully elastic. Whenever magic methods fail to secure the desired control of events, an excuse is always ready to hand—the ritual was not properly executed, the spells not quite right, the occasion not propitious, another magician was making more powerful magic. . . .

The second mode of organising mythical thought may be called the projective, in which personality is projected into the external world.

After the primary infantile phase in which the baby lives in a world of his own emotions, the next step in experience is the awareness of personality—first other people's, beginning with the mother's, and later his own. Personal beings are recognised, and are found to influence the world of desires and emotions by their control of events. The natural and apparently inevitable consequence is for the child to personalise events and objects which arouse emotion and favour or frustrate his desires.

Lewis Mumford, in his admirable book *The Conduct of Life,*[4] has stressed the fact, too often neglected by the intellectualism of logicians and philosophers and the materialist 'scienticism' of empirical scientists and practical technicians, that the infant's early world is a world of feelings and people,

[4] Harcourt, Brace, New York, 1951.

in which objects are not separately distinguished, but are apprehended only as part of an emotional experience. This being so, it is inevitable that primitive thinking should operate in terms of emotional powers and personal agents.

Only later, with the aid of words as mental tools, can the child categorise experience in terms of things and ideas, and start thinking objectively and intellectually. And even then, objects and events often remain charged with the emotional forces and projected personalities of earlier modes of thought. Indeed language itself is primitively charged with such emotional and personal significance: the progress of human science and learning has been bound up with the development of appropriate language, more objective and more rational. Mathematics, of course, represents the fullest expression of such emotionally uncommitted language, while the arts have concentrated on emotionally charged and often non-verbal symbolism.

In any case, the projection of personality into external things and events provides the basis on which the daimonic phase of early human thinking was organised. Projective thought peopled the universe with demons, spirits, devils, ghosts and gods. And under the outer pressure of accumulated experience and the inner pressure of man's exercise of logical reasoning, these cultural entities proceeded to evolve in fantastic multiplicity.

The third mode of mythical thought may be specifically called the mythological, which sets out to give theoretical explanations of phenomena, especially explanations of their origins, whenever factual knowledge is insufficient. To do this, it requires language and must wait on reason applied to experience; and so, like the later creation of gods by projective thinking, it can only operate when, with the aid of speech, the infant has become a child.

Just as magic becomes intertwined with daimonic thinking, so gods are frequently involved in mythology: the three modes of mythical thought, though apparently successive in origin, remain entangled for much of history. Sometimes, indeed, as with culture-heroes, mythology makes a novel use of the god-hypothesis as part of its explanation. All mythical thought is purposely interpretative, and attempts to confer significance on reality. The trouble is that, since it always starts from incomplete knowledge and almost always from false premises, its significances are usually wrong, distorted or misleading.

In passing, it should be noted that elements of the mythical modes of thinking may survive in naturalistic and scientific thought. Hypostasised 'forces' and 'principles' are de-emotionalised refinements of personalised thinking; and cosmological speculations like that of continuous creation are myths dressed up in scientific guise and expressed in the naturalistic mode.

I have spoken of the origin of gods: it remains now to consider the fascinating subject of their subsequent evolution.

In biological evolution, we find many different types, characterised by different plans of organisation (for instance insect *versus* vertebrate, or mammal *versus* reptile). Every successful type evolves into a large group, characterised by a rapid increase in numbers and in variety of sub-types. During its evolution, it shows gradual trends towards improvement—sometimes improvement in general organisation, sometimes in this or that specialised efficiency. In the great majority of cases, these trends eventually become stabilised. In plain language, they come to an end, and the type (if it does not die out) continues indefinitely on the same level of organisation or specialisation: it has exhausted its inherent possibilities of major improvement.

Further, every type of course finds itself in competition with other evolving types: and such competition may modify the course of its evolution, restrict its improvement, reduce its numbers and variety, and sometimes even lead to its virtual or total extinction. And large-scale biological progress occurs through the replacement of one successful or dominant type by another, as in the classical example of the replacement of the cold-blooded reptiles by the warm-blooded mammals and birds as the dominant type of land animals at the close of the Mesozoic about sixty million years ago.

Gods are not organisms, but they are organised cultural entities: like other cultural entities, they can and do evolve, and in a way which shows many points of resemblance (though also of difference) to the biological evolution of organisms. Substantially, they are organisations of human thought which seek to represent, canalise, and give a comprehensible interpretation of the forces affecting human destiny: formally, they are organised in the guise of personal beings.

The forces affecting human destiny that underlie the construction of gods are immensely various. They include the elemental forces of nature and its catastrophes, from earthquake to pestilence; the phenomena of growth and reproduction, plant, animal and human; the emotional forces aroused by the terrifying and the mysterious, and by the sense of sacredness experienced at the crises of human life, like birth and death, puberty and marriage; authority, of father and family, of priest and king, of law and church, of city, tribe and society at large; the power of conscience, of ideals, of the forces of light struggling with the forces of darkness; the power of all compulsions, whether external or internal.

In his religions, man starts with variety and gradually organises it into some sort of a unity. In certain stages, every society has multiform gods, often of different degrees of importance, representing different special bits of destiny and its forces. Particular objects or places may be deified; or separate aspects of nature like sea, sun, or storm; or different aspects of human natures as in the later Greek pantheon; the city may be represented by a god as in ancient Mesopotamia, or the tribes as in early Judaism, or the household as in ancient Rome; human individuals may be deified or divinised, whether for their mythical exploits like hero-gods, or by traditional virtue of their office like the Egyptian Pharaohs, or deliberately like Roman Emperors, or in their rôle as saviours like Jesus or the Buddha. There is, in fact, as in biological evolution, a proliferation of specialised variety.[5]

Improvement of the type also takes place. In the first place, gods are transferred from the natural to the supernatural world, from the material to the non-material or spiritual. It is no longer the tree or the rock, the animal or the image which is worshipped, but the spiritual being behind the object or above the phenomena. At the same time, gods are spiritualised: in their make-up, less emphasis is laid on the crude forces of physical nature and life, more on the human ideals of justice and truth, benevolence and wise but firm authority, compassion and love. The conflict between the unimproved and the improved type of god is familiarly exemplified by the struggle of the Hebrew prophets against 'idolatry'.

This also illustrates another kind of improvement—the trend from variety towards unity or at least some degree of unification. A first approach may be made by erecting one god in a pantheon to the position of chief ruler, as occurred with Zeus in Greek religion; or by divinising a human ruler

[5] Homer Smith's *Man and his Gods* (Little, Brown, Boston, 1952) gives a vivid picture of the evolution of gods during human history.

as symbolising the unity of a vast empire over and above the variety of other gods and cults which it contains, as with the Roman Emperors.

A further radical step may take place by the conversion of a tribal god into a universal deity, as in Judaism. Or the universality and singularity of the deity may be proclaimed from the outset, as with Islam. Or finally the difficulty of embodying all attributes of divinity in a single person may be met by that brilliant device of Christian theology, triunity— the tripartite unity of the Trinity.

During cultural as during biological evolution, there is a struggle for existence between ideas and beliefs. There is not only a struggle between gods, but gods in general come into competition with other cultural entities which are seeking to interpret a similar range of phenomena, and so compete for the same area of ideological territory. The most important of these competitors are scientific concepts concerning various aspects of man's destiny, beginning with the world of physical nature in which that destiny is cast, and gradually invading the field of human nature.

The so-called 'conflict between religion and science' results from, or indeed is constituted by, this competition. In broadest terms, the competition is between two dominant types of cultural entity—the god hypothesis organised on the basis of mythical thinking, and the naturalistic hypothesis, organised on the basis of scientific method.

As a matter of historical fact, the results of this competition have been to expel gods from positions of effective control, from direct operative contact with more and more aspects of nature, to push them into an ever further remoteness behind or beyond phenomena. Newton showed that gods did not control the movements of the planets: Laplace in a famous aphorism affirmed that astronomy had no need of the god hypothesis: Darwin and Pasteur between them did the same for biology: and in our own century the rise of scientific psychology and the extension of historical knowledge have removed gods to a position where they are no longer of value in interpreting human behaviour and cannot be supposed to control human history or interfere with human affairs. Today, God can no longer be considered as the controller of the universe in any but a Pickwickian sense. The god hypothesis is no longer of any pragmatic value for the interpretation or comprehension of nature, and indeed often stands in the way of better and truer interpretation. Operationally, God is beginning to resemble not a ruler, but the last fading smile of a cosmic Cheshire Cat.

There has been other competition too—from the progressive secularisation of the sacred. Many areas of life once unquestioningly recognised as God's domain, many activities originally regarded as pertaining solely to the service or worship of gods, have now been secularised. In ancient Mesopotamia, economic affairs were a province of the god of the city, and astronomy was practised only by his ministers. Government was originally a divine prerogative: the Pharaohs of Egypt ruled as gods, and the Divine Right of Kings survived into modern times. Drama was first liberated from religion in classical Greece, and Sunday still belongs almost entirely to God in parts of Scotland. For the Jews, morals were the edict of Jehovah. Only in high civilisations does art become emancipated from religious or pseudo-religious domination. The Bible was for long regarded as the Word of God: we all know how this notion of divine revelation has impeded the growth of knowledge.[6]

This secular competition has also modified the evolution of gods during history. The relations with social activities have become progressively restricted. Today, gods are no longer spearheads of history, as they were in early Islam or in the Spanish conquest of the New World; they no longer operate in international politics as the Christian god did in the medieval days of the Holy Roman Empire; they no longer enforce opinion and doctrine by war or punishment, torture or death as in the Albigensian Crusade or the early days of the Inquisition or in Calvin's theocracy, nor are they effective in inciting large-scale persecutions, as against witches; they no longer have much say in laying down the curriculum of universities, or in dictating how citizens shall spend their time

[6] The grave results of authoritarianism based on the arrogant assumption of possessing the sole and absolute religious truth are well documented by Paul Blanshard in his trilogy, *American Freedom and Catholic Power; Communism, Democracy and Catholic Power;* and *The Irish and Catholic Power;* while the alarming effects of idolising a sacred book are shown in Marley Cole's study of *Jehovah's Witnesses* (1956).

Eric Fromm, in his brilliant book *Escape from Freedom,* has pointed out how human timidity and the desire for reassurance at all costs have inhibited the rational approach and encouraged the growth of authoritarian systems of belief which claim to have all the answers.

on Sundays; they no longer dictate economic behaviour, as
for instance by prohibiting the lending of money at interest
in medieval Christendom.

There are of course local exceptions, such as the Scottish
sabbath I have already mentioned, or the invoking of God to
justify *apartheid* in South Africa; and sex has not yet been
secularised, at least in respect of marriage, divorce, and birth-
control, for Roman Catholics. But by and large, in the Western
world and in various other countries too, they have been
forced out of public affairs and everyday activities, and their
dominions have been in large measure taken over by the
secular arm: their functions are now largely confined to providing individual salvation and assurance and—what is clearly
of the greatest importance—awareness of a reality transcending customary limitations of time and space, more embracing
than the nation, more enduring than any present organisation,
larger than humanity.

But though their direct social and political functions have
been diminished, they still continue to exert a powerful indirect influence on affairs. If men think about their destiny
in terms of the god hypothesis it is impossible to avoid certain
conclusions and practical consequences: belief in gods inevitably influences human conduct and the course of history.
Among innumerable examples I may point to the rise of the
Egyptian priesthood to powerful land-ownership; the weakness of the Aztec empire; the discouragement of many
branches of science by the Church; and in our own day the
effect of the Roman Catholic view of God on divorce, education, and population, or the attempts to impose a Koranic constitution on Islamic countries. T. D. Kendrick's admirable
little book *The Lisbon Earthquake* gives a particular example
of the practical effects of a theological as opposed to a scientific hypothesis of the causation of natural disasters.

The last major feature of biological evolution is progress
by replacement of old by new dominant types of organism.
This too is paralleled in cultural evolution. In the ideological
field, as we have seen, cultural entities and systems concerned
with destiny are of three main types—the magic, the divine,
theistic or daimonic, and the naturalistic, the first organised
on the magic hypothesis of pervading non-material power and
magic influence, the second on the god hypothesis of supernatural beings, the third on the scientific hypothesis of comprehensible natural forces.

Some time in prehistory gods replaced magic as the dominant type of belief-system, though magical concepts continued to play a considerable but increasingly subordinate rôle. The naturalistic type of belief-system made a premature appearance in the classical Greek world: but its organisation was then inadequate to compete with the god-system, and after a limited and primitive flowering, it went through a long period of repression and subordination. Only when it achieved an adequate plan of organisation, with the conscious formulation of scientific method in the seventeenth century, did it begin to play any significant rôle on the stage of cultural evolution. But from that time on, its rise was assured.

There is a striking parallel with the biological evolution of a new dominant group such as the mammals. The earliest mammals appeared in the Triassic. But they were only proto-mammals, which had not achieved fully mammalian organisation. As a result they remained small and unimportant for the best part of a hundred million years. It was not until the reptiles had become stabilised and perhaps over-specialised, and the mammalian organisation at the same time radically improved, and after a world-wide climatic revolution had removed many competitors, that the mammals began their rapid rise to dominance.

Cultural evolution, however, is never identical with biological. Evolving biological entities are separate organic types. A single original organic type can produce a group by branching into a number of distinct sub-types, the ramifications remaining separate down to the level of species. A dominant group is one in which this process of diversification has produced a large variety of sub-types and a very large number of species: it is a biological entity defined on the one hand by the common ancestry of all its separate members, and on the other by its evolutionary success.

In cultural evolution, however, convergence and fusion are increasingly superposed on divergence and separation. Originally separate cultural elements may diffuse from one culture to another, ideas and practices arising in one segment of cultural life may invade other segments. Accordingly any cultural entity or system dealing with a major social function, like law or religion or education, is bound to be in some sort of a synthesis, containing elements from other systems and other cultures.

For the materialistic and scientific approach, there is no such thing as religion in the abstract, only a number of actual religions. And all actual religions are organs of man in society for dealing with the problem of destiny on the one hand and the sense of the sacred on the other. If you like to combine the two, you can say that religion attempts to deal with the problem of destiny considered in the light of our sense of its essential sacredness and inevitable mystery.

Destiny confronts us in particular events of our individual lives—sickness, falling in love, bereavement, death, good or ill fortune. It is involved in the ordering of our personal existence on earth and the great question-mark of our continuance after death. In national guise, it confronts us through war, or hardship, or social evil that makes us ashamed. Finally, destiny extends beyond the nation to humanity at large; and beyond humanity to all of nature. Destiny confronts us in our ideals and our shortcomings, our aspirations and our sins, in our questioning thoughts about what is most comprehensive and most enduring, and about all that remains unknown. Perhaps most embracingly, destiny is apprehended in the confrontation of actuality with unrealised possibility, of our sense of guilt with our sense of sacredness, of our imperfections with our possible perfectibility.

The time is ripe for the dethronement of gods from their dominant position in our interpretation of destiny, in favour of a naturalistic type of belief-system. The supernatural is being swept out of the universe in the flood of new knowledge of what is natural. It will soon be as impossible for an intelligent, educated man or woman to believe in a god as it is now to believe that the earth is flat, that flies can be spontaneously generated, that disease is a divine punishment, or that death is always due to witchcraft. Gods will doubtless survive, sometimes under the protection of vested interests, or in the shelter of lazy minds, or as puppets used by politicians, or as refuges for unhappy and ignorant souls: but the god type will have ceased to be dominant in man's ideological evolution.

However, this will not happen unless the emerging naturalistic type of belief is fully adequate to its task: and that task is the formidable one of interpreting and canalising human destiny. Thus the short-lived Goddess of Reason of the French Revolution was a non-viable hybrid between the naturalistic and the god type of belief.

Already some non-theistic belief-systems have emerged to dominate large sections of humanity. The two most obvious are Nazism in Germany and Marxist Communism in Russia. Nazism was inherently self-destructive because of its claim to world domination by a small group. It was also grotesquely incorrect and limited as an interpretation of destiny, analogous to some of the primitive products of the theistic type, such as deified beasts, bloodthirsty tribal deities, or revengeful divine tyrants.

Marxist Communism is much better organised and more competent, but its purely materialist basis has limited its efficacy. It has tried to deny the reality of spiritual values. But they exist, and the Communists have had to accept the consequences of their ideological error, and grudgingly throw the churches open to the multitudes seeking the spiritual values which had been excluded from the system.

Before an adequate naturalistic belief-system can develop, scientific method must have been applied in all the fields contributing to human destiny: otherwise the system will be incomplete and will merely provide one of the premature syntheses that Gardner Murphy [7] rightly stigmatises as standing in the way of fuller comprehension. To be adequate, it must include scientific knowledge about cultural as well as cosmic and biological evolution, about human nature and social nature as well as about physical and organic nature, about values and gods, rituals and techniques, practical moralities and religious ideals as well as about atoms and cells, moons and suns, weather and disease-germs.

Only when scientific knowledge is organised in a way relevant to our ideas about destiny can we speak of a naturalistic belief-system; and only when the scientific knowledge concerns all aspects of destiny will the belief-system begin to be adequate.

[7] *Proceedings of the Columbia Bicentennial,* 1954.

I will not cease from mental fight,
    Nor shall my sword sleep in my hand,
Till we have built Jerusalem
    In England's green and pleasant land.
                                    —WILLIAM BLAKE.

We cannot kindle when we will
    The fire that in the heart resides,
The spirit bloweth and is still,
    In mystery the soul abides.
But tasks in hours of insight willed
May be through hours of gloom fulfilled.
                        —MATTHEW ARNOLD, *Morality.*

But at my back I always hear
Time's wingèd chariot hurrying near;
And yonder all before us lie
Deserts of vast eternity. . . .
. . . Let us roll all our strength and all
Our sweetness up into one ball,
And tear our pleasures with rough strife
Through the iron gates of life.
                —ANDREW MARVELL, *To his coy mistress.*

    . . . Not for these I raise
    The song of thanks and praise;
But for those obstinate questionings
Of sense and outward things,
Fallings from us, vanishings;
    Blank misgivings of a Creature
Moving about in worlds not realised,
High instincts before which our mortal Nature
Did tremble like a guilty thing surprised.
                —WILLIAM WORDSWORTH,
                    Ode on Intimations of Immortality.

4

Personalia

I have hesitated for some time before writing this chapter of a personal nature. It is not without reluctance that one sets down incidents of one's private and personal life in public black and white. Not only that, but I felt that many of my readers might and probably would think that any such incidents were uncalled for in a book of this kind. However, after deliberation, I have come to the opposite conclusion, and this for various reasons. I write as one who is not and has never been a member of any organised church. I do not know if any body of men and women share my views in whole or in part. In any case, I have arrived at them by myself. I have been helped, of course, by talk with friends and critics, by books, by the accidents of my life and events of the larger world, by much good fortune, and by much also that at the time seemed and indeed often was bad fortune: but, with all the help, the conclusions are my own and not those of any organisation.

Now religion, whatever else it may be, is certainly a matter involving all sides of the personality. Also religion, even old-organised religion, is in its highest manifestations a function of the individual, an affair of the single soul, attempting to relieve or to transmute its loneliness, to communicate its joy, or to support its longings. I therefore felt that to speak, even briefly, of some of my own personal experiences which are religious or bear upon the problem of religion, would be useful. It would in the first instance give a concrete background which might by some be easier of apprehension than impersonal analysis, and would certainly throw light on the analysis. Secondly, it would serve to introduce me, I hope, as someone who has felt religion's problems as vital problems, who has had the course of his life altered and often perplexed by the attempt to find a way out of the religious difficulties that beset him, whose will and emotions as well as his intellect have been concerned in the business.

That is my excuse for this chapter. I hasten to add that it is purely supplementary to the rest of the book, which I have tried to make as complete in itself as is possible in such small compass.

*

Both inheritance and family tradition alike made it pretty certain that I should take an interest in religion, and, further, that my approach would not be an orthodox one. My grandfather, Thomas Huxley, although represented during his lifetime as a prince of infidels and arch-enemy of religion, was in reality (as I have set down elsewhere) [1] a man deeply and essentially religious by nature. His was a puritan and iconoclastic spirit, but one with profoundest capacity for reverence. That capacity he expended chiefly in reverence for truth and for moral virtue; and it upheld him in a life's work almost superhuman in its arduousness. Naturally, that Huxley tradition was in the air I breathed, with its implications of high but hard thinking, plain but fiery living, wide intellectual interest and constant intellectual achievement, great outspokenness and moral courage, and, back of all, this sense of the ultimateness and supreme value of truth and goodness. Perhaps the air of that tradition was a trifle tonic for a diffident and romantic child. It may have helped, by the very height of the achievement which it embodied, to encourage the growth of what psychotherapists call an inferiority complex, leading to those oscillations between self-distrust and self-assurance, despair and elation, so familiar to many growing minds. But in any case it set a standard which from very early times was of the greatest value to me.

On the other side of my descent there entered a very different strain and tradition, also religious, also moralist, but of quite other character. My great-grandfather was Thomas Arnold of Rugby, a man often abused or laughed at nowadays, but at all events one of strong religious conviction and great moral force, and a born teacher. He was able to repose his religious life quite whole-heartedly in a mildly liberal and low-church orthodoxy.

---

[1] 'Thomas Henry Huxley and Religion—The Modern Churchman,' 1925, reprinted in J. S. Huxley, *Essays in Popular Science*, Chatto & Windus, 1926.

Perhaps it was due to his beautiful Cornish wife, in the lines of whose portrait there can be seen ineffable qualities of human graces and of a tender mystic sense which are lacking in his more rugged face and more straightforward character, but whatever the cause, certain it is that most of his numerous children were endowed with a combination of qualities, which, though valuable and rich, did not promote peace of mind or assurance. The best known of these was Matthew Arnold; and his combination of an aristocratically moral temperament with strong religious leanings, an acute critical faculty, an artistic and mystical capacity which in his case found outlet in poetry, a somewhat sardonic humour, and considerable learning, may serve as typical of the family. His brother, my grandfather, had the same kind of ingredients, but in different proportions. The result in his case was that he was one of the few men who have not once but twice left the Anglican for the Roman Church. His religious conscientiousness was undoubtedly great, for on each occasion of his leaving one church for the other he knowingly lost his position and means of livelihood. He was a friend of Clough's, who has used him as the peg of reality on which to hang the figure of the hero of his long poem 'The Bothie of Tober-na-Vuolich'; and the thoughts of that hero well illustrate the conscientious scruples, moral and intellectual, which seem to have tormented him all his life; while his idealism is illustrated by his decision, which was actually put into practice, to cap a brilliant university career by emigrating to New Zealand as a settler in order to be away from the horrors of industrialism and to be able to help in the founding of a new world.

The same moral-religious-literary combination reappeared in many of the next generation too, the obsession with the relation between theology, truth, and conscience, the desire both to teach and to serve either by writing, or socially, or scholastically. This generation was best typified by Mrs. Humphry Ward, her earlier novels such as *Robert Elsmere* and *David Grieve*, and her strenuous work on behalf of the Passmore Edwards Settlement and the play-centres for London children. The influence of her books and, still more, her personality, and that of Matthew Arnold's writings on critical and religious subjects, were among the most potent influences among which I grew up.

Any education we had which could be called directly religious was of the slightest. Very simple prayers introduced us to the mysterious word *God*. We were told the history of

Jesus. I vividly remember being shown the pictures in Tissot's *Vie de Jésus* and puzzling my small brains over them and the imaginations they raised. Otherwise we were encouraged to read whatever we liked (I recollect reading most of *Sartor Resartus* at the age of eight, and, though comprehending little, being fascinated by its grandeur and sense of mystery), and had our youthful curiosity encouraged rather than repressed. Moral ideas, particularly of truth and unselfishness, were strongly impressed on us; and not only that, but I certainly acquired from my early years a sense that certain ideas were, in some not fully understood way, sacred. I do not subscribe to Matthew Arnold's definition of religion as 'morality tinged with emotion'; but that certainly formed part of the atmosphere of my upbringing.

As I search about for definite incidents of childhood bearing upon religious development, I find only disconnected memories, both disconnected in time and unorganised in thought. I had that common childish love of pure speculation, and can remember very well, for instance, the spot where, seeing a rolling fives ball oscillate into immobility, I concluded that, since one could not tell exactly when motion stopped, motion must continue for ever, getting continuously and infinitely smaller and smaller. But such speculation was mostly about things which I could see. I certainly had no special or vivid intuitions about God, nor did I find myself prompted to logical questionings on the subject. The only such ideas which came to me unprompted were very vague, and consisted in the feeling that there existed a something, call it a power if you like, which came in contact with my life by being responsible for such external phenomena as the weather.

I had no picture of this power, no belief that it was personal. On the other hand, I felt about it that it somehow worked by contraries and was concerned not to let poor mortals have too good a time—that same feeling which finds it unlucky to say that a child is pretty, which mistrusts too much happiness, and especially mistrusts the mention of it, the arousing of which in ourselves makes us oppose an argument for the mere reason that the other man has put it forward. If, for instance, I was extremely anxious to have a fine afternoon, I would not like to confess it openly, even in thought, but would feel that if I said, or ostentatiously thought, the opposite, I might get what I wanted. This idea of going by contraries is widespread among all races and almost all classes;

and yet, if I may trust my own recollections, it was in my own case a quite spontaneous rationalisation, whose logical implications (of a malicious personal power in control of events) were, however, not followed out: most likely it arises with equal inevitableness elsewhere and equally remains in one of the mind's watertight compartments.

Freud tells us that a father-complex acquired in infancy is the chief or sole reason for our personification of the forces of nature as a personal god. It may be so: but even Buddhists have fathers, and even animistic and polydæmonist savages, who see a god in every nook and cranny, have no more than one natural father! My own case too makes it very difficult for me to believe that this view is generally applicable, since although I experienced a certain feeling of awe towards the uncomprehended idea of God, I never thought of God as personal. In addition, I have no grounds whatever for supposing that I ever had a father-complex; however, this to a good Freudian is no evidence, since he would assert it merely showed that it had been successfully driven into the subconscious. But I make my assertion for what it is worth.

Although the religious teaching which I received was wholly unorthodox in quality, and, fortunately for any later interest of mine in religion, extremely small in quantity, yet not only it but casually overheard conversation of my elders and passages in the gloriously miscellaneous reading of a book-addicted child naturally put into my mind many ideas that intuition never did. Naturally also, the contrast between the ideas and practices of our unorthodox household and those of our church-going neighbours did not escape my observation. We children went to church at Christmas, at Easter, and on one or two other special occasions like Flower Sunday or the Harvest Festival (and, it may be parenthetically remarked, enjoyed the infrequent experience largely for the reason that it was not frequent); the nieghbours' children went to church once or even twice every Sunday in the year. The fact of this general churchgoing on the part of the British public; the inherent mysteriousness, on their intellectual side, of the ideas one heard in church; the feelings of sanctity and awe which it seems impossible for a young mind not to feel at first contact with the topics of religion (unless they are driven out by means of an opposite feeling, such as ridicule)—these in unanalysable combination conspired to give me an interior puzzlement, an unsatisfied sense of emotional and intellectual mystery; this remained an unresolved complex, growing with me and within me like a thought-tumour, part of my being and yet not assimilated into the rest of my mental self.

At this stage, however, these feelings and ideas played no very important part in my life. On the other hand, I very clearly recall various more spontaneous actions related to religious development. One in particular I would like to record, as it seems to me, looking back on it, to be as good an example as one could find of 'natural religion'.[2]

On Easter Sunday, early in the morning, I got up at day-break, before anyone else was about, let myself out, ran across to a favourite copse, penetrated to where I knew the wild cherry grew, and there, in the spring dew, picked a great arm-ful of the lovely stuff, which I brought back, with a sense of its being an acceptable offering, to the house. Three or four Easters running I remember doing this.

I was fond of solitude and of nature, and had a passion for wild flowers: but this was only a general basis. It will not account for my acting thus on Easter Day, and only then: I never went off gathering wild cherry or any other flowers before breakfast on other days; if I did feel prompted by the fineness of the day to get up early, it was to read in a favourite perch in an oak-tree. But somehow, it seems, I found Easter Day a holy day. Naturally I was not at that age concerned to enquire very fully why or how it was holy, whether simply because other people regarded it as holy, or because of some intrinsic quality in the day; but it was a fact that it was so to me. That mysterious and sacred quality impressed itself on my mind, and had a double effect upon my actions. The holy day became as it were a lightning-conductor on to which could be concentrated those apprehensions which a child may have of something transcendent in the beauty of nature, that dim and vague sense of what can best be called holiness in material things. This, in everyday intercourse with other children and with grown-ups, is mixed up with so many other sensations and ideas that it is difficult to talk about; the world, even the child's world, inhibits it. But when sanctity is in the air, as at Easter, then it can have free play.

In the second place, the sanctity of the day not only drew out these suppressed feelings. It also lent special significance

2 For a similar example of 'natural religion' in a child, but in this case associated with fear and the quality of 'bad-sacredness', see Tristram Hillier's autobiographical *Leda and the Goose* (Longmans Green, London, 1954), p. 2.

to the actions I performed; and the beauty of the morning, the flowers I brought back, and indeed the whole pilgrimage, became invested with a special significance. How, in such cases, that significance becomes attached is matter for the psychologist to determine; but that it did so with me is a fact, and it is also pretty evident that the same psychological machinery contributes to the genesis of religious nature-festivals (from one of which, of course, Easter takes its partial origin).

In my childhood, as would seem to be the case in the childhood of man in general, morals, though often a difficult enough problem in all conscience, did not on the whole become early connected up with any religious belief or feeling. The only exception, and that a partial one, concerned those topics which I may refer to as tabooed. Certain subjects and actions were met by our elders and betters, not with the simple fiat of Authority, but by an atmosphere in which Authority took shelter behind Mystery, or was itself obviously shocked. Childhood is very quick to detect such differences of atmosphere, and it seems probable that any subject whatsoever could have this mysterious horror woven around it as it develops in a child's mind. We escaped invocation of the fear of Hell and the wrath of God in relation to the ordinary delinquencies of boyhood; we escaped, in another sphere, the terror of ghosts and all the rest of the fears generated by superstition. But sex and in a lesser degree swearing both came to have taboo-feeling attached to them. Since I certainly, and I think all the rest of the family, were very shy on intimate matters, the mere feeling that a subject was sacred, whether positively like the idea of God, or with what one may call the negative sacredness of taboo, was enough to keep it in any ordinary circumstances from being mentioned, far less discussed. I imagine that this sort of 'sacred horror' is a very common cause of undue reticence and undue repression in a very large number of human beings. It certainly was so in my own case; and, not I think by any particular incident but by this general atmosphere, the small beginnings of another possible 'complex' were established. The main psychological failing from which I came to suffer was a self-distrust and shyness which was often agonising: this deserves mention because so far as I can see some such feeling is frequently a contributory cause of the more specifically religious 'sense of sin' and spiritual incompleteness and unworthiness which is so frequent an accompaniment of adolescence. In my own case, it amalgamated itself with the other complexes which were forming within me to make a considerable and serious bit of mental organisation which was undergoing repression.

This particular weakness was accentuated when I went as a day-boy to a preparatory school, and still more when I went on to a public school and was thrown on my own resources in a society composed almost wholly of other immature human organisms. At least it achieved one thing for me—it helped foster a love of solitude, to which and the meditative habit of mind so engendered I owe a great deal of my intellectual development.

At Eton, I was one of the comparatively few boys (judging from conversations then and in later years) who on the whole enjoyed the chapel services. This had nothing whatever to do with belief in the ordinary sense, since I decided, on the matter being left entirely in my choice, not to be confirmed. The whole Christian scheme, theologically considered, remained wholly incomprehensible—I could not for the life of me understand how anyone with the background of the time could come to accept it. And yet there was the patent fact that the great majority of those around me did accept it. Doubtless a great many did so because everyone else did so; but none the less there were plenty who were not only sincere (which one can quite well be even if one's convictions are ready-made), but had thought hard and deep about the whole question. This made me feel that there must be some difference between me and others, a difference which eluded me, but, owing to the natural instinct of the young for solidarity, made me feel mentally uncomfortable, and deepened that natural sense of mystery which surrounds religious topics into one which was unnatural.

In spite of this, as I say, in spite of all my intellectual hostility, the chapel services gave me something valuable, and something which I obtained nowhere else in precisely the same way. As I look back, this simple personal fact illustrates, better than could whole reams of argument, the extreme complexity of religion, and the ease with which watertight compartments are established in the religious life, as indeed within the mind in general. Indubitably what I received from the services in that beautiful chapel of Henry VI was not merely beauty, but something which must be called specifically religious. The flights of Perpendicular Gothic; the anthems and organ voluntaries; the poetry of the psalms or lessons—these doubtless were contributory factors. But, once the magic doors were opened and my adolescence became aware of literature

and art and indeed the whole emotional richness of the world,
pure lyric poetry could arouse in me much intenser and more
mystical feelings than anything in the church service; a Beethoven concerto would make the highest flights of the organ
seem pale and one-sided, and other buildings were found more
beautiful than the chapel. It was none of the purely æsthetic
feelings which were aroused, or not they only, but a special
feeling. The mysteries which surround all the unknowns of
existence were, however dimly, contained in it, and the whole
was predominantly flavoured with the sense of awe and reverence. In addition there was the fact of the service's being communal, and of its long historic past. Just as in childhood I had
found Easter already sacred, a day which, regarded from the
standpoint of existing society as a whole, and not from that of
any single individual only, nor from that of abstract reason or
rightness, did have a definite sentiment attached to it, and so
was a holy day; so here in later boyhood I was confronted
with a place, a liturgy and a ritual which presented themselves
to my mind inevitably as wearing a mantle of reverence,
bathed in a special atmosphere, or, to put it most unequivo-
cally, as in some immediate way possessing holiness, through
the fact that so many individual people had in that place experienced awe, found in that liturgy an outlet for their desires
for righteousness, expressed their inner religious feelings in the
physical acts of that ritual.

It is, of course, perfectly true that experience, or reason, or
a sceptical temper, may and often does discount these feelings.
If not, we could never get progress in religion, and iconoclasm
would be unknown. But let it be remembered that iconoclasm, for instance, is only possible because reforming zeal
recognises the facts of which I have just been speaking, but is
enraged because this garment or atmosphere of holiness has
been thrown round objects which to it seem unworthy. True
also that maturer judgment may come to realise that in any
and every case the atmosphere of holiness has come where it
is because the human mind has put it there. But what is for
the moment of importance, and what is too often forgotten
by rationalising enthusiasm, is that when the mind first perceives this quality of holiness in things, it does really feel it
inhering *in the things*, in a way no different from the way in
which, for instance, it finds and feels the quality of beauty
inhering in things.

Thus the emotional side of the religious life was in me re-
inforced by the flowing sap of adolescence; but the intellectual

side, in conspicuous isolation from the emotional, was inhib- ited, driven back upon itself, and led into a mood of perma- nent and unsatisfied questioning by the inacceptability, to my growing intellectual interest, of any Christian theology prof- fered to me, and the failure of any person or any book to come to the rescue with any more intelligible or more accept- able scheme.

Meanwhile, again at the outset in isolation from the other two, the moral problem forced itself upon me with new inten- sity. There can be very few human beings upon whom adoles- cence does not force a new intensity of moral problems. Not only is the whole emotional life vivified and new capacities of feeling revealed, but also reason and the growing sense of maturity arouse new ideals or raise old ones to new heights. And yet at the same time the unsuspecting mind finds itself the prey to new impulses of passion generated within the or- ganism by the automatic changes of physiology, only partially comprehensible to most human beings until they receive their highest satisfaction, and yet doomed to remain unsatisfied, or to an incomplete, distorted, or unblessed satisfaction, for a period which to the rapid mind of youth seems wellnigh infinite.

At the same time, or generally a little later, youth wakes to the fact of social inequality, and, if not one of the tough- minded, to remorseful distress at its own privileged position, or envy of the position of others, or both at once.

I did not escape the usual fate; in fact, on comparing notes with others I seem to have taken the complaint in a form more virulent than usual. The contrast between the new-found pure ecstasies of the spirit, whether over poetry or music or in the passion of that romantic love expressed for all time by Dante in the *Vite Nuova,* and the equally new-found insistence of unvarnished animal passions obtruding into and sometimes obscuring the more spiritual part of the mental life, led to con- flict and to an exaggerated horror of sex the intruder. Thus conflict was intensified in two of the main departments of my life, the intellectual and the moral, and the two conflicts of course made connections and became one many-sided conflict.

So far as I can see, the main difference between primitive and developed religion lies in the fact that the latter attempts to resolve the conflicts which the former either is content to leave unresolved or simply does not see. Primitive religion is content to accept the sacredness of certain things and events and ideas as given, and to react to each such individual holiness in the way which seems most immediately appropriate. But the reflective mind is not content with this, and demands that its religious life shall be a whole. It must be a whole intellectually, strung together upon a consistent theology; a whole morally, based upon a coherent moral philosophy and a recognised scale of values; and a whole emotionally, related to an æsthetic sense which demands the fullest beauty and rejects unworthy feelings. And, if possible, it must be a whole in respect of uniting these three aspects; the moral scheme must not be incredible, the intellectual scaffolding must not have implications which offend the moral sense, the emotions must not hang *in vacuo,* detached from all relation with practice and with thought.

The conflict can never be resolved once and for all by the mere acceptance of a formula or a cut-and-dried scheme of salvation. It must work itself out in each individual life— whether to failure, to a precarious equilibrium of hostile forces, or to the full equilibrium of activity based on underlying peace. All that organised religion, with its doctrines and practices, can here do, is to proffer help to the individual in this task. It is doubtless true that without this help the individual would fail; but the same is true in every other department of life. Only through the accumulated experience of the race, proffered in daily intercourse, in tradition, in formal education, can the individual, however keen his striving, come to realise the possibilities that are in him.

So it was with me. The next stage in my development was largely taken up with attempts to solve the conflicts which, actively and violently, though far below the surface, persisted in fighting themselves out to a conclusive decision. Looking back on that time, with personal experience as well as some reading of modern psychology to guide me, I see how the battle raged at different levels. That spatial conception, of levels of the mind, though dangerous if taken in any stupidity of literalness, is yet a vital one. Perhaps one day some thinker, helping in the great task of 'the transvaluation of all values', will translate the great vision of Dante's *Divina Commedia,* with its superposed circles of being from the base of hell to the summit of paradise, into psychological terms, substituting for an unreal exterior vastness the equally vast realities of the microcosm. In any case, those conflicts of which we are speaking may sometimes be going on in the sight of others, or sometimes hidden under a blanket of reserve. They may sometimes take place in the full glare of consciousness, at others but dimly perceived, at others below yet another surface, not only below the surface which conceals them from the observation of others, but below that which conceals them from our own. There, in the circle of the unconscious, events may happen which only later obtrude themselves upon our conscious knowledge; there the springs of our energy may be sapped without our knowledge or comprehension, by a constant strife.

I was animated by passionate fervours, beliefs in the supreme value of certain ideas and activities. These in theological parlance are called Faith. They were none the less violent in me because not fixed upon the orthodox objects of religion; they drove me on to austerities of life directed towards the moral perfection which was at once so sacred and so elusive; to concentrated bursts of work towards mastery of the science in which I ardently believed; to withdrawals into solitude in search of illumination, and wanderings through countries and through books on a quest for what to me appeared of supreme value, the stuff of which great poetry is made, in which both truth and beauty join hands. But this 'faith' was not yet grounded in experience or linked with all the potentialities of my self. It was as prejudiced and bigoted (I can say, looking back) as any narrow religious faith.

I do not propose to emulate the unreticent candour of a Barbellion or a Marie Bashkirtseff, interested in self-analysis, nor the Pepysian interest in complete record of all facts centring on self, nor the self-revelation, undertaken for the advancement of a particular creed, of the great St Augustine. I am only concerned to show that, contrary to the express or implied assertions of many upholders of revealed religion, belief in revelation or in a personal God (let alone in the details of orthodox Christian theology) is in no way indispensable to religious experience, religious struggle, and religious development; and, since at the same time I am concerned to show that I am not writing from the completely detached viewpoint of the man who attempts to discuss what he cannot fully describe or understand, through his having no experience of or sympathy with the inner felt realities which give it importance and life, I have been constrained to combine the two aims in one by referring to what of my own experience seems to bear upon these questions.

I need only say that the conflict existed, that I was unable to dismiss it or suppress it, that so long as it remained unresolved it refused to remain stationary but became more serious; and that, aggravated by outer circumstances, it rendered

me profoundly miserable, as well as paralysing my energies
by threatening to tear my mental being in half. Such conflicts
are perfectly familiar to nerve-specialists and psychiatrists,
and to those who, through study or profession, are brought
in contact with religious psychology; they are none the less
tragic and huge to those in whom they take place. In my
own case, as I expect in many cases, things were made worse
through the contrast between what by others I was presumed
to be and the reality. At the end of my time at Oxford, I
suppose that to others I must have appeared a fortunate young
man enough, with physical health, a certain talent, lucky in
the opportunities of the best that upbringing and education
could give, and with enough of juvenile achievement behind
me to give me assurance of being able to push forward
towards a career. The reality was a young man feeling this
all acutely, forcing himself to intense activity of work to
make up for the assurance (intellectual as well as, or rather
combined with, moral) of which a divided self is robbed, and
applying to himself the terrible words of Walt Whitman,
which, casually read one day, printed themselves fierily upon
his mind as a description of his own state: 'Hell under the
skull-bones; Death under the breast-bones'.

Life would have been intolerable but for glimpses of the
alternative state, occasional moments of great happiness and
spiritual refreshment, coming usually through poetry or
through beautiful landscape, or through people. I had been
used, ever since the age of fifteen or sixteen, to have such
moments come to me naturally, without effort, in the ordinary
course of a full life: and ever since, they had been the things
which seemed most valuable in my existence. But now that
they were becoming of more vital importance to that life, as
assurances that I was not doomed to a miserable existence
through having lost the very faculty of experiencing this kind
of rapturous or deep joy that permeates and strengthens the
mind, they were vouchsafed in diminishing measure, and (although sometimes with very great intensity) more fleetingly.
It was of no use trying to force these experiences of peace, or
reconcilement, or rapture, or those in which supreme value
seems within grasp; they came at their sweet will or not at all.
Such independence of our volition, on the part of those bits of
life which we value most, is, I take it, one of the most important of the facts which in the sphere of religious experience
have given rise to the doctrine of divine grace as something
which is granted from a source wholly outside ourselves.

I also suspect that the great intensity of these experiences of value when they did come was based upon a piece of psychological machinery which is of some general interest in the religious sphere. It is, so far as I can see, a fact that any intense conflict, especially when accompanied by repression, automatically results in far greater intensity of feeling for either of the conflicting tendencies in their periods of temporary victory. Almost all religious mystics have passed through a period of conflict and discipline, in which the body and its desires are to be mortified. This process may eventually be accomplished and the discipline become perfect, but it involves in its earlier stages a great deal of repression; and I suspect that even in the end the 'mortification' of desires is not literal, that they are repressed from their normal outlet and harnessed in new ways. In any case, the possibility that conflict may contribute to the intensity of desired states of mind should, I think, be considered in discussing the psychology of mysticism.

But to return to myself. The deprivation of these periods of spiritual satisfaction was to me perhaps most serious in a sphere that at first sight seems remote from the scene of struggle—I mean nature and natural beauty. But ever since the age of fifteen or so I had found in natural beauty a satisfaction which was not only a rest and refreshment from any distress of every day, but one which was complete, and truly mystical (because irrational, given, and so transcending itself as to cause every highest and deepest fibre of the mental being to vibrate). Many men have experienced such feelings: Wordsworth and Ruskin are two Englishmen who have given it adequate expression, Richard Jefferies another who has cast his expression in a cruder, more pantheistic mould.

And now, just when most needed, this source of comfort was cut off. Wordsworth too has lamented the failing of the radiant experience:

> I cannot paint
> What then I was. The sounding cataract
> Haunted me like a passion; the tall rock,
> The mountain, and the deep and gloomy wood,
> Their colours and their forms, were then to me
> An appetite, a feeling and a love . . .
> . . . That time is past,
> And all its aching joys are now no more,
> And all its dizzy raptures.

or the whole opening of the famous Ode:

The things which I have seen I now can see no more.
Whither is fled the visionary gleam?
Where is it now, the glory and the dream?

What he laments is a spiritual blindness wholly analogous, in the sense of deprivation which it brings, to the physical blindness lamented by Milton:

> *Thus with the year*
> *Seasons return; but not to me returns*
> *Day, or the sweet approach of ev'n or morn,*
> *Or sight or vernal bloom, or summer's rose,*
> *Or flocks or herds, or human face divine;*
> *But cloud instead and ever-during dark*
> *Surrounds me . . .*

I lamented it the more since it was not only refreshment, but medicine for a sick soul. Thousands, I know, pass through some such experience every year: but that does not lessen the misery, nor the shut-in sense of isolation, nor the uniqueness to each separate individual.

Meanwhile, it must be emphasised that such experiences are identical in their nature with some of the experiences recorded by the religious mystics, the only essential difference being that those of the mystics are related to and focused upon definite theological conceptions, while mine (like those of Wordsworth) were not; essentially the same feelings were present in both cases, and were sacramental in their nature; but in the professed Christian they sanctify the spirit which is thirsting to feel some assurance of oneness with the power which it feels outside itself and chooses to worship, while in what we may call the nature-mystic they sanctify the visible external world and at the same time the mind which can receive the sacramental impression.

Not only this, but the sense of being forsaken, unable to summon back all that one feels of highest value, is common enough too in the realm of theistic religion. Mystics have called it 'the dark night of the soul', and describe it as an abandonment of the soul by God.[3] Again, however, it does not matter whether you believe that a divine being who used

---

[3] See Victor Gollancz's interesting anthology *From Darkness to Light*, Harper, New York, 1956, where many mystics have described their passage through this terrifying blackness to eventual peace and illumination.

to visit you now no longer comes, or whether, as with me, there is no reference of the distress suffered to the action of any personal or supernatural being whatever. In both cases the feeling (to judge in the only way in which one can judge, from the writings of those who have been through the experience) is similar. In both cases it is a feeling of terrible blackness, of loss, of loneliness and abandonment, the dark and the loss and the shut-in solitariness appalling the soul through having on the negative side just that same quality of transcendence, of being connected with ultimate reality, which when positive gives to the mystical experience of god or of nature (or of love for that matter), with its radiance and richness and sense of communion, its equally disproportionate but real value.

The only difference of importance is that in the one case the feeling is related in thought to an all-embracing intellectual framework which the mind has thought through for itself or at least accepted ready-made from its religion, while in the other case no such framework exists in the mind, or if it does no such connection is made, and the feeling is experienced untranslated into intellectual symbols.

Whatever the precise cause may have been, the phase of conflict ended with that crash known generally as a nervous breakdown. From the standpoint of the psychologist who observes them, most disorders of this type are apparently paralyses of action caused by the mental house being divided against itself, and squandering all its energy in civil war; this is combined, for most of the time at least, with extreme depression, worry, and self-reproach. To the sufferer they are the extremest blackness of the soul's night, a practical demonstration that not only heaven but hell is within us, and that neither the one nor the other need seem deserved. Job, in extremity of external suffering, would have cursed God and died. The breakdown patient has not even the energy to curse; but he knows, or thinks he knows, himself accursed, and finds his thoughts set upon self-destruction, as the only way of removing the cause from himself and the accursed life from being a burden to others.

I do not suppose that those robust-minded persons, full of common sense and practical virtues, who have not only never suffered from any such breakdown of the self, but who regard it as a symptom of radical inferiority of character and nature, can appreciate what it means to return to a normal universe after thus inhabiting the bottomless pit. They have always found the world a comfortable enough place to live in, and so have not troubled themselves to arrive at any real consciousness of how or why life is worth living. But to discover that life *is* worth living when for long months you had obstinately and against all reason been compelled to feel and believe the reverse—that is to be made very forcibly conscious of the values inherent in the commonest things and acts, and to gain a new sense of life's significance.

For myself, I was content, once the tyranny of civil war within the self was over and the blackness of the night passed through, to accept the variety of the world, to let it flow in upon a mind no longer too preoccupied with its own affairs to be disinterestedly concerned with existence. On the other hand, this same contentment and readiness to be interested in whatever turned up, though it made all life a picaresque adventure, dulled the edge of the desire for external achievement or for internal development, and allowed the seeds of the old conflict to slumber instead of prompting the eradication of the brood. I had learnt humility, but not yet learned to translate humility into achievement or work.

To this period, however, I certainly owe much which either directly or indirectly contributed to eventual religious development. I spent three years teaching in a newly founded university in Texas. Living thus in a foreign country made me realise that all the familiar institutions and ideas of my own country were not the inevitable and permanent things that they had seemed (and that they seem all life long to those who do not make themselves, or are not made to, reflect upon them) but relative, a product of time and place and circumstance interacting with a particular brand of human nature; and this, combining with my biological training, made me see in this kind of relativity—biological relativity, I may call it—an essential and general principle. It also taught me to substitute for the natural intolerance of youth a tolerance which, from being at first a mere matter of practical convenience, became at length a reasoned principle. Most important of all, by throwing me on my own mental resources among all sorts and conditions of men, it taught me to value Terence's words 'nihil humanum alienum a me puto,' to feel the bond between myself and, not humanity, but individual human beings of every kind, race, or station; and again, building on this, to come to see as a leading principle that there existed nothing of which we have any cognizance, higher than the individual man, his thoughts, faculties, aspirations, and what these have produced.

Browsing in the public library at Colorado Springs, under the shadow of Pike's Peak, while waiting to go into hospital for an operation, I came across some essays of Lord Morley, in which there occurred the words, 'The next great task of science will be to create a religion for humanity.' I was impressed that a man of Morley's intellectual power and rationalising tendencies should have been so much interested in a religion for humanity; I was fired by sharing his conviction that science would of necessity play an essential part in framing any religion of the future worthy the name; and I was impressed too with his use of the impersonal word *Science*, as implying that any real progress in religion nowadays would be the slow product of generations of thinkers and workers reacting on the common thought and practice of the times, much more than the creation of a single personality, in this respect reversing the historical process which had seen the traditional and communal religions of primitive peoples give place to the great historical religions—Buddhism, Christianity, and Islam—with their individual founders.

Other passages in his essay forcibly reminded me of how all great minds—writers, painters, men of science, organisers —all make their contribution to religion, even if one may have to translate their contribution into a different language to fit it to oneself and one's own time. But in spite of the opposition of sects and bigots and of those who fix their eyes only upon the past, religion does slowly change, through great men's thoughts and actions.

Morley's words made the more impression upon me, since already I had conceived some half-hearted idea of attempting to restate the realities of spiritual values which my experiences had forced upon me in terms of an intellectual framework drawn from my scientific training; I was aiming at a harmony which, although only vaguely perceived, I yet felt must exist, and, if it existed, and could be found, would not only bring satisfaction to myself, but might save others from some of the conflicts and pains which I had been through.

Morley's words confirmed me in my resolve to try to contribute to the task he envisaged. The time, however, was not yet. More than tolerance and acceptance, more than interest and good-will was required before I could even to my own preliminary satisfaction resolve either my intellectual or my

moral difficulties and see the way clear to unity: and only
when I had achieved some sort of unity could I desire or
think or act with any confidence.

When as a young man at Oxford I read Goethe's *Faust* for
the first time, I found the conclusion of the second part very
little to my taste. It seemed an anticlimax of the first water
that Faust, having run through all human knowledge, sinned
on the grand scale and greatly repented, enjoyed supernatural
power, and been inducted into the mysteries of cosmic workings, should devote his declining years to the draining of a
marsh. But Goethe was not Goethe for nothing. In later years
I came to realise forcibly enough how personal experience for
the mere sake of personal experience was not satisfying, how
sentimental desires to do good might tangle the wings of
action in their syrup, how not only did thought practised
alone and for its own sake tend to become imprisoned in an
intellectual void, but how action was able to help thought to
richer life just as much as thought could guide action to better
ends. I came round full circle from the intellectual arrogance
of youth (my youth as well as Faust's!) which is not content
with loving knowledge for its own sake but insists on despising
utility and practical considerations; and came to understand
that, at least for minds like mine in a civilisation like ours,
the only salvation must include constant work and activity,
not by any means necessarily directed to immediate practical
ends, but based in the conviction that it is bound up in some
way and in the long run with practical results.

It was perhaps inevitable that Faust, with his particularly
self-concentrated youth and prime behind him, should have
found final satisfaction in action of direct social and utilitarian
value: but if he be regarded as a special case, it is a special
case of a principle of general application, the gospel of work,
with its obverse, the putting of value and meaning into work
for those who must labour at work not of their own choice,
whether they like it or no.

Meanwhile public events contributed their quota to my
private story. The first World War came, and with it the
accepted bases of existence dropped away, and all had to be
faced from the beginning again. The war revealed human
nature as nothing else could have—human nature in all its
supreme of heroism and folly; cool organised driving force
and credulous, prejudiced suggestibility; self-sacrifice and
brutality; ideal aspirations and savage desire to win and
punish. To one who had breathed the international atmos-

phere of science, and had lived a considerable part of his active life in foreign countries, forced by circumstances to discount the natural prejudices aroused by different habits and strange ways of thinking, who had learnt to consort familiarly and on friendly terms with Italians, Germans and Americans, some of the problems of the war were especially acute. Was there, for instance, one morality for the nation, another for the individual? I shall never forget the disgust and aversion I felt one day in the United States when I heard quoted for the first time (and quoted with complete approval) the cele-brated dictum of an American soldier, 'My country, right or wrong'—and the rest of the rigmarole, words which are im-mortal as the fittest inscription on the pedestal of the golden calf of self-hero-worship.

It seems pretty evident that, if human necessities are to be supplied, and the practical working of the social machine is to be made smooth and expeditious, international and economic morality cannot be as exigent as individual morality. In any case, they *are* not so exigent and never have been; and it is difficult to see how the three could ever be the same, since a man in solitude is different from the same man with family or friends, or the same man as a unit in a mob or an army, or the same man in his business or public capacity. That is not merely matter of common observation, but must be so, in the same way that 'the same' atom is actually in a different state according as it happens to be *solus,* or in this or that chemical combination.

But, this being so, what becomes of your Absolute in morals, your *summum bonum,* your Categorical Imperative? They disappear as external rulings or as fixed standards. True that they can be retained in a certain psychological sense—the categorical imperative is the moral need, itself absolute, to act in one way rather than in another in a particular set of circumstances; the *summum bonum* is the highest goal of good which you, a particular individual, can actually set be-fore yourself as guide; to speak of the Absolute in morals may be interpreted to mean that all particular acts can and should be referred to an abstract and general standard. But these senses are very different from the usual sense, and their acceptance implies a relativity of morals which at first blush is to many people very disquieting.

If on the other hand the relativity of morals is a fact, it must be accepted, and its implications worked out. The war forced this problem upon me, and made me complete my ideas of biological relativity as regards structure and instinct, which had been impressed on me as a biologist through the facts of evolution, by extending them into the sphere of human morality.

Further, the war released an academic person like myself from the grooves of thought in which he was professionally bound. Whereas even members of the learned professions tend to fill their time, outside their actual work, with substitutes for thought, such as dancing, smoking, gossip, or reading; in the war there were not only more occasions of hard thought, but more opportunities (often they seemed too many!) for thinking when no substitute was at hand. The war, itself a senseless denial of thought, was a great promoter of thinking.

Now that my brain was freed from the routine of an intellectual profession I began to use it and my leisure on the religious problems which were still constantly at the back of my mind. There was still in my thought an unresolved mystery over the matter, and I was determined to get to the bottom of this if I could. It was impossible that the problems which for nineteen centuries Christian theologians had been discussing could have no meaning whatever. It was impossible that the considerable number of my friends and acquaintances who had taken Holy Orders should not be describing something which was perfectly real to them in terms of the vocabulary of which they were the heirs. It was impossible that I, brought up in the same age and country as they, in some cases for years in the self-same atmosphere of school and university, should not have had experience of the same reality.

Was the fact of our mutual unintelligibility a mere matter of terms? or of false interpretations on the one side or the other? or of wilful blindness on my part or unjustifiable imaginations on theirs? or of all three blended?

I set myself, in the intervals of military training, to read a number of books of a theological character with the intention of seeing how much of them I could grasp in terms of the evolutionary-naturalistic scheme at which I was then arriving. A great many of them have completely faded out of my recollection; but I well remember reading the essay by Gore in *Lux Mundi* under canvas while stationed near Canterbury, and being at the same time both fascinated by the delicacy and beauty of character which it (and other essays in the same volume) revealed, and repelled by what to me was the sheer intellectual perversity of its attitude and that of the book in general.

Another incident of the same year remains vividly with me. We were doing night exercises between Aldershot and Fleet: the warm June night was scented with broom: the monotony of exercise, enforced silence, and darkness, combined with the beauty of the hour, impelled to aimless meditation.

Suddenly, for no particular reason, without apparent connection with other thoughts, a problem and its solution flashed across my mind. I had understood how it was that two views or courses of action could not only both be sincerely held as good, but both actually could *be* good—and when the two came into contact, the one could both appear and be evil. It can be so when both are aiming in the same general direction, but the one is moving so much more slowly that it becomes a drag on the other's wheel.

Ideas and facts, particular examples and their general meaning, the tragedy of bitter conflict between two fine realities, two solid honesties, all jostled each other in my mind in that moment of insight, and I had made a new step towards that peaceful basis for action which is expressed by the French proverb, 'Tout comprendre, c'est tout pardonner'.

It also had that definite quality of being thrown into consciousness, implied in the term revelation, which has been described for purely intellectual discovery by many mathematicians and men of science, notably Poincaré in his essays on scientific method. It was an exaggeration of the sense that comes when one suddenly sees a point which had eluded comprehension, but without any accompanying sense of effort. The same general sense in the sphere of feeling one may have when one is suddenly transported to a complete peace and satisfaction by some sudden view of distant hills over plain; or by a sudden quality of light—'the light that never was on sea or land', and yet is suddenly here, transforming a familiar landscape; or by a poem or a picture, or a face. But only once before had I had such a complete sense of outside givenness in an experience—the only occasion on which I had had a vision (of a non-hallucinatory but amazingly real sort: such, of a religious cast, abound in the records of mystics such as St Theresa). This of mine had no connection with morals or religion; it was a seeing with the mind, a seeing of a great slice of this earth and its beauties, all compressed into an almost instantaneous experience. Mozart describes something of the same sort with music, when, after finishing the composition of a symphony, he would experience an intense pleasure, the intensest which he knew, in an interior 'hearing' of the whole work almost simultaneously.

How, precisely, these experiences are generated, psychology and nerve-physiology must learn and tell us. I can vouch for the fact that the experience is felt as intensely real and intensely valuable. It is, I suppose, a realisation, by means of the intuitive faculty, of a great deal which the conscious mind has been striving towards but has never yet held all at one time, an indivisible whole, in its grasp.

Those two experiences, in two different fields of the mind, made me realise, perhaps incompletely, the quality of mystic vision, whether artistic or religious; they drove me to read a good deal on mysticism and the descriptions given by visionaries of their own experience; and made me realise how stupid it was to dismiss all such happenings with the word 'pathological'.[4]

Clearly experiences of this general nature may be pathological from the start, or may be over-emphasised and exaggerated into morbidity; but so long as they are beautiful and satisfying in themselves, lead to a strengthening instead of a weakening of the self, are not pursued so that they lead to neglect of other things, and leave no harmful after-effects, it is a mere misuse of words to call them pathological. They are exceptional rather, experiences difficult of attainment but to be desired, only to be attained by a mixture of fortunate endowment and previous discipline of the spirit.

They and my reading also convince me, however, that the revelation of the mystic vision, about which so much is written, is revelation only in a psychological sense, not literally. There need be no supernatural being or force making the revelation; nor is the revelation one of an external reality. The desires and aspirations of the mind conspire with its organising faculties (which we all know well enough in dreams) to organise vital experience on a new level, above that of the ordinary self, above that of all merely discursive activity, in which new intensity is gained through so much more than usual being seen and felt together in a single organised moment of spiritual perception. To me the statement that moral revelations or mystic visions are the result of communication by personal supernatural beings is merely one way, and an erroneous way, of interpreting the undoubted facts.

---

[4] For a record of the experiences of mystics in all parts of the world, with a penetrating commentary, see Aldous Huxley, *The Perennial Philosophy*, Harper, New York, 1945.

Most of the war passed in occupations very alien to such experiences and reasonings. After the war came the need to buckle to and refurbish the very rusty equipment of my peacetime profession. It was now, with the young Faust-spirit satiated, the spirit which demands experience for experience' sake, that I arrived (half unconsciously and under the pressure of professional circumstances) at the 'gospel of work', of which I have already spoken, as the only satisfactory practical basis for an active middle life; and I threw myself with all the energy I possessed into my own subject. Two or three years later circumstances decreed that I should take up once more the still-tangled threads of my thoughts on religion, and try to clarify them. I was asked by friends whose judgment I trusted, to write a paper on *Science and Religion* for delivery at a summer school at Woodbrooke. After some hesitation (since no one knew better than myself what an amount of clarification there still remained to be done in my mind) I consented. The effect, for myself at any rate, was another justification of the gospel of work. I was, through having undertaken the task, forced to hammer at my difficulties, to think out conclusions, to find where loose threads would connect, to examine what I really did mean by this or that casually-used term. The final result was an essay which appeared in my *Essays of a Biologist,* published in 1923.

The two main conclusions to which I found myself logically driven from my premises were concerned with the definition of religion and the definition of God. Religion, after trying to see as best I could what various religions and religious people had in common, I felt impelled to define as the reaction of the personality as a whole to its experience of the Universe as a whole. Dean Inge, in a review of my book, quoted this definition of religion as one of the best he had come across. In spite of this approval, however, and in spite of the sense of advance in comprehension which this way of looking at the matter gave me at the time, I now realise clearly that it was both incomplete, and also too vague and general.

Somewhat similar objections I now see to my definition of God. There are three recognised ways of approach towards intellectual comprehension and definition of the term God. One may simply point to the so-called revelation of Scripture. Since this to me and to most educated men and women to-day is simply an appeal to mythology, I did not concern myself with it. Or one may attempt the philosophical approach, the definition by metaphysics. Here, by close process of abstract reasoning, the philosopher attempts to see what Absolute, or First Cause, or Final Principle, is in his opinion necessary to ensure the coherence or the reasonableness of the universe, and this he (or, sometimes, others for him) calls God. One of the notable attempts in this field is that of Professor White-head, who, after a brilliant opening on psychological aspects of religion and the religious life, suddenly takes wing for the realms of metaphysics, and concludes that God is the prin-ciple of rationality which prevents the world from being chaotic and unreasonable. I quote his own words (p. 90) : 'The actual but non-temporal entity whereby the indetermination of mere creativity is transmuted into a determinate freedom. This non-temporal actual Entity is what men call God—the supreme God of rationalised religion'; or again (*Science and the Modern World*, p. 250), 'We require God as the Principle of Concretion,' and (p. 257) 'the nature of God is the ground of rationality.'

My objection to this, as to all the metaphysical approaches to Deity which have ever been made, is that the God which they claim to reveal (I say *which*, not *whom*, for it is always immensely impersonal) has no relation, so far as can be observed, with the various gods or aspects of God which humanity in its thousands of millions has actually wor-shipped. This of course does not say that the metaphysical God may not be the true one; or may even be both true and in reality identical with the God of the common men's reli-gion. But in the first case it would be much better to call it by another name; and in the second, there would still remain such a huge unbridged gap between the two aspects of the one truth that the problem can scarcely be regarded as much nearer solution than before.

The third method of approach is the humbler, simpler, but perhaps surer method, already adopted in other fields with considerable success, which we call the method of Natural Science, and it was to this that I pinned my faith. This of course consists in the refusal to accept authority as such, in an insistence upon the study of facts, and upon inductive reasoning from the facts as its main method, and therefore in a rejection of all purely *a priori* schemes or those which start with deduction before they are ready with an inductive basis. In our particular example, the method of science is to look round and find what are the types of gods which actually are being or have been worshipped (or, if you prefer it, what various ideas of God human beings have held); to classify and compare these gods and these ideas; to analyse them in terms of all available kinds of knowledge—knowledge of sociology, of history, of psychology, of the non-human sciences; and, as a result of all this collection, classification, comparison, and analysis to try and understand, not what man *ought* to have worshipped and felt in worshipping, but what it is which man *has* actually experienced in his religious moments, and what he *has* actually worshipped.

I had already in 1923 come to see to my own satisfaction that, if we proceed in this way, it becomes pretty clear that man has actually worshipped certain aspects of the powers which he sees and feels operating in and through outer nature and his own life. Some of those powers turn out to be the blind forces of nature; others the ideals and emotions of his own soul; others are the half-mechanical, half-personal forces of society. Whatever their nature, they bear singularly little obvious relation to the Absolute of the philosophers.

These powers, however, almost without exception, man has chosen to personify as supernatural beings. We are used to discounting the river-gods and dryads of the Greeks as poetical fancies, and even the chief figures in the classical Pantheon—Venus, Minerva, Mars, and the rest—as allegories. But, forgetting that they once carried as much sanctity as our saints and divinities, we refrain from applying the same reasoning to our own objects of worship. It was precisely this step, of stripping divinity (whether a mere *genius loci* or the single beings of monotheist religions) of the personality which man had projected upon it from himself, which I found myself forced to attempt as a logical conclusion from my premises. Once more, the sense of relief in having attained another step in comprehension, and in bringing together whole realms of fact, all equally real, which had hitherto seemed poles apart, was so great that I neglected to observe incompletenesses in my view.

I suppose that these incompletenesses were dimly realised; but it was not until I had been asked to write this present book, and had begun drafting it, that I discovered how great they were. I found myself again in the state, familiar to all who are searching for a comprehension which they know is possible but which eludes them, of feeling plunged into a hole in one's subject, and there being swirled round and round in a whirlpool of thought without being able to catch on to the one and only possible landing-stage, which one knows is there, but cannot discern.

A chance reference in an article by that fine character and teacher, Estlin Carpenter, put me on the track. I had been too general, too much preoccupied only with theology and reason; and had neglected the specific psychological basis of religion. That is to be found in the sense of holiness or sacredness. From this as starting-point all religion takes its flight, and only gradually (though inevitably) do the moral and the intellectual become attached to it and fight their battle for completeness and unity.

This conception (doubtless it is also incomplete, but definitely giving me the sense of a real further advance in comprehension), together with some of the evidence leading up to it and the conclusions to which it points, I have set forth as best I could in other parts of this book. For intruding this personal chapter, now that it is written and I read it over, I make no apology. Pure generalities in any subject often slip off the mind like water off a duck's back; and if my primary object has been to assert my right to meddle in these high matters, as one who has suffered from their compulsive force, and has for many years been drawn to resolve their problems in his mind, I have in attempting this been able to make the presentation of some of my general thesis easier, by linking abstract and general ideas on to concrete happenings of a particular mental life, and so, I hope, made them seem less remote, more actual, than might otherwise have been the case.

Our age is retrospective. It builds the sepulchres of the fathers. . . . Why should not we also enjoy an original relation to the universe? Why should not we have a poetry and philosophy of insight and not of tradition, and a religion by revelation to us, and not the history of theirs? . . . The sun shines to-day also. There is more wool and flax in the fields. Let us demand our own works, and laws, and worship.
—RALPH WALDO EMERSON, *Essays.*

Whatever the world thinks, he who hath not much meditated upon God, the human mind, and the *summum bonum,* may possibly make a thriving earthworm, but will most indubitably make a sorry patriot and a sorry statesman.—Bishop BERKELEY, *Siris.*

Incomprehensible? But because you cannot understand a thing, it does not cease to exist.—PASCAL, *Pensées.*

When we review the various forms in which men think of divinity and express their reverence, we involuntarily ask, 'Which of these is better, and which worse?' . . . An effort should be made, perhaps, not so much to give a definite and direct answer to the question, as to offer some of the standards for judging rival forms of religion. . . . First would come this, that *the pure and continued expression of any single religious motive is undesirable.* For, indeed, religious motives, like muscles, work best in opposition. . . . Yet such a thought should be supplemented at once, inasmuch as while retaining each and both of two opposing motives, *one motive may well be dominant.* . . . The supreme virtue of thought, however, is not its balance and vigour and richness, but its veracity. Accordingly a third rule to guide our judgment may be that *the assertions of religion, as to what is real, should be true.* And this at once brings us to a distant region where we are met by Pilate's question; and also by the thought that it is not the office of religion to *know,* but only to be loyal, that if there be avenues to truth, they lie not in religion, but in science and philosophy.
—G. M. STRATTON, *Psychology of the Religious Life.*

Common sense and a respect for realities are not less graces of the spirit than moral zeal. . . .
. . . They [the Nonconformist Churches] saw the world of business and society as a battlefield, across which character could march triumphant to its goal, not as crude materials waiting the architect's hand to set them in their place as the foundations of the Kingdom of Heaven. It did not occur to them that character is social, and society, since it is the expression of character, spiritual. Thus the eye is sometimes blinded by light itself.—R. H. TAWNEY, *Religion and the Rise of Capitalism* (1926).

Like the celestial order, of which it is the dim reflection, society is stable, because it is straining up.—R. H. TAWNEY (on the mediæval religious view), *Ibid.*

In so far as it knows the eternity of truth and is absorbed in it, the mind *lives* in that eternity. In caring only for the eternal, it has ceased to care for that part of itself which can die.—GEORGE SANTAYANA, *The Ethics of Spinoza.*

5

Some Fundamentals

It is my next task to attempt some account of the realities on which religion is based. Obviously, this task is much the most difficult which I shall have to undertake. Theologians and mystics alike, the one group approaching religious reality from the side of intellect, the other from that of intuition and emotion, agree in finding this reality, in the last resort ineffable, not to be fully described in words, not to be completely apprehended by the human mind. In passing, let it be noted that this holds good also for other realities than the religious. Even the great poet can only adumbrate his experience in words; and the experience of falling in love should be enough to convince the intellectualist sceptic of the incommunicability and limitlessness of some very real and very common experiences.

But, however difficult, the task must be undertaken. It can only be even approximately successful if reader co-operates with writer by the goodwill of sympathetic imagination. No work of art can be appreciated unless the imagination, even grudgingly, goes out to it; this is all the more so if the poem or picture be difficult, or deal with unfamiliar things, or with familiar things in unfamiliar ways. When we first travel abroad, the chief feelings are almost invariably those of amusement and disdain, not infrequently mixed with unreasoning hostility, towards human beings who conduct the business of life in ways so different from those to which we are accustomed. These feelings can be broken down slowly by time and use, or quickly by the sympathetic imagination; and then, though we may still sometimes smile, we no longer are disdainful or hostile without cause. So here I must demand the same co-operation, however unfamiliar or unattractive my way of approach or my conclusions may seem, and ask that my readers take for granted my sincerity, my desire to reach beyond the appearances of the surface to realities below, and an absence of any wish to make debating points or to score a barren victory of mere argument.

It is often stated that the essential of religion is belief in God, meaning by that in a personal or superpersonal Divine being, or at least a belief in supernatural beings of some kind. This, however, is manifestly not true. There are whole religions which make no mention of God. The most notable example, as already mentioned, is that of Buddhism. Not only that, but even in countries where a theistic religion is current, and even among the most devoted adherents of such religions, there exist, normally and regularly, acts and thoughts and experiences which most certainly must be called religious, but which equally certainly do not of themselves demand explanation in terms of God. However, owing to the fact that the idea of a divine being has already, and on other grounds, come to occupy a foremost place in the religion, these experiences and acts do, as a matter of fact, come to be interpreted in terms of the current theology, although they could with equal or greater propriety be described in pure psychological terms, as involving the feeling of holiness, no less and no more.

This indeed is and has always been one of the two besetting vices of religious systems, to over-exalt the purely rational and therefore communicable elements of religion at the expense of the non-rational but deeper intuitions and felt experiences which are unique and personal, difficult or impossible of easy communication to others, and yet the true material of religion. It has led to the setting-up of creeds and dogmas as the supreme standard in religion, and to the belief that salvation may be assured by adherence to an intellectual statement of belief.

Two simple examples may be given of the way in which current intellectual explanations, which were later abandoned by general consent (at least among educated men), have influenced the interpretation of perfectly definite facts. In the time of Jesus, and for many centuries afterwards, certain mental disorders were ascribed to possession by supernatural beings, regarded as demons or evil spirits. We can now say with perfect confidence that this was perhaps a natural explanation, but certainly an erroneous one. Or again, it is almost universally found that savage peoples and those in the early stages of civilisation ascribe natural events, and in particular great catastrophes, such as earthquakes, floods, droughts, storms, or eruptions, to the direct activity of supernatural beings, and that much of their religious practice is therefore concerned with propitiation of these beings by sacrifice, offerings, worship, or prayer, so that they may not allow catastrophes to occur. The old view still lingers in such observances as prayers for rain in a season of drought, and is of course widespread in backward countries—an earthquake shock will bring half the population of Naples down on their knees, and even in the last great eruption of Vesuvius, religious processions headed by priests with relics and sacred emblems marched as near as they dared to the advancing lava-flows in the futile attempt to make them change their course. But any moderately educated person now knows perfectly well that catastrophes differ in no essential way from the humblest and most ordinary natural events, and that both alike proceed according to the routine of natural laws: over these natural processes prayers and sacrifices will have no effect, though patience in the acquisition of knowledge and effort in its application may enable us to control or palliate them.

I propose therefore to leave the idea of god on one side for the present, as an interpretation or explanation by theology of certain ultimate and irreducible facts which we may call the facts of religious experience. Let it not be forgotten that our knowledge of the thoughts and inner nature of other men and women, even of those who are nearest to us, is indirect, an interpretation or explanation of their actions, of their expression, of the arbitrary symbols called words which they employ. We know directly no human consciousness save our own.[1] Thus if, in common with liberal thinkers within the churches, we reject the idea of direct revelation as merely the crude symbolism of an earlier age, our simplest and most direct idea or experience of god will also involve an interpretation, and a very much more difficult and indirect one than that by which we recognise the existence of minds in our fellow-men. It will be an interpretation of facts of outer nature and of the human spirit and its experiences.

We now approach the crux of the matter, namely, the

[1] The only possible way in which direct experience of another's consciousness could occur would be by means of telepathy, should this be proved to exist. Those who assert that we can have a direct intuition of others' personality, apparently not by means of telepathy (e. g., Baron von Hügel), are simply misusing the term and mistaking the faculty of intuition, which is a marvellously speedy and unitary interpretation, for a non-interpretative faculty, mysterious in its nature, of direct knowledge.

question of the reality at the basis of religion. In attacking this question, it will be of service to pass in review a few definitions of religion.

There have been many attempts to define religion; and the number of definitions produced is almost as great as the number of men who have attempted definition. What is more, many of the definitions are mutually contradictory, and many seem to have no common ground at all with others.

Matthew Arnold defined religion as 'morality tinged with emotion.' Salomon Reinach, that learned and sceptical French Jew, calls it 'a body of scruples which impede the free exercise of our faculties.' Professor E. B. Tylor proposes 'the belief in spiritual beings' as a minimum definition of religion. Max Müller, on the other hand, preferred to say that 'Religion consists in the perception of the infinite under such manifestations as are able to influence the moral character of man'. Sir James Frazer, who, next to Freud, has done more than any man since Darwin to change the thought of the world, seeks his definition along wholly different lines. He says that religion is 'a propitiation or conciliation of powers [which he elsewhere defines as "conscious or personal agents"] superior to man which are believed to direct and control the course of nature and of human life'. Jevons in his *Idea of God* says 'the many different forms of religion are all attempts to give expression to the idea of God'. It should be noted, however, that Jevons is willing to extend the idea of god to cover the numerous spirits of the animistic stage of religion, and even fetishes.

Professor Whitehead, who embodied in his one person the rare combination of philosopher, man of science, man of letters, and mathematician, has given us (in spite of great obscurity in his main construction and in his philosophic approach to theology) some illuminating phrases on religion. As a preliminary to definition, he contrasts human activities such as arithmetic with religion. 'You *use* arithmetic, but you *are* religious.' He then goes on to say that 'Religion is force of belief cleansing the inward parts. . . . A religion, on its doctrinal sides, can thus be described as a system of general truths which have the effect of transforming character when they are sincerely held and vividly apprehended.'

In passing, I should like to point out that Whitehead is here making the common mistake of employing for religion in general a definition which can really only be applied (but there with some force) to developed religion. He is substituting

his ideal of religion for the actuality, which often not merely
falls far short of the ideal, but is of quite another nature.
He later says 'Religion is what the individual does with his
own solitariness,' in this again neglecting the highly social
nature of almost all religions.

Two further sayings deserve quotation. 'Religion is the art
and theory of the internal life of man, so far as it depends on
the man himself, and on what is permanent in the nature of
things.' This again is beautiful and true, but only if applied
to developed religions, and to their best side to boot.

Later he says that religion 'runs through three stages, if it
evolves to its final satisfaction. It is the transition from God
the Void to God the Enemy, and from God the Enemy to
God the Companion.' This is pregnant with meaning, both
for the student of comparative religion and for the man
desirous of developing his inner religious life.

Stratton, in his very suggestive and broad-minded book,
The Psychology of the Religious Life, gives three tentative
definitions: 'One might say that religion is the appreciation
of an unseen world, usually an unseen company; . . . or perhaps it might better be described as man's whole bearing
towards what seems to him the Best, or Greatest—where
"best" is used in a sense neither in nor out of morality, and
"greatest" is confined to no particular region'. Finally, he says
that religion is 'the effort to maintain communion, not with
the infinite, but with that which possesses supreme worth—
which is perhaps but a deeper kind of infinitude'.

All these appear to me to suffer from the same fault as
those from Whitehead and many others, of being applicable
only to ideal or, at best, to developed religions.

St James wrote: 'Pure religion and undefiled before God is
this, to visit the fatherless and widows in their affliction, and
to keep himself unspotted from the world'. This of course
does not claim to be a general definition of religion; but even
as a definition of the ideal in religion it is incomplete, in that
it fails to include many aspects of the religious life.

T. H. Huxley, after speaking of 'the engagement of the
affections in favour of that particular kind of conduct which
we call good', continues, 'I cannot but think that it, together
with the awe and reverence, which have no kinship with base
fear, but arise whenever one tries to pierce below the surface
of things, whether they be material or spiritual, constitutes
all that has any unchangeable reality in religion'. This by

its form does not claim to be a general definition: but it is interesting as one of the earlier attempts at a psychological interpretation.

Donald Hankey is stated to have defined religion as 'betting your life there is a God'. Professor Wallace, in less trenchant language, but perhaps with a not dissimilar real meaning behind his words, wrote that religion is 'a belief in an ultimate meaning of the universe'. Lord Chesterfield's dictum, that religion was 'a collateral security for virtue,' can hardly aspire to be considered a definition, but well illustrates the utilitarian statesman's view of orthodox religion's social function. E. S. P. Haynes, in his book *Religious Persecution*, talks of a religious creed as 'a theory of man's relation to the universe,' which is an excellent definition on the purely intellectual side. John Morley's definition, which applies rather to developed religion than to religion in general, was 'our feeling about the highest forces that govern human destiny' (*Rousseau*, p. 278). James Martineau, in spite of this unorthodoxy, had not emancipated himself from the theistic views which surrounded him. He wrote (*A Study of Religion*, p. 1) that religion is 'the belief in an everlasting God, that is, in a Divine Mind and Will ruling the Universe and holding moral relations with mankind'. Professor McTaggart, that eminent philosopher, was more cautious. In *Some Dogmas of Religion,* he says 'Religion is clearly a state of mind. . . . It may best be described as an emotion resting on a conviction of harmony between ourselves and the universe at large'.

These examples could be multiplied: but they will have served to show what diversity of thought exists on the subject. All the definitions so far given are incomplete, emphasising one aspect of religion to the exclusion of others. But the essential religious reality, the experience which seeks to embody itself in symbols and to find intellectual expression in theologies—what is it? Is it not the sense of sacredness? And is not this sense of sacredness, like the feeling of hunger or the emotion of anger or the passion of love, something irreducible, itself and nothing else, only to be communicated by words to others who have the same capacity, just as the sensation of colour is incommunicable to a blind man? [2]

As Estlin Carpenter says: 'An encyclopædic account, however, should rest rather on an exterior definition which can serve as it were to pigeon-hole the whole mass of significant

---

[2] In modern psychological parlance, this 'sense' or 'feeling' should be called a *sentiment*.

facts. Such an exterior definition is suggested by M. E. Crawley in *The Tree of Life,* where he points out that neither the Greek nor the Latin language has any comprehensive term for religion, except in the one ἱερά, and in the other *sacra,* words which are equivalent to "sacred things" '; and he concludes, 'we may define, then, the religious object as the sacred'.

This central, psychological definition has been adopted, with various modifications, by a number of writers, such as the Swedish Archbishop Söderblom and the American anthropologist Lowie, by Dr R. R. Marett, and Dr Rudolf Otto. I can best amplify the conception by quoting from these last two authors.

Dr Marett, surveying the religions of primitive peoples with the dispassionate gaze of an anthropologist, writes as follows: 'We must admit that in response to, or at any rate in connection with, the emotions of Awe, Wonder, and the like, wherein feeling would seem for the time being to have outstripped the power of "natural," that is reasonable, explanation, there arises in the region of human thought a powerful impulse to objectify and even personify the mysterious or "supernatural" something felt, and in the region of will a corresponding impulse to render it innocuous, or better still propitious, by force of constraint, communion, or conciliation'. Or again, speaking of variations in certain primitive forms of the worship of sacred stones, 'underlying all these fluctuating interpretations of thought there may be discerned a single universal feeling, namely, the sense of an Awfulness in them [the objects of worship] intimately affecting man and demanding of him the fruits of Awe, namely, respect, veneration, propitiation, service'.

Dr Otto, a well-known German Protestant theologian, wrote *The Idea of the Holy,* which was acknowledged in theological circles to be of first-rate importance. He finds in the direct experience of the holy in events, persons, things and thoughts, not only the origin of religious feeling and beliefs in the past of primitive tribes, but the kernel of all that is of value in modern Christianity, as elsewhere in the religious life. He points out with some emphasis, not only that sacredness is in its origin quite remote from any moral associations or intellectual interpretations, but that even in developed religions, like Christianity, in which morality and intellect have come into close connection with religious feeling, the experience of sacredness is something *sui generis,* a direct experience like that of beauty or logical correctness, and that to substitute for it a rational moral feeling or an intellectual theological comprehension is to rob religious experience of its central core and the well-spring of its feeling.

Speaking of this feeling in a developed religious consciousness, he writes: 'Let us consider the deepest and most fundamental element in all strong and sincerely felt religious emotion. Faith unto Salvation, Trust, Love—all these are there. But over and above these is an element which may also on occasion, quite apart from them, profoundly affect us and occupy the mind with a well-nigh bewildering strength. Let us follow it up with every effort of sympathy and imaginative intuition wherever it is to be found, in the lives of those around us, in sudden, strong ebullitions of personal piety, . . . in the fixed and ordered solemnities of rites and liturgies, and again in the atmosphere that clings to old religious monuments and buildings, to temples and to churches. If we do so we shall find we are dealing with something for which there is only one appropriate expression, *mysterium tremendum*. The feeling of it may at times come sweeping like a gentle tide, pervading the mind with a tranquil mood of deepest worship. It may pass over into a more set and lasting attitude of the soul, . . . until at last it dies away and the soul resumes its "profane," non-religious mood of everyday experience. It may burst in sudden eruption up from the depths of the soul with spasms and convulsions, or lead to the strangest excitements, to intoxicated frenzy, to transport, and to ecstasy. It has its wild and demoniac forms and can sink to an almost grisly horror and shuddering. It has its crude, barbaric antecedents and early manifestations, and again it may be developed into something beautiful, pure, and glorious. It may become the hushed, trembling, and speechless humility of the creature in the presence of—whom or what?—in the presence of that which is a *Mystery* inexpressible and above all creatures'. I have quoted from Otto at some length, because both the non-rational fact of religious experience and its psychological basis are so clearly put by him.

The power which religious feeling has to transform life is also vividly stated (though not perhaps so vividly as by Victor Hugo when, in *Les Misérables*, he wrote of the old housekeeper Mme Baptistine, 'Nature had created her merely a sheep; religion had transformed her to an angel').

Sir Francis Younghusband's remark in his *Light of Experience*, apropos of the lasting effects of even a transitory religious exaltation, is also worth quoting here:—'In the same way, a man cannot always be "in love"; but life is a different thing for him after having been in love once'.

Apropos of primitive religions Otto says of this feeling: 'It first begins to stir in the feeling of "something uncanny," "eerie," or "weird". It is this feeling which, emerging in the mind of primitive man, forms the starting-point for the entire development of religion in history. "Daemons" and "Gods" alike spring from this root, and all the products of "mythological fantasy" are nothing but different modes in which it has been objectified, and all ostensible explanations of the origin of religion in terms of animism or magic or folk psychology are doomed from the outset to wander astray and miss the real goal of their inquiry, unless they recognise this fact of our nature—primary, unique, underivable from anything else—to be the basic factor and the basic impulse underlying the entire process of religious evolution'.

But this feeling, and the supernatural power which is assumed to explain it, are not necessarily good. The actual feeling, the 'religious thrill,' to borrow Lowie's phrase, is morally quite neutral, and, as Otto points out, may be debased or refined, experienced in relation to things in themselves either evil or good. And the supernatural power assumed to reside in objects thus felt sacred, the 'theoplasm' of which gods are later made, is supposed to manifest itself for evil as well as for good ends, to be utilisable for black magic as well as for promoting fertility, to cause plagues and catastrophes as well as human blessings, to be the wrath of god as well as his love.

For this reason, Marett prefers not to call what is experienced 'the sacred' or 'the holy,' since these to us almost invariably connote only goodness, but to borrow the Polynesian word Mana, which is actually employed to-day to denote the mysterious power assumed to be resident in all objects, good or evil, desirable or to be shunned, which arouse this awe-ful sense. In the same way, Otto feels constrained to coin a word for the experience of sacredness, and uses numinous, from the Latin numen, a divinity to be worshipped.[3] It is not without significance that these similar results should have been reached by two very different minds, approaching the subject by wholly different routes. Marett is an anthropologist, trying to make sense of the accounts given by travellers,

[3] Such an acute writer as R. W. Hepburn, in his Christianity and Paradox (Watts & Co., London, 1957), agrees in regarding the numinous as the irreducible hard core of religious experience.

missionaries, and men of science, of the tangled workings of the primitive mind. Otto is a Protestant divine, attempting to make the theology of Christianity fuller and more accurate. The one is making an external approach to primitive religion, the other is dealing with the highest organised religion, and from within. And yet both alike come to the conclusion that there is an ultimate category of religious experience, which is defined by this sense of mystery and awe. The one important difference between them is that Otto goes the farther of the two. He not only points out that the numinous may be felt in evil as well as good things, but that *normally*, whether in evil or good things or in neutral, the feeling involves both attraction and aversion, both fascination and fear.

One thing is clear from my list of definitions, that feeling and action and belief, all three, must be, or at least usually are, involved in religion. Even Reinach's cynical phrase, negative though it be, implies feelings capable of important influence upon action. But without the aid of the psychological key provided by the definitions of Crawley, Marett, and Otto, it would be extremely difficult to see how these three components—emotional, practical, and intellectual—were fitted together in religion, and what common component of all religions there might be to which the term religious could be applied. What makes religious emotion religious and not merely æsthetic? What makes us say that one motive or reaction is religious, another moral? What is it that brings one piece of ceremonial or ritual within the pale of religion and leaves another outside? Why is it that we call one belief scientific and another religious?

We may put it in this way. The normal man has an innate capacity for experiencing sanctity in certain events, just as (on a lower and more determinate plane) he has for experiencing red or blue, fear or disgust or desire, or as he has for experiencing beauty, or the validity of logical proof, or for feeling love or hate, or judging good and evil. Some have this in an overmastering degree, and will be haunted all their days by their experiences of holiness and the felt need of conforming their life to them. The majority, on the other hand, have it much less intensely. They will, in their degree, understand holiness when it is pointed out to them, but be incapable of the pioneering discoveries or the power of expression of the exceptional few. These few are like the few creators in the world of poetry or music, the rest are like those who can and do respond to the creation of the poets and musicians and value it, while themselves remaining dumb. Finally, there are undoubtedly some who, either congenitally or through their upbringing, are wholly unable to appreciate what is meant by the sacred or the holy, just as there are a few men who are incapable of appreciating music, a few who are born with defect of the retina leading to colour-blindness, a few who are born imbecile, unable to follow a logical chain of reasoning, a few born moral imbeciles, incapable of appreciating what is meant by right or wrong, and many more in whom upbringing or their own mode of life has deadened or wholly distorted this moral sense.

Not only does the normal man have this capacity for experiencing the sense of the sacred, but he demands its satisfaction. This may come through the services of an organised Church, as is shown by the Russian peasants who in many places insisted on building new churches in place of those that official Bolshevism had destroyed or turned to other uses; or through artistic expression; or through a religiously-felt morality, the necessity of which to some minds has been so finely put in *Romola* by George Eliot that I cannot forbear from quoting: 'The highest sort of happiness often brings so much pain with it, that we can only tell it from pain by its being what we would choose before everything else, because our souls see it is good'.

I use the term 'sense of the sacred' or 'sense of the holy' for want of a better. Had it not been overlain by all sorts of alien and irrelevant ideas, *religious sense* or *sentiment* would have been preferable.

Thus the powers that are behind nature; the mysteries that confront the inquiring mind; the great moments of man, his birth, his marriage, and his death; the revelations of art and knowledge; the moral ideal and the practice of good—all these and many others may be objects of religion, but are not so of necessity. They only come within the ambit of religion in so far as they are touched with sanctity by the mind, in so far as they are thought of and felt as sacred.

So we may have holy joy and sacred sorrow; sanctified revenge, religious war; sacred rite and sacred art; morality tinged, not simply with emotion, but with this one particular emotion or sentiment of sanctity; intellectual arts which, because fused with a feeling of awe, are religious. Any and every activity of man, whether cruelty or kindness, love or hate, bigotry or enlightenment, bestial rite or most lovely expression of thought, may be experienced as sacred, tinged with this quality of the holy, and so become and be religious.

The sense of the holy is a highly complex frame of mind. One of its chief psychological accompaniments is awe, which is itself complex, with fear, wonder, and admiration all entering into it as ingredients. Reverence, into which there also enters submissiveness as an element, is a frequent if by no means invariable accompaniment. But mystery may probably be regarded as its real essence, with awe as necessary, and reverence as common, ingredient. The mystery may be merely the vulgar mystery of the unusual or strange. The mysteriousness of this may be wholly removed by education and knowledge. But, be it noted, comprehension, in the ordinary sense of understanding the past casual sequence by which such and such an event or organism came into existence, or of analysis of event or organism into its component parts, with an understanding of how they work—this does not by any means necessarily rob the being or thing considered of mystery; but now it is a mystery which no longer appeals to the untrained but only to the educated sense. Precisely the same thing, of course, is to be seen with art. Many birds and animals are attracted by bright colours; so are savages and children, who also love the bizarre and the crude, indulging their fancy without reference to any consciously or unconsciously held body of principles. With the maturing of the mind, however, taste changes. It finds raw or trivial what delighted it before; but, though it may despise that by which it was once captured, it finds new beauties to love, and, what is more, still loves them by means of the same faculty—only new-disciplined, matured and entered into relations with reason, experience, and other emotions—which in childhood loved a bright patchwork of colours or in adolescence the most sentimental of pictures.

Another characteristic of the sense of mystery in the disciplined mind is that it tends to find its objects more and more in the familiar, less in the merely unusual. This, too, has its parallel in art. It is only a temporary and uncompleted phase of art which gives us programme-music, subject-pictures, the purely narrative poem or story, the building which is striking at all costs. The great artist can make a kitchen table contain more beauty and meaning than a second-rate hand can infuse into a picture of the greatest event in history;

and the finest works of art deal often with the simplest and
most familiar human verities.

So with religion. The gaping spirit which needs to be stimulated by extravagance, miracle, or catastrophe, gives place
to the insight which finds in the commonest facts materials
for reverence, wonder, or love. As Wordsworth put it, describing his wife and his love for her:

> She was a phantom of delight
> When first she gleam'd upon my sight.

Later, with full knowledge,

> And now I see with eye serene,
> The very pulse of the machine. . . .
> . . . and yet a Spirit still, and bright
> With something of angelic light.

When the fact of existence has become itself a wonder,
there is no room for miracle in the vulgar sense.

There is still another point in which religion resembles art:
good intentions are not enough. A man with a good natural taste, or with one that has been well trained and
disciplined, will find certain attempts at artistic expression
definitely *wrong;* they are to him not merely crude or immature or incomplete—those qualities can be readily for-
given—but they arouse in him a definite feeling of hostility
or distaste owing to their stressing the lower at the expense
of the higher, or distorting the whole scheme of values so as
to become, to him, without value or even with a negative
value. When sickly sentiment takes the place of genuine feeling, when vulgarity takes the place of humour, when unreal
motives are exalted at the expense of the strong reality of
every day—then the result is intolerable to the man who
knows better, in the same sort of way as it is intolerable to
hear or see something which to us is supremely valuable
greeted with a snigger or a leer.

Similarly, there are whole religions, as well as the religious views of many individual persons, to which the man
who is acute or sensitive in his religious perceptions and
emotions reacts simply by a feeling of repulsion, so incongru-
ous or so pretentious do they appear.

Precisely the same is true of their moral aspect; and no

amount of sincerity can condone, to those who have higher standards, the sanctification of evil through religion. For one or other of these reasons, many religions and religious actions are bound to seem repulsive or wicked to the developed religious consciousness. Nothing can make the religious sacrifice of human beings by the Aztecs seem anything but evil to us. We are filled with horror when we find that they took pleasure in representing, in their sacred art, the victim biting clean through his tongue in the moment of agony, presumably since the greater the pain of the victim the more would the God appreciate the sacrifice. On the other side, those who feel anything of the austerity of religion cannot but look with active distaste at the deliberate cultivation, by certain representatives of certain Christian bodies, of a religiosity of sentiment, especially among emotional women, which takes the undisciplined overflow of adolescence and sexual feeling, directs it on to religious objects, and in so doing not only encourages morbidity but degrades the objects of worship themselves.

*

The chief ways in which religion has been moulded seem to be somewhat as follows.

In the first place, man demands some sort of explanation of the world and of his place in it. He dislikes to leave a mystery completely unexplained, though he prefers leaving it with some mysteriousness, and not wholly explained in a banal way. His attempts at explanation of facts which give rise to religious feeling are mythology or theology. First of all, these atttempts are either crude rationalisations or else myths—in other words, they are attempts to provide rational support for a desire without having real evidence or reasons at hand. In the case of myths, the desire is primarily the desire for explanation itself: to this there may also be added desire to explain in terms which gratify other desires, such as that for immortality. Logic and experience both then set to work on these 'explanations', and proceed to improve them. Logic improves by attempting to make them more complete, by trying to remove inherent contradictions; experience tries to mould the explanations into greater conformity with observed facts.

It is true that in origin religion has nothing whatever to do with belief in a God or gods, or with abstract good as against abstract evil, or with the salvation of souls, or with obedience to this or that revelation. These are all later growths, more elaborate dwellings for the religious spirit. But it is equally true that, inevitably and universally as man's accumulated experience grows and his logic comes into play, he will find certain things and ideas to which this quality of sacredness seems of necessity to adhere.

The sense of the sacred is only the root of the matter. Religion as it is developed—perhaps even from the first—has involved intellect and morals and ritual as well as feeling. Further, it has attached its feelings of sacredness to all sorts of objects and ideas.

Logic and experience do not always tend in the same direction, since logic will very often take certain premises for granted as self-evident (e.g., that a personal God exists) and then draw conclusions from them. The conclusions may bear no relation to facts, or may even contradict experience; but such conclusions of logic are often preferred by humanity to the conclusions of experience.

One process which from the beginning makes itself felt is the transference of the feeling of sanctity experienced in relation to certain objects or events, to the explanation later advanced to account for the objects or events. This is due to the principle of association so fundamental in the human mind. So theology becomes sacrosanct, taboo to alteration, in a way not found with scientific doctrines. This accounts for the fact that there is such irrational but strong resistance, on the part of religious people, to theological changes—the proposals made are not weighed on their intellectual merits, but are met by a current of feeling. In addition, the force of authority is introduced. This comes about in two ways. For one thing, the mere fact of immemorial tradition becomes in itself sacred, and the fact that things have been done in one particular way for generations in the past becomes a valid reason for continuing to do so in the present and the future. And, secondly, the desire for reinforcing the sanctity of beliefs leads frequently to the assertion that they have been revealed, directly or indirectly, by supernatural authority. Religious conservatism is thus aided both by the authority of tradition and by that of revelation.

The foregoing shows how two separate bodies of explanation of phenomena can grow up side by side—theology and natural science. The one has grown up round objects experienced as sacred; the other has grown up round common objects, not regarded as worth consideration by religious intellects. But, unfortunately, explanations cannot be kept to localised regions of reality. Conclusions drawn from sacred science or theology overflow into everyday life and demand application to quite ordinary objects, while natural science, pursuing its humdrum methods, eventually comes to apply them to objects regarded as sacred as well as to ordinary ones.

It is thus probable that in the development of civilisations there will always come a time when science and theology will find themselves in conflict. Science and theology start in different regions of experience; the men who pursue the one are generally of very different type from the devotees of the other; and the emotional backgrounds of the two are quite different. But both inevitably grow, and therefore inevitably invade each other's territory. The only possible solution, save an indefinite prolongation of the conflict, is for religion to admit the intellectual methods of science to be as valid in theology as everywhere else, while science admits the psychological basis of religion as an ultimate fact.

The first point we have made is that the process of association can and does bring intellectual explanation, or at least certain attempts at a certain kind of intellectual explanation, into connection with religion, and so cause these explanations to become invested with the specific religious quality of sanctity.

In precisely the same way, moral ideas can and do become linked by association with religion, and therefore sacred. Morals appear to acquire religious associations in several separate ways. In the first place the 'negative sacredness', of which taboo is the developed form, becomes directly attached to actions which are found to shock one's own feelings or those of the community; these will include actions calculated to disturb any accepted sense of sacredness, like laughing in church, or quarrelling at a graveside; and also actions which run counter to the accepted standards of the community, as when a member of a warlike tribe shows cowardice, a member of a respectable Puritan family obtains a divorce, or a member of the aristocratic class, in Victorian days, expressed a desire to become an actor or a professional violinist.

Thus a great deal of what we may call tribal morality and custom, merely for the reason that it is generally accepted, traditional, and prescribed by authority rather than reason, comes to have a certain religious, or at least a psuedo-religious sanctity attached to it, although without necessarily being thought of as having any connection with supernatural beings.

Meanwhile, however, the belief in supernatural beings is in existence. If they exist as personalities in any way like us, they too must have their morality—they are responsible for the governance of the world, they cause events to take place in accordance with their wishes.

The more man's reason gets to work on his religious problems, the more difficult does he find it to ascribe low moral motives and insight to his gods. At any particular time in history the moral character of his gods comes largely to reflect his own moral ideas; but various peculiarities are added. Logic gradually compels the idea that the moral, like the intellectual and other qualities of God, is absolute and complete—that God is not only more powerful, better, and possessed of more knowledge than we, but all-knowing, omnipotent, and absolutely good. On the other hand, evil exists; and its existence is a challenge to God's moral character. Two distinct tendencies have, as a matter of fact, resulted from these two aspects of the problem. Either man, in his theology, prefers to see a God of absolute good perpetually in conflict with a Devil or supernatural being of evil nature; or else (which better satisfies the desire for logical unity), he ascribes to God wisdom and kindness infinitely transcending our own, so that evil of all sorts, including pain and misfortune, but especially moral evil, which seems so intolerable to us and so repugnant to our moral sense, is to God's absolute knowledge a necessity for our spiritual development, to his transcendent wisdom an obligatory move in the working out of the cosmic plan.

The two ideas are combined in an extremely curious way in Milton's *Paradise Lost*. Satan is a prominent personage of the cosmic drama, but the conflict between him and God is not a fair fight, like that in Persian theology between Ormuzd and Ahriman. We are soon let in to the secret, which the Devils do not know with certainty, that the Almighty is omniscient and omnipotent, and that all the machinations of the Fiend are therefore foredoomed to failure as certainly (though for a different reason) as those of the villain in a good old-fashioned melodrama. It is this hard incongruity which makes Milton's great epic take rank below Homer's or Vergil's or that other great poem of cosmic scope, the *Divina Commedia*.

Freud believes that the reason why the forces of nature are personified as a paternalist ruler or divine father is to be sought in a universal infantile father-complex. The matter does not, I confess, seem so straightforward to me. On the other hand, once theistic personification has been accomplished, it would be natural for any ideas and emotional forces which might arise from infantile complexes concerning parents, to be transferred to the theological sphere. I think it very probable that certain views about and still more feelings towards God may owe a great deal to this cause. Thus family relations and the morals of family life are likely to acquire connection with religious feeling in several different ways.

It has frequently been maintained that religious belief is needed as a buttress to private and still more to public morality. Matthew Hales, a noted judge at the close of the seventeenth century, could write: 'To say that religion is a cheat is to dissolve all those obligations whereby civil societies are preserved.'

This idea has been, however, so often exploded that it is not worth while slaying the slain and going over once more the ground so well covered by Lecky, Westermarck, and others. I will content myself by quoting E. S. P. Haynes' dictum, that 'if morality did really depend on other-worldly sanctions, the religious changes of the last fifty years would by now have dissolved society at large'. But apropos of the question of divine personality it is worth while recalling, with Santayana, that 'what makes for righteousness, the conditions of successful living, need not be moral in a personal sense, any more than the conditions of a flame need be themselves on fire'. And let us also remember that the undue association of morals with religion has tended to surround morality with such a coat of untouchable sanctity that too often for this very reason moral progress has been unduly retarded.

The final upshot is a compromise. By the time morals begin to be thought about instead of accepted as necessary tradition, the idea of a supernatural being in control of religious affairs has come into being. Logic, applied to man's developing moral sense, tends to make this supernatural being a model of moral perfection. On the other hand, the facts of life, including the problem of evil, had long previously claimed attention and demanded, if possible, some explanation; and various theological myths had been invented for this purpose. Very frequently these myths involve actions or ideas of deity which are hardly consistent with a more developed morality. In these cases there is a cleavage between two views of God, a logical and moral difficulty which is sometimes openly acknowledged and discussed, more often simply slurred over. In the Book of Job the difficulty is faced. It is the problem of evil in its simplest form, in the form in which it haunted the practical mind of the early Hebrew, set upon this life rather than the next, upon national success and survival rather than any personal immortality. Why do the wicked prosper, wax fat and kick; why do misfortunes fall upon the innocent or those who have done their best to be upright? Job poses the question as applied to his own plight. His three friends answer, with the simple but crude faith which believes what it thinks ought to be so, 'because you have deserved it'. But Job knows this is not true. He appeals to Jehovah himself. And he is answered by Jehovah himself. The answer is as simple as that of the three comforters; it is not much more comforting: but it is sublime instead of puerile, it symbolises a true fact instead of a false hypothesis. The answer is, 'Because I am the Lord; because my ways are not your ways; because you cannot understand the divine purpose; because ultimate reality is and always will be a mystery, to be feared as well as loved'.[4]

On the other hand, sublime as this idea may be, it still involves all sorts of difficulties on the theistic plane which are avoided if religion does not personify its objects of worship.

*

In this chapter I have attempted to advance two main ideas, both largely unfamiliar. One is that the essence of religion springs from man's capacity for awe and reverence, that the objects of religion, however much later rationalised by intellect or moralised by ethics, however fossilised by convention or degraded by superstition or fear, are in origin and essence those things, events, and ideas which arouse the feeling of sacredness. On this point, with the testimony of anthropologists and archbishops to back me, I hope to have convinced my readers.

The other is that the idea of supernatural divine beings,

[4] Cf. Spinoza's words: 'He who truly loves God cannot wish that God should love him in return.'

far from being a necessity to any and every religion, is an intellectual rationalisation which was necessary, or at least inevitable, at a certain primitive level of thought and culture; which was then, the crucial assumption once made, worked on by man's intellect and by his ethical sense to give such high conceptions as that of the God of the Hebrews after the Exile, or the God of most modern Christian churches; but which now must be abandoned if further religious progress is to be made.

These ideas, I know, are unfamiliar to the great majority. I know also that when a man has been accustomed to approach a problem from one angle and is then asked to approach it from another wholly different angle, the result is usually bewilderment, or annoyance, or both. The mental constructions we have built up have their foundations and top storey, their roots and branches, their feet and head: to demand a new approach often seems like asking us to turn our house on its side before living in it, or to make our ideas go about standing on their heads. None the less, the history of thought shows clearly enough that thus to turn an idea upside-down may be fruitful and necessary, and that it is of the greatest importance that humanity should now and again take out its beliefs for spring-cleaning. In pure science an example is afforded by Mendelism, which makes the idea of invisible units the starting-point in a study of heredity, instead of thinking backwards from the visible characters of the plant or animal. Darwin's great idea of Natural Selection was another case of reversal of current thought; the delicate adaptation which was previously hailed as proof of purpose in a divine artificer was now approached from the other side and seen to be the necessary outcome of non-purposeful variation and selection. The present position in philosophy, arisen largely through the development of Einstein's relativity theory, is another case in point. Most people are so used to taking space and time as a necessary and fixed external framework that they feel the basis of their thought shattered when asked to think of them as relative and as a method of thinking rather than as externally real. Or, to take an example from the ethical sphere, to the average barbarian, the average Jew, or the average Roman, at the beginning of our era, maxims such as the duty of loving your enemies must have seemed complete topsy-turvy-dom. It was the duty of the good tribesman, the good Jew, the good citizen to hate his enemies. The Jew at least had plenty of divine authority for smiting them. And yet even opponents of Christianity would be compelled to admit that the world, however incompletely it has carried out the precept, has found it to contain deeper truth than its opposite.

*

But if religion is not essentially belief in a God or Gods and obedience to their commands or will, what then is it? It is a way of life, an art like other kinds of living, and an art which must be practised like other arts if we are to achieve anything good in it.

Religious emotion will always exist, will always demand expression. The ways in which it finds expression may be good or may be bad: or, what seems hardly to have been realised, they may be on the whole good for the individual worshipper but bad for the community. Man's scale of desires and values, his spiritual capacities, dictate the direction of his religion, the goal towards which it aspires; the facts of nature and life dictate the limits within which it may move, the trellis on whose framework those desires and emotions must grow if they are to receive the beams of truth's sun, if they aspire above creeping on the ground. It is our duty to know those outer facts truly and completely, to be willing to face all truth and not try to reject what does not tally with our desires: and it is our duty to realise our own capacities, to know what desires are to be put in command, what desires are to be harnessed to subordinate toil, to place our whole tumultuous life of feeling and will under the joint guidance of reverence and reason.

In so far as we do this, we prevent the man of devout religious feeling from being subordinated to a system which may organise the spirit of religion in opposition to discovery or necessary change, or may discharge its power in cruelty and persecution; and we help religion to help the progress of civilisation. But in so far as we neglect this, we are making man a house divided against itself, and allowing the strong tides of religious feeling to run to waste or to break in and devastate the fruit of man's labour. And the choice is in our own hands.

Tantum religio potuit suadere malorum.—LUCRETIUS.

> There's naught, no doubt, so much the spirit calms
> As Rum and true Religion.
> LORD BYRON, *Don Juan.*

The life of Reason alone is free from Magic.—PLOTINUS.

The diversity of the world is natural. Yet not less natural is this liability to accept its own diversity. It is by limitation—the limitation which all art involves; for experience seems to show that these diverse forms cannot accept each other. I recall the critical, disdainful gaze of a small terrier as he stood still to watch a great goose pass by. Let us, therefore, accept with joy the diversity of the world, and with equal joy its inability to accept its own diversity. For that also is delightful.—HAVELOCK ELLIS (*The Forum*, 1924).

A God, like a man, can only be judged by the standard of the age to which he belongs; for experience seems to show that the ethical code of a deity is seldom superior, and may be distinctly inferior, to that of his human contemporaries.—Sir JAMES FRAZER, *Folk-Lore in the Old Testament.*

> Peor and Baalim
> Forsake their Temples dim,
>   With that twice-battered god of Palestine,
> And moonèd Ashtaroth,
> Heaven's Queen and Mother both,
>   Now sits not girt with tapers' holy shine,
> The Libyc Ammon shrinks his horn,
> In vain the Tyrian maids their wounded Thammuz mourn.
>   —JOHN MILTON, *Hymn on the Morning of Christ's Nativity.*

When I mention religion, I mean the Christian religion; and not only the Christian religion, but the Protestant religion; and not only the Protestant religion, but the Church of England.—Parson Thwackum, in FIELDING'S *Tom Jones.*

Thus men forgot that all Deities reside in the human breast.
> —WILLIAM BLAKE.

Many people . . . have been extremely religious and extremely wicked. —R. H. THOULESS, *Introduction to the Psychology of Religion* (1922).

It is the attempt to punish, as God is supposed to punish, that largely accounts for the hideous record of religious persecution.—ANON.

A religion which personifies unworthily the Power behind things will do far more to retard than to advance the highest welfare of the race.
> —Canon B. H. STREETER, *Reality.*

Du gleichst dem Geist, den du begreifst.—GOETHE.

> The Vision of Christ that thou dost see
> Is my vision's greatest enemy.
> —WILLIAM BLAKE, *The Everlasting Gospel.*

The children of the mind are like the children of the body. Once born, they grow by a law of their own being, and, if their parents could foresee their future development, it would sometimes break their hearts. —R. H. TAWNEY, *Religion and the Rise of Capitalism* (1926).

6

Comparative Religion

It will be as well to give some further account of religion from the dispassionate point of view of the student. There are those who have a genius for religion, as others have a genius for poetry, or for lawn-tennis. They will be saints as surely as the others will be poets or champions. But religion differs from the other activities we have mentioned in that it is not exhausted in its own performance, like a game, nor is it even like art, whose direct efforts are confined to its own sphere. For it is not only individual, but social; and it is not only emotional, but overflows in action. In these respects it is like politics, for instance, or science. A man may be a great scientist although his scientific beliefs are in the main erroneous. He will be great in so far as he has seen some new fact or principle hitherto hidden. But the logic of his discovery (sometimes true logic, sometimes false) will be embodied in action by lesser men in ways of which he never dreamed; and these logical principles all the time demand new checking, new facts, new vision. The alchemists were rightly excited over the transmutation of one substance into another wholly different substance in their crucibles under the influence of heat or of mixture with some other material: but the conclusions which they drew from this—that the elements were indefinitely transmutable, and that materials existed capable of turning any base substance into a noble one—these resulted in an extraordinary waste of human effort and expense. Pasteur was one of the greatest men of science who have ever existed. His full proof that not even microscopic life was generated except from existing life, his discovery that many diseases were produced by the presence of bacteria or microscopic animal parasites, and his further discovery that immunisation against bacterial disease was possible —these opened the door to a vast and beneficent increase of control over human suffering. But time alone will show whether the pushing to their extreme of the conclusions to be drawn from these discoveries, at the expense of other avenues to discovery, may not have led to a very considerable waste of time and energy, and even in some directions have led to loss of health and life instead of to gain. The stressing of the parasite as 'the cause' of disease, and of artificial immunity as the best protection or cure, led to the comparative neglect of all other causes, prominent among which are the variations in disease-resistance due to variations in health and physiological state and those which are congenital.

So (though of course with a difference) in religion. Religion is in one sense an individual illumination; it is a holy and a beautiful way of living one's own life. But the individual illumination can only light up what is there; the bright light in the soul lights up the room in which the soul lives— its time and place, the thought of that time and that place; and the picture thus made, by illumination and thing illumined, is what influences other men. Indeed, it is more than that, for the illumination itself is not something absolute; its very character has in part been derived from its surroundings.

Like science, too, religion is never complete. It advances: and a religious advance is like a scientific advance—the 'revelation' is the discovery of something both new and good, but not of all the unknown, or of the complete good. However, the thought of the time, with all its limitations, sets itself to push conclusions to their furthest possible limits; and, just as in science, these conclusions often turn out to be wrong or impossible, simply because they take no account of other truths and other aspects of reality which had not then been discovered or recognised.

Thus, if a religious life is in one way like a great work of art, expressing to others just its own uniqueness and value, in another way it is like a scientific discovery, which compels to further theory and full working-out, and in still another way like a political principle, which must express itself in the organisations and institutions that confine and mould daily life.

And for all these reasons it is imperative that the bases of religion should be dispassionately analysed, for only so shall we have the hope of utilising the driving-power and the fertilising flow of its current to the best purpose, and indeed without doing positive harm.

The chief ways in which such an analysis will be profitable are by a comparative study of religion in different people at all possible levels of culture; by some attempt at an understanding of the psychological mechanisms underlying religious experience; by an examination of theology, which aims at being reason's scaffolding for religion, with reason's fullest freedom; and by an inquiry, in the light of all our experience and our whole scheme of values, as to what place religion ought to take in the life of a community of civilised people. This is a formidable task; and in this volume I can do little beyond introduce my readers to a few leading ideas and lines of thought, and then refer them to the works of the authorities on the several subjects. But so great and so rapid is the accumulation of knowledge, so extreme the specialisation of thought at the present time, that even this twisting together of the threads of thought will be of value if it is rightly done. Without it, the threads lie loose, each breaking if even a small load is placed upon it; but if the loose threads be twisted into cords, and one day the cords into a rope, that rope may be strong enough to bear the weight of those who, for lack of any rope of thought, are unable to climb out of chaos.

Comparative religion is the study of the religious beliefs and practices of mankind, conducted in the same spirit as comparative anatomy, which is the comparative study of the structure and plan of animals and plants. It notes the facts, the differences and the resemblances between one religion and another; it seeks to trace the family history of beliefs and rites, their evolutionary origins; to explain the presence of this or that practice as a survival from past times; to correct the theorisings of those who lay down what religion ought to be by showing them what it actually and in hard fact is.

Tylor and Frazer are perhaps the classical figures in this field; but they have had helpers and rivals too numerous to cite. What demands mention is a few of the main conclusions to which the study leads. In the first place, then, as we have already set forth, to the idea that religion has grown out of, and indeed originally consists in, the activities of mind and body aroused by the feeling of sacredness. Further, that this sacredness need not and does not at the start have the restricted meaning which we give to it, of 'good-sacred' only, but may include 'bad-sacred' also (e.g., the powers supposed to be invoked in black magic). In other words, that this feeling which we are trying to describe is in its pure original form unattached to moral ideas, may either attract or repel, or both at once, may be either positive or negative or ambivalent in respect of goodness.

Various words exist in primitive languages to denote this sacred power, such as the Polynesian *mana*, the North American *manitou* and *maxpé*, the West African *njomm*, the Moroccan *baraka* (see Westermarck, *Ritual and Belief in Morocco*, 1926), and so forth; while we have seen that a modern theologian has coined the word 'numinous' to denote all that falls into this category.

An example of how the word *holy* may even in modern English be applied to something morally neutral is afforded by Coleridge's description of the site of Xanadu:

> *A savage place, as holy and enchanted*
> *As e'er beneath a waning moon was haunted*
> *By woman wailing for her demon lover.*

On the combination of admiration and fear, fascination and horror, in the feeling of sacredness, little need be said. We need only remind ourselves that one of the great achievements of Christianity, or rather of Jesus, was to show how this fear could be cast out or transmuted into the nobility of awe —by being dominated by an admiration raised to the higher level of love. True that it has been the perverse triumph of sect after sect to render this achievement of little account by their hideous emphasis on a real Hell of eternal torture; but this does not lessen Jesus' great discovery.

It is an entire mistake to conceive that the objects of this religious feeling are essentially or primitively beings of the nature of gods. Some things, some events, some ideas are sacred, numinous, full of *mana*: that is all. Their relationship to the later concept of gods lies solely in the fact that something of spirit, in the broadest sense, is supposed to inhere in them: but, so far as we can gather, primitive man prefers to interpret most phenomena in terms of spirit, projecting that nature with which he is most familiar—his own—into all other natures.[1]

One of the best-known examples of 'negative mana' is

[1] Hartland has coined a suggestive term in this connection. This idea of the supernatural, this mana, this numinous quality in things, he calls *theoplasm*—the stuff of which gods are made. The more the idea is reflected on, the more pregnant does it become.

taboo, that sacred prohibition which in many primitive tribes attaches to various places and actions. Taboo is more than usually prominent among the Polynesians. The sacredness of a chief was such that he was dangerous to touch, being as highly charged with sacred power as is a high-tension wire with electricity. This sacredness even communicated itself to what he had worn or touched or eaten from; a Tongan chief could not give his discarded garments to his inferiors—they would bring disease or danger. Conversely in Hawaii, if a man's shadow fell on the King or even on the King's house, he was put to death.

It is of some interest to find that when the Polynesians are converted to Christianity their habituation to a life of taboo shows itself in their exaggerating every possible taboo in their new religion. The Tongans become, for instance, the most virulent Sabbatarians, and they even invent new taboos, ascribing such sanctity to the house of worship that they are frightened to use any water from a church roof.

Very numerous are the food taboos of primitive religion. A number of these are set forth in Leviticus and Deuteronomy.

We, to-day, are not without our taboos; and a study of them is not without interest. Our greatest taboo has been on the discussion of sex. The child who begins to ask awkward questions and to display its perfectly natural curiosities on these as on all other matters, is, for the most part, simply told not to, and in a shocked voice. Here, on the one hand, is the natural desire of curiosity, on the other, repression by authority, and by authority mixed up with ideas of right and wrong. Thus here, in a sense artificially, are attraction and repulsion combined, and there is generated a mystery which at one and the same time both fascinates and frightens. Later, when inevitably morals and religion become intermingled, this other mystery, of God, will come in to reinforce the first. But there will be a mystery even if the child has been fortunate enough to have parents who have not added ideas of God and supernatural anger to the inevitable burden on his unfledged mind. Even without this a taboo will have been brought into existence.

It would appear that the taboos of early religion range from some such vaguely mysterious social prohibitions as this, up to those which are armed with all the supernatural force of godhead.

Another constant feature of primitive religion is its belief that man's life is surrounded by powers or forces which can and do influence it for good or evil. The relation of these forces to objects which are sacred is not always quite clear. Sometimes the sanctity or mana is itself the force, which can be made to discharge itself in this way or that. This is so with the sacred stones of certain Polynesians, which, according to them, have power to make crops grow; and, at the other end of the scale, with miracle-working relics, round and on which the supernatural force is supposed to have accumulated. At other times, the supernatural forces are supposed to be hovering round, waiting for the chance of exerting their power; this they can do more readily at certain special times, such as birth or marriage, when the soul for one reason or another is exposed to spiritual danger. A very large collection of facts concerning the supernatural dangers which are believed to be run at marriage, and the steps taken to avert those dangers, is to be found in Crawley's *Mystic Rose*.

In such cases, it is essentially the event which possesses some mysterious 'negative sanctity' (as well, often, as sanctity in our positive sense); and the powers which can at this time do harm may be as neutral, from the standpoint of sanctity, as the bacteria which invade a man when his resistance is lowered. They may be regarded just as we may regard luck, with superstition but without reverence or awe. On the other hand, the powers may be themselves endowed with mana—ghosts of the dead, mysterious nature-spirits, bad luck deified. This whole attitude has its watered-down counterpart to-day in all kinds of superstitions concerning luck, and is based on a very simple psychological reality. The psychological reality is that when we are undertaking an unusual or unique event, or making a decision or embarking on a venture of importance, we are inevitably wrought up in one way or another, unusually receptive to outer impressions and strange inner thoughts. Whatever general system of ideas about our life and its relation to the rest of the world we have allowed to take root in our minds, will influence us at this moment. How many superstitions of good and bad luck still crowd round the wedding-day in twentieth-century England; how seriously some of them are taken; and how difficult it is not to take some of them seriously!

This brings us on to the question of magic and its relation to religion. There are authorities who deny that magic has any real, essential relation with religion, and see in it rather the prelogical germ of science. Most, however, who have considered the question carefully, although some may be prepared to admit that the fountain-head of magic may reside rather in the region of intellect (however incomplete and distorted) than in that of religious feeling, insist, and I think with reason, that primitive magic and primitive religion were from the first so intertwined, and so gradually did the connection between them loosen, that it is both difficult and unprofitable to attempt their separation.

Most magic is based on the idea of sympathetic influence. No one in attendance on a Moroccan woman in childbirth must tie a knot, or have their clothes tightly laced: to do so would impede easy delivery. In Rossetti's poem, 'Sister Helen,' the woman makes a waxen image of the lover by whom she has been deserted, and by slowly melting it, brings about his death: this magic method, in one form or another, is extremely widespread both among savages and in moderately civilised societies, such as that of classical Rome or the European Middle Ages. Many of the so-called Nature Festivals seem to have been in their origin ceremonials for inducing fertility of the soil by sympathetic magic. Quite obviously of this type are many of the rites practised by hunting tribes to secure success in hunting. One of the most remarkable objects left to us by prehistoric man was found in a cave in the Pyrenees. It is the headless body of a bear, modelled in clay: in its neck is a hole, as for a stick, and between its paws lies a real bear's skull; the clay body is marked with gashes from sharp instruments. It can with considerable probability be assumed that this object originally had the bear's skull attached to it, that the whole was then covered with a bear's skin, and that to the accompaniment of some ritual, the hunters pierced the counterfeit bear with their spears to ensure success in their hunting of the real cave-bear, which was one of their main sources of food, perhaps 20,000 years ago. The Australian natives practise magico-religious rites to-day to ensure the multiplication of their food-animals and success in hunting.

Dr Marett, in his *Primitive Religion,* gives an illuminating discussion of the probable origin of the belief in sympathetic magic and its efficacy. He further shows how, in a world like that of primitive man, magic could not fail to borrow sacred or religious power from the reservoir of mystery and mana which the savage feels all round him, any more than religious feeling could help borrowing the ideas and methods of magic to help it in the task of propitiating the sacred powers. In this way, other forms of magic than that of influence by sympathy have grown up.

So was cemented the alliance between magic and religion, the alliance which is by no means yet broken. Exorcism is magic: the Rumanian poltergeist medium, Eleonore Zugun, whose case was investigated in London, was the subject of exorcist rites by Rumanian priests. Belief in the miracle-working power of relics or holy places is belief in magic. Cures of certain types of disease may be effected through such agencies, but this is by means of the suggestibility of the patient, not through any mysterious supernatural power emanating from the objects or places themselves.

The evil eye is magic: a stranger cannot pry inquisitively round the streets of Naples without having the sign of the horns, infallible warder-off of the influence of the evil eye, made at him. Witchcraft is magic: in 1926 a Devonshire farmer so firmly believed that a neighbour had bewitched his beasts, that he assaulted her, and was tried and sentenced for it, protesting the truth of his assertion to the last.

Aulard, in his interesting study of religion during the French Revolution, states that the more he goes into the history of the time, the more he is convinced that only a small minority of the French nation were either devoted Catholics or devoted adherents of the Religion of Reason or of Patriotism: the bulk of the people, if left to themselves, would simply have relapsed entirely into the beliefs in paganism and witchcraft, a magico-religious system which, even under a veneer of Christianity, they had for centuries chiefly practised and lived by.

Religions, like living animal and plant species, are the product of evolution. Again, like animals and plants, they have evolved into a number of bizarre and wholly unexpected and unpredictable forms. The old story of the yokel who, after seeing a giraffe for the first time, exclaimed that he was now confirmed in the belief that there was no such animal, has its real applicability. A giraffe; a deep-sea angler-fish; a giant spider-crab; a stalk-eyed fly; a praying mantis; a matamata terrapin—these and many other creatures are really very improbable—much less like fact than fiction. And the same is true of religions. The Toda religion; the whole amazing elaboration of totemism; a revival meeting; prayer-wheels; entire societies dominated by religious magic; monasticism

run mad, as in Tibet or Mount Athos; asceticism run mad,
as in Thebaid or in Indian fakirism; human sacrifice; sacred
self-mutilation; temple prostitution—these phenomena among
many others at first sight seem too strange to be believed.
And yet they exist and, what is more, exist wrapped in the
odour of sanctity.

It should, of course, never be forgotten that the selective
process in evolution will not do more than ensure survival in
existing circumstances, as economic pressure does not ensure
that an object manufactured for sale shall be the best of its
kind or even good of its kind. All that economic pressure
ensures is that the object shall somehow sell itself; all that
biological pressure ensures is that the animal or plant shall
survive and reproduce itself; all that social pressure ensures
with religion is that it shall somehow or other satisfy to a
reasonable extent the religious needs of its votaries.

Nearly a million species of animals are already known. Of
these, only a few thousand are endowed with anything which
can be called intelligence, only a few tens with high intelligence, and only one with conceptual thought. In the same
way, there are hundreds of known religions; it had better be
left to more orthodox writers than myself to enumerate those
which can be called high religions.

Animal evolution witnesses to a central upward trend of
biological progress; it also shows us the retention of low types
along with high, the throwing out of blind-alley side-branches
of specialisation at every level, and sometimes even degenera-
tion. Religious evolution also shows a central progress—but
equally the production of bizarre side-branches, the permanent confining of the religious spirit in low-level embodi-
ments, its projection into every conceivable cul-de-sac, its too
frequent bending over from upward to downward growth.

Flaubert, in his *Tentation de St Antoine*, gave an amazingly vivid picture of a thousand-and-one fantastic manifestations of the half-baked religious spirits jostling each other in
the morning of civilisation. Frazer's great *Golden Bough* gives
a portentous scientific résumé, carefully documented, of similar but, on the whole, more primitive manifestations.

*

One of the facts which emerge most clearly from a survey
of our own and others' religious life is that crude beliefs and
superstitions with their attendant practices may survive along-

side of the highest and purest developments of monotheism and religious morality. In organic evolution we find that in spite of general upward progress, all grades of living creatures, advanced, primitive, and degenerate, manage to exist perfectly well side by side.

In both cases, however, the balance of the picture is changed during evolution, and low-level types which were once dominant in later ages become subordinate.

We should therefore not be too discouraged at the fact that in spite of nearly two thousand years of Christianity, in spite of the labours of the scholastics and other religious philosophers, in spite of the broad-mindedness of modern liberal theology, the present age, even in countries like England or the United States, France or Germany, let alone Italy, is still permeated with superstition, bigotry, intolerance, and crude religions of various kinds.

Every advanced religion must experience some hostility towards religions at lower levels of development, whether intellectual, moral, or emotional; it is impossible for it to remain neutral. The ideal of religious tolerance is probably the best which the State can adopt, but even where it has been adopted it has only been between certain limits. England to-day permits freedom of religious belief and practice—but if a religious sect which practised human sacrifice or ritual prostitution were to attempt to establish itself in the country, it would receive short shrift. As a matter of fact, Britain engaged in putting a stop to head-hunting in certain parts of Burma, although this practice was based on religious grounds; we can all remember the unfortunate end which overtook the Rev. Smith-Pigott and his 'Abode of Love,' and the prohibition of polygamy to Mormonism both in this country and the United States; while the difficulties of Russia and Canada with the anti-social but extremely religious Doukhobors have been by no means light.

To take a final example on a more exalted plane, most States do not give full freedom of action even to those who during a war, however genuinely, have a true religious objection to fighting. It is demanded that they should do something useful, or be shut up.

So long as States exist, it is clear that religious toleration cannot, or at least will not, be permitted in cases where religious belief aims at or tends towards the overthrow of the State or the principles on which its existence is grounded.

When, however, we come to the upholders of this or that religious system, the possible grounds for hostility to other beliefs become much greater. In the same way democratic States (though not totalitarian States) find it both necessary and desirable to tolerate diversity of political party; but the political parties themselves must be in some degree hostile, or politics would degenerate into a game of log-rolling.

Religion being of necessity a spring of action, and also bound up with a scale of values, no man of genuinely religious feeling can be perfectly indifferent towards religions which to him seem to turn his values topsy-turvy, and so inevitably in the long run to lead to actions which to him seem wrong. He may even see clearly that other religions have very good points, and yet be forced to judge them adversely because, in his opinion, they move less quickly towards the good than his own. But in all questions of toleration the old though too frequently disregarded principle of tolerating the man but attacking the ideas should at least be adopted.

In conclusion, I would like to try some comparative analysis of separate features of religion. To continue the parallel from animal life, the evolutionary zoologist may not only describe outstanding divergent types of animals as examples of what evolution can and does bring forth, but he may also attempt a historical analysis. Here he may either try his hand at phylogeny, when he will discuss the ancestry of different actual types and their relationship to each other; or at evolutionary comparative anatomy and physiology, in which he takes one by one the different aspects and functions of life, describes the structure and working of the various kinds of organs which subserve these different functions, and attempts to discover the main trends to be discerned in the evolution of each and in their interrelation one with another.

These are matters of considerable difficulty for religion, and I must refer my readers to anthropological works for a treatment of the subject. However, even if it is difficult or impossible to trace the precise early evolution of particular religions, it is practicable to distinguish a number of main religious levels, and to arrange them with a considerable degree of probability in their evolutionary order.

At the base comes the stage in which the main object of religious feeling is mysterious or supernatural power, not usually personified, but conceived of as residing *in* particular objects and events. Thought is in this stage pre-scientific, and is content to remain in a number of more or less watertight compartments. The logical faculty may be well developed in particular instances or fields, but is not concerned to be complete or to apply itself to the whole field of thought, so that beliefs may often be mutually contradictory. The theological side of religion is therefore represented by mere rationalisations in the form of myths, often of a vague and fluid nature. At this stage magic is inextricably mixed up with religious belief and practice. This is the stage of animatism and early animism.

A certain school of writers, prominent among whom is Levy-Bruhl, claim that savages think in an essentially different way from civilised men, and would characterise their thought as pre-logical or a-logical. It is, however, generally admitted that this is an error. Their thought may be extremely logical, but often gives us the impression of illogicality because it is founded on wrong premises. Apart from this, the chief difference between savage and civilised thought is in the completeness of logical attack, the lengths to which it is pushed, and its use to break down the barriers between different compartments of experience. The main differences between the low stage and our own consist in the primitive man's failure to have grasped the value of scientific method, and his failure to unify the different aspects of his mental life; otherwise the differences are mainly differences of emphasis and of premises.

The next main level is one on which the mysterious power is generally conceived of as not *in* but *behind* objects and events. This is almost always combined with the personification of its different aspects as supernatural but more or less manlike or animal beings. The further personification proceeds, the more will rites of propitiation, sacrifice, prayer, and worship come to overlie the more primitive rituals based upon magic, although of course the two sets of activities long remain interwoven. At this level, there is still very little unity apparent in thought, religious or other. A multiplicity of sacred beings exist, their attributes often overlap, the mytho-theology which professes to give an account of them and their relationships to each other and to the world of things and men is frequently self-contradictory. In particular, the relation of religion and its gods to morality is at this stage almost always very feebly defined.

At the next level, general ideas have begun to make

morality reasoned and to link this reasoned morality firmly with religion. At the same time the pure logical reason begins to play over the rationalisations of mythology, to attempt the sweeping away of self-contradiction and the achievement of coherence; it tries to complete and strengthen the intellectual side of belief, and to link this also more firmly with religion's central core of feeling.

This stage is one of conflict and transition. Both reason and the ethical sense, once pursued with thoroughness towards whatever goals may appear in the quest, reveal a host of intellectual and moral inadequacies in accepted religion. On the other hand, the theological chaos of the lowest levels is often in this stage replaced by an ordered hierarchy of gods.

This period of transition, familiar to us in two very distinct examples, the religion of classical Greece and that of the early Jews when Jehovah was still a mere tribal god, gives place to a more stable phase in which these general ideas, in one form or another, have become dominant, and religion accordingly becomes definitely unified. The most familiar result to us is the emergence of monotheism from cruder religious views.

The religions of classical antiquity show tendencies in this direction, by elevating one of a hierarchic pantheon of gods— Zeus or Jupiter—to a position of supremacy over the rest; the same is true of the old Scandinavian religion, with Wodin as head god over the other gods and goddesses. From this, it would be not a great step to elevate the head god to be sole god, while degrading the rest to the position of saints or angels or other subordinate spiritual beings. As a matter of fact, however, the transition to full monotheism in Europe was mainly effected in another way. The early Jews had already arrived at an approximation to monotheism, but it was a local and tribal monotheism. Jehovah was their only, or at least main, god, but he was one among a number of other some-what similar gods belonging to other primitive tribes. The transition here came through the spiritual logic of the Hebrew prophets; they perceived that if Jehovah was a true God, he must have attributes which would make him true universally, and not only for the Jewish nation. The nationalism of the Jews, however, resisted the implications of this view, and it was left for St Paul to rescue early Christianity from similar narrowness, and to proclaim that its god and its salvation were universal, for Jew and Gentile, Roman and barbarian, free and slave.

Buddhism in its pure theoretical form has adopted a quite different method of arriving at the same general level; it has aimed at the merging of the personal soul in an impersonal flood of spirit. But it, also, arrived at the idea of a universal spiritual ground of things.

The emotional side of religion meanwhile, of course, persists, but it too becomes transformed and often harnessed in new ways. The desire for the mere acquisition of magic power becomes transformed into a desire that some of the holiness of the divinity shall become transferred to the worshipper, or into a desire for pure righteousness, which, however, is still supposed to be obtainable only by supernatural means. The preoccupation with taboos, ceremonials and rituals which are more or less meaningless, but must be adhered to for fear of offending supernatural power, gives place to a preoccupation with an ethical morality which is regarded as sacred. The Decalogue is three parts of the way towards the achievement of this; while Leviticus and Deuteronomy represent a backsliding towards the multiplication of magico-religious or purely ritual morality.

Finally, the preoccupation with morality and personal religion leads to the attachment of greater importance to the ideas of salvation and of a future life. Immortality as conceived by all primitive peoples, including the early Greeks and the early Jews, is a very second-rate existence: the departed spirits lead a life very like their life on earth, but are encumbered with various disabilities, and their survival is often not even permanent. Frequently, only certain privileged men can expect to survive death. The idea of salvation in a modern sense is unknown; in so far as the ideas which underlie it exist, they are equated with worldly success or with the acquisition of supernatural power in this life. Even to the writer of the Book of Job, through whom primitive religion receives its highest expression, the idea of a blissful eternal life as the reward of righteousness is wholly unfamiliar.

But with the arrival of universal or general ideas as dominant in religion, there comes a change. The logical reason (as opposed to science, which is concerned primarily with 'brute fact,' as Whitehead puts it) pushes on to complete all possible conclusions from the premises provided her. If nature is a unity, there are not many gods but one God. If he is really God, he is all-powerful, all-wise, and all-good; if he is all-good, he cannot permit evil to triumph and good to go unrewarded;

if he is fully supreme he is eternal, and can grant eternity to others, and so forth. By this sort of process, the notions of an eternal life which shall be the reward or the punishment for actions in this life grew up, and the idea of salvation became transmuted from the present attainment of supernatural power or the immediate thrill of the experience of grace, holiness, or communion, to the acquisition of the privilege of admission to a future paradise.

This was the main trend of events in Europe and the Near East, culminating in the Christian and Mohammedan schemes of salvation. In India, on the other hand, the trend was different. Here, too, the acquisition of sanctity and the rewards of religiously right living were in the forefront of ideas; but while this life with its burden of sin, trouble, pain, and imperfection was despised by both Eastern and Western religions at this stage, yet the East went further than the West, and envisaged all personal life, in this world and the next, as always and inevitably a limitation, and not only what we call evil desires but all desires as bad. The most sacred end of life is therefore the suppression of desire, which will permit the soul to cease its transmigrations and the personal being to return to the impersonal and greater reality whence it was derived. Both systems are alike in advancing their main spiritual concern from the present to the future, from the particular and present to the eternal and the general, but they seek to achieve their end in divergent ways.

This comparatively stable period was in its turn followed by another period of transition, which is that of Western civilisation to-day. This transition was largely effected by the rise of the scientific spirit to dominance.[2] No human society of course exists which does not manifest the scientific spirit in some form; every consciously observed sequence of cause and effect, every attempt to check the flights of logical reason or illogical desire against brute fact, and to understand and control fact by the aid of reason, is in its degree science. But the rise of the scientific spirit to play a dominant or even an important part in thought and affairs dates back only some three hundred years. With the Greeks there was a dawn of science; but the Greek spirit was much more the spirit of pure reason, philosophy, and generalisation than of science; the idea of a growing

[2] Social and economic changes, of course, also played their part, though they too were themselves largely the product of the fundamental change of outlook.

body of solidly-tested knowledge, based primarily upon induction, as the kernel and foundation of thought and practice, did not emerge until the seventeenth century, with Bacon and Galileo as its two first pillars.

Just as the generalising properties of man in the fields of reason and ethics revealed all sorts of inconsistencies in the accepted religions of the time, so the acquisition of scientific knowledge and the application of the scientific spirit, with its incessant demands for tests of verification and its insistence on the need and virtue of humble agnosticism if verification is not possible, have revealed other inconsistencies on the new level of religious thought.

The chief ways in which the scientific spirit is making its influence felt are its uncompromising hostility to all the magical, semi-magical or superstitious elements in religion; its insistence upon natural law, both in inorganic and organic nature, with the consequent relegation of supernatural power (long previously banished from a position within phenomena) to a position even further and further removed behind objects and events; its achievements in controlling nature, which are being more and more taken as an earnest of fuller and more general control to come, with a consequent greater emphasis on the rôle of religion in this life to the detriment of concern in another life; its successful appeal to the authority of fact in opposition to all other authoritarianism, which has naturally weakened all religious appeals to the authority of sacred books or revealed codes of conduct or miracles and of traditionalism in general; and, finally, in its narrowing down the field of the supernatural towards a vanishing point.

If the process continues—and in spite of conflict there is every appearance of its so doing—religious thought is due to enter on a new phase of relative stability, based upon the naturalistic and humanistic outlook brought in by the scientific spirit.

The great achievement to be hoped for from this would be the achievement of unity. At present we are the slaves of a dualistic system of thought which continually produces false antitheses, as between soul and body, or between natural and supernatural. The savage's animism or animatism was a crude attempt at a unitary view; philosophic idealism and materialism are one-sided efforts which achieve apparent unity by leaving out half of the picture; science is now providing the basis for a single-minded naturalism. Its immediate aim would be the husbanding and harnessing of man's spiritual forces, its twin goals the development of the individual soul (development as from a grub to a free winged creature) and the greater good of the human community. Scientific knowledge would provide the necessary firm soil in which the airy growths of spiritual values may root themselves and the scientific outlook would prevent the religious imagination from the excesses to which, unguided, it is too prone.

Swiftly I shrivel at the thought of God,
At Nature and its wonders, Time and Space and Death,
But that I, turning, call to thee O soul, thou actual Me,
And lo, thou gently masterest the orbs,
Thou matest time, smilest content at Death,
And fillest, swellest full the vastnesses of space.
Greater than stars or suns,
Bounding O soul thou journeyest forth.
                              —WALT WHITMAN, *Passage to India.*

We judge the acts of others by our own sympathies, and we judge our own acts by the sympathies of others, every day and all day long, from childhood upwards, until associations, as indissoluble as those of language, are formed between certain acts and the feelings of approbation or disapprobation. It becomes impossible to imagine some acts without disapprobation, or others without approbation of the actor, whether he be one's self or any one else. We come to think in the acquired dialect of morals. An artificial personality, the 'man within,' as Adam Smith calls conscience, is built up beside the natural personality. He is the watchman of society, charged to restrain the anti-social tendencies of the natural man within the limits required by social welfare.
                              —T. H. HUXLEY, *Evolution and Ethics.*

                              (The Mystic)
O thou undaunted daughter of desires!
By all thy dower of lights and fires;
By all the eagle in thee, all the dove;
By all thy lives and deaths of love;
By thy large draughts of intellectual day,
And by thy thirsts of love more large than they;
By all thy brim-filled bowls of fierce desire
By thy last morning's draught of liquid fire. . . .
                              —R. CRASHAW (on Saint Teresa).

The spirit can for the time pervade and control every member and function of the body, and transmute what in form is the grossest sensuality into purity and devotion.—THOREAU, *Walden.*

Nothing but habit could blind us to the strangeness of the fact that the man who believes that morality is based on *a priori* principles, and the man who believes it to be based on the commands of God, the transcendentalist, the theologian, the mystic, and the evolutionist, should be pretty well at one both as to what morality teaches, and as to the sentiments with which its teaching should be regarded.
                              —ARTHUR BALFOUR, *The Foundations of Belief* (1894).

Religion has no doubt already at the savage stage begun to influence moral ideas even in points which have no bearing upon the personal interests of Gods; but this influence is known to have been not nearly so great as it has often been represented, and it seems to me to be a fact not to be doubted that the moral consciousness has originated in emotions entirely different from that feeling of uncanniness and mystery which first led to the belief in supernatural beings.
                              —E. WESTERMARCK, *The Goodness of Gods* (1926).

Men were thought of as free—in order that they might be judged and punished; but consequently every action had to be regarded as voluntary, and the origin of every action had to be imagined as lying in consciousness. In this way the most fundamentally fraudulent characteristic of psychology was established as the very principle of psychology itself.—F. NIETZSCHE, *The Twilight of the Idols.*

7

Psychology and Religion

Modern psychology, like so much of science, has given man reason to feel humbler and less self-assured than in the 'good old days.' On the other hand, again like other scientific advances, it has shown him how, if he takes its lessons to heart and disciplines his mind in the light of the new knowledge which it has given, he may attain a more limited but more secure confidence, a less ambitious but also less dangerous outlook. It would be presumptuous to attempt a full attack on religious psychology in a single chapter. I shall therefore content myself with a discussion of a few special points of interest, followed by a brief attempt at some general conclusions.

First and foremost come the consequences of evolution and its acceptance. If man's body has evolved, then so has his mind. Our mental powers are not only relative, developed in adaptive relation to the world around us, but there is no reason whatever for supposing them in any way complete. I do not mean theoretically or logically complete—all are agreed upon their incompleteness in this respect; but practically, from the standpoint of evolution, there is no inherent reason why the average or the best present human minds should represent the limit of possibility. The mind even of a stupid man can grasp and deal with problems entirely out of the range of a cat's mind; and the problems with which the mind of a great mathematician, or indeed of any genius, deal are at least as high again above those which our stupid friend can tackle. Even if we leave genius on one side, the world would be a very different place if the average inborn ability of men were as high as the average of the most able ten per cent of the population to-day. But there is no reason to leave genius on one side, nor to refuse to face the possibility that mind could be developed by selection to a pitch which would bring its owners to the same height of incomprehensibility to us at our present level of mind, as

133

is our present level to the cats and dogs who sit by the fire and hear us talking, but cannot comprehend.

The relativity of our mental faculties should also be remembered. It was Bergson who first pointed out that on evolutionary principles we must think of reason as being adaptive, that it was a mental organ developed *ad hoc,* for the convenient handling of that kind of reality, those sorts of relations, which most commonly occur around us, and not necessarily for handling any and every reality or dealing with all kinds of relations. It is an organ adapted to its functions, as a limb to locomotion or an eye to sight.

Then again, in a different outer world, our eyes would have been different. Our eyes are only sensitive to one octave of light-waves; but that is the octave in which the sun is emitting the greatest energy. Without a doubt, had the sun been emitting rays of longer average wavelength when life evolved, our eyes would have been attuned to those conditions.

The mind is not static; it grows like the body; but its transformations after birth are much more considerable than those of the body in the same period, and are comparable in extent to prenatal bodily changes. In addition, the range of transformations possible to it is very great, unlike the narrowly-determined development of body. Like the body, it must be adapted to its environment; but unlike the body, it is not given us with its adaptations automatically prepared, but adaptation has to be achieved by each individual during his lifetime. The adaptations may be on a low and incomplete plane, permitting only limited control, or on a high plane and far more complete, permitting much greater control and also much greater freedom and creative power: on either high or low plane they may be beautifully adjusted, or there may be maladjustment and friction.

The great problems of mental adaptation are threefold—to adapt the inner urge of instinct and impulse, longing and desire, to the actualities of the environment, social and natural, in which the individual has to live; to discover means for achieving greater conscious control over the environment, and greater independence and freedom for the individual and the expression of his individuality; and to achieve an integration of personality.

All that the individual is provided with in infancy are certain broad innate tendencies or instincts, certain capacities of sensation and perception, and certain capacities of remembering, learning, and profiting by experience. There are no such things as innate ideas: the mind is a blank slate, not yet written upon. On the other hand, differences in the qualities and strengths of the innate tendencies, differences in the capacities for observation, attention and learning, help largely (together with the environment) to determine what shall be written there.

Thus the development of the mind is a gradual organisation of the several separate and often opposed instincts and impulses, with the separate and often contradictory lessons of experience, into some sort of unity.

As Santayana writes, commenting upon Spinoza: 'Given the propulsive energy of life in any animal that is endowed with imagination, it is clear that whatever he finds propitious to his endeavours he will call good, and whatever he finds hostile to them he will call evil. His various habits and passions will begin to judge one another. A group of them called vanity, and another called taste, and another called conscience, will arise within his breast. Each of these groups, in so far as they have not coincided or co-operated from the beginning, will tend to annex or overcome the others. This competition between a man's passions makes up his moral history, the growth of his character, just as the competition of his ruling interests with other interests at work in society makes up his outward career. The sort of imagination that can survey all these interests at once, and can perceive how they check or support one another, is called reason; and when reason is vivid and powerful it gives courage and authority to those interests which it sees are destined to success, whilst it dampens or extinguishes those others which it sees are destined to failure. Reason thus establishes a sort of resigned and peaceful strength in the soul, founded on renunciation of what is impossible and co-operation with what is necessary.'

The foundations are laid in early childhood, but the memory of this period fades before a continuity of remembered mental life is attained. The other great critical period for the mind's development is and will always remain that of adolescence, because then new and powerful instinctive impulses come into prominence, and also because the individual is then leaving the sheltered life of childhood and being confronted with the problems of the environment in more serious form. The consciousness of self grows with the degree of organisation of the mental life, but is present from an early stage.

*

A word is due on the remarkable tendency of primitive thought to express itself in images rather than in concepts, in forms which appeal to the senses and emotions rather than to the intellect, by means of symbolic rather than rational representation. This is combined, very frequently though by no means always, with that other tendency of low-level thought to give free rein to its wishes instead of checking them up against hard fact and ethical standards.

These are matters of very familiar experience in dreams, when the higher centres, which attempt to deal with hard fact by means of conceptual thought, are fatigued and out of action. They are also very familiar to those who have studied hypnosis and so-called mediumship. In genuine trance, ideas almost always 'come through' in the form of pictures or stories; and the same is often true of day-dreaming and reverie.

The amazing power of these subordinate brain-centres to produce a scene complete in every detail, to fuse it with the most intense emotions, and to pass from scene to scene with incredible swiftness, is familiar to every dreamer.

The modern theory of dreams and visions is far from complete, but it may at least be said that these faculties of imagery, when released from control by higher centres, have the power of taking an idea presented to them and translating it into imagery, symbolic or otherwise, which is usually loaded with a profusion of detail and charged with a strong feeling of conviction.

Furthermore, it may also be safely said, without committing oneself to the details of any of the rival theories such as those of Freud or Jung or Adler, that in the passage of the idea towards expression in the guise of imagery (a passage which is entirely in the realm of the subconscious) it may make contacts with various emotional tendencies, some favourable and some hostile. Further, as a result of the impact of these associated ideas and tendencies which are thus called into action, the idea may get distorted in its passage, and become symbolised in quite a different guise from what would otherwise have been the case. To these distorting and modifying agencies Freud has given the rather unsatisfactory name of the censor.

All the religious mystics, whether they be Christian Europeans or Indian Yogis, seem to stress, in the same general way, the need for putting the intellect to sleep before the mystic experience, of whatever type, is vouchsafed.

The vividness and directness of visions and symbolic imagery give this method of thinking, if thinking it can be called, an advantage over the more laborious methods of conceptual thought, which can only attain its greatest triumphs by cutting down the fringe of undefined meaning round its words and ideas to a minimum, making them standardised counters instead of pictographs, and substituting an efficient machinery of thought to grind out its results, for the imagery which aspires to be intellectual method and emotional expression all in one.

This psychological advantage is all the more reason for being very careful to restrict the scope of imagery within its own proper sphere, and for mistrusting it whenever it claims to usurp the functions of the intellect.

*

I may now pass to some of the specific psychological experiences of the religious life.

Suggestion is always of great importance; and correspondingly religious ritual and service are often arranged so as to promote suggestibility. The dim light, the familiar words, the fixed postures, the isolation from other influences, the general sense of awe—the whole atmosphere is such to promote a receptive or suggestible state of mind. Authority itself helps to suggest the truth of what it so firmly asserts, and, the receptive state once induced, the words of the prayers tend to be impressed upon the mind and themselves to exercise some authority there after the fashion of a suggestion given in hypnosis. The fact that religious instruction is usually begun very young, buttresses it with all kinds of alien strength and makes certain religious feelings and ideas take root so deeply and so unconsciously that it is extremely hard for the growing mind to break away from them without great difficulty, and often indeed a profound sense of sin. This depends partly on the greater suggestibility of the child, partly on the fact that impressions made in childhood gather round themselves all sorts of strong emotional associations.

Suggestibility is also increased by whatever tends to weaken the natural control of the higher centres of the brain. Thus, fasting and long vigils will prepare the mind to receive unquestioningly what at such a time may enter it.

This brings up a second important set of facts, namely, those depending on the graded organisation of the mind into what has been called a hierarchy of different levels, with the degree of dominance of the higher levels varying from time to time. When the control exerted by the higher centres is weakened or removed, the lower centres have free play in ways which are not possible when they are acting in subordinate capacities. On the intellectual side, the highest type of thought is conceptual, using words and abstract ideas tied together by logic and reason; when this is in abeyance, the mind tends to think in a succession of images or symbols, connected only by the loose bonds of association. On the volitional side, conscious purpose is on a higher level than mere impulse. As regards morality, the actions, often painfully learnt, which take in the claims of others, are on a higher level than those based on primitive desires; and coping with reality is on a higher level than indulgence in phantasy or giving rein to one's wishes. In the field of perception and intuition, the conscious act which comprehends a great many facts and aspects of reality together and at once, is on a higher level than the crude faculty which can only deal with them separately.

The commonest result of the relaxing of the higher centres' control is for conceptual thought to give place to imagery, and for the imagery to express the fulfilment of some normally inhibited desire. The imagery is often distorted, owing to conflict of higher and lower in the mind, so as not to express the desire in too crude and stark a form. All these features, as we have seen, are frequently met with in dreams.

*

The same sort of thing, but naturally with many differences, occurs in many so-called mystic experiences—hallucinations of sight or hearing, interior visions or auditions, or ineffable sense of grace or communion. In certain ways it may be said that the mystic experience is on a lower plane than logical thought or moral effort—for it generally substitutes images for concepts, and is also in many cases a wish-fulfilment rather than a wrestling with fact. On the other hand, it is only fair to say that the gradual perfection of the mystic experience, which so many of the mystics record, represents a raising of the level in regard to another aspect of mental life, namely, the embracingness of the experience, the comprehension of many aspects of reality in one mental act, the integrated resolution of conflict.

All agree in general that meditative prayer is a preliminary stage: this passes over with practice from a state when it is accompanied by normal, directed thought (a 'prayer of understanding') to a state known technically as the 'prayer of simplicity', in which connected or logical thought is in abeyance.

After this, visions and auditions often make their appearance, and the worshipper usually goes through an experience known generally as mystical conversion, in which the struggle between the individual's 'natural' will and all those other tendencies described as the Will of God comes to resolution through the total submission of the individual. In later stages, so far as can be judged from the mystics' descriptions, the experience becomes more ineffable, more and more one of being *possessed by* some knowledge, or of directly feeling and perceiving what is felt and perceived as divinity, less and less one of its perception at a distance or of thinking about it, however clearly. It is interesting to note that many mystics record a sense of 'blackness' or 'night' as they first approach this stage, and find themselves giving up their familiar and clear processes of thinking to an as yet unpractised, confused, and fitful faculty of this direct perception.

The earlier stages after mystic conversion are sometimes called the prayer of quiet. As the sense of direct perception and the emotional intensity of the experience grows, voluntary control over the mental state diminishes. The mystic experience can no longer be relinquished by a simple act of will as formerly; it so fully possesses the mind that it has to be dispelled, if necessity arises, by active bodily movement. This is the stage described by St Teresa as the 'prayer of union'. Some mystics finally lose even this control, since during the experience they cease to be able to move their limbs at all, and may be wholly oblivious to the ordinary impressions of sense. This is the state technically known as true ecstasy, in which the body is in a cataleptic state, but the mind is caught up to full and deep experience. A further state is sometimes attained in which the soul is in a permanent state of illumination, the inhibitions on sense-impression and bodily movement are removed, and, on the contrary, an extraordinary impulse to activity in ordinary work is experienced; this is described both by St Teresa and Madame de Guyon.

It would seem thus that more and more of the mental life comes to be involved in the experience under the dominance of the ideas of divinity and love, until finally even the activities of everyday life, which at first were completely hostile to the mystic experience, themselves too become subordinate to the same dominant system of thought.

In passing, as emphasising the strange inter-relations of body and mind, it may be remarked that Madame de Guyon, one of the celebrated mystics, records not only considerable changes in her capacity for mystic experience with her monthly periods, but also a marked intensification of the blissful sense of peace when she was pregnant.

Many symptoms of undoubted hysteria can be directly paralleled from the lives of the great mystics, for instance St Catherine of Genoa. A good discussion of this point is to be found in *The Mystical Element in Religion*, by that remarkable character, himself a mystic, Baron von Hügel.

Mysticism makes one of the most interesting chapters of religion. The mystic's private certitude and frequent disregard of all outward conformity and of good works have often been a great stumbling-block to the ordinary devout but non-mystical churchman. In addition, where mysticism is valued, a regular epidemic of it tends to spring up by imitation and suggestion. Religious authorities themselves assure us that much so-called mystic experience is dangerous or even, in their terminology, from the Devil instead of from God; St Teresa herself, throughout a long period of her life, met with great opposition from her religious superiors.

The mystic experience clearly may be of extraordinary beauty and value to those who experience it; and may also be the truest refreshment of the soul wearied with conflict and with work.[1] But with it are involved two dangers—the danger of spiritual selfishness, of prizing the experience at the expense of all else; and the danger of distorted mental development, of forcing the soul into pathological, low-level, or one-sided activities, if the thoughts and desires back of the experience are themselves undisciplined, crude, or feeble.

*

The reader will have noted that the mystics themselves and religious writers in general apply the term *prayer* to all kinds of experiences to which its ordinary use in the sense of petition could not be applied. This brings us to some consideration of ordinary or petitionary prayer such as is prescribed in the Book of Common Prayer and is habitual morning and evening with most Christians. On reflection, it will be seen to have two functions; one which only has meaning if the worshipper has a real belief in a personal deity who can influence the

[1] 'What fruit dost thou bring back from this thy vision?' is the final question which Jacopone da Todi addresses to the mystic's soul. And the answer is: 'An ordered life in every state.' (Evelyn Underhill, *Mysticism*, p. 23.)

course of events; and another which only has meaning in so far as the worshipper has a real desire for his own spiritual alteration, or for experience of those attributes which he associates with this deity, attributes of sanctity and awfulness, of power and tremendous mystery, of goodness and love, of beauty and wisdom. These two motives are inextricably mixed in the prayers of Christian churches and indeed of most theistic religions.

Without some of the second element, prayer is in itself valueless as a spiritual exercise, and tends, by a natural psychological process, to degenerate. For if prayer is a mere petition, nothing should matter so long as it is in due form, and reaches its destination. All the other functions of prayer, however, are in reality functions of contemplation and meditation rather than petition. The contemplation may be of some intense desire of the worshippers, such as the desire for purity, and so be cast in the form of a petition; but the psychological machinery will not operate unless the idea permeates the mind. Prayer of this contemplative type is one of the central kernels of developed religion. It permits the bringing before the mind of a world of thought which in most people must inevitably be absent during the occupations of ordinary life: it allows the deepest longings of the soul, driven down below the surface by circumstance, to come into action: and it is the means by which the mind may fix itself upon this or that noble or beautiful or awe-inspiring idea, and so grow to it and come to realise it more fully.

It is thus partly a method of auto-suggestion, partly a means of refreshing the spirit. It differs psychologically from the banal methods of auto-suggestion as described by M. Coué and his followers, in that it insists on attempting to contemplate some spiritual fact or idea in all its glory. In so far as the soul succeeds in this, it will be tapping sources of spiritual peace and vitality which cannot be gained by the mere repetition of a formula.

In what I have been saying, I have spoken of contemplative prayer at its best. Like every other religious activity it may fall short, be deflected from its true aim through the distorting power of false reasoning, or become secondarily degraded. If the worshipper's earnest desire is not fixed, either directly or indirectly, upon spiritual beauty and truth or his own improvement, but upon some material benefit or some change in the course of nature, then his theology is deluding him and his effort is vain. Or he may fix his thoughts on revenge or some other desire of low spiritual quality, and thus degrade instead of elevating his soul. If he allows prayer to become simply a ritual of agreeably familiar words, the mere recital of which is felt to exert some mysterious power, then he is allowing both the petitionary and the contemplative aspect of prayer to sink to the level of magic. It should also not be forgotten that for many people art and literature help nowadays to accomplish many of the functions of meditative prayer. Good music to many listeners brushes away all the cobwebs of everyday, and opens the ivory gates of meditation, while at the same time 'taking the mind with beauty', imposing a dominant loveliness and reverence upon the spirit. Tolstoy's description, in *War and Peace,* of the effect of music on the troubled mind of Nicholas Rostov, is an admirable instance of this effect in its simplest and most immediate form. Good literature, among other functions, brings both dormant and wholly new ideas to the mind's front door, and helps to comprehension. It also often provides a means whereby the mind works off its own repressions of fear or desire through imaginative participation or realisation of them as portrayed in the doings of others. In fact, it may be safely said that the frank discussion and portrayal of every side of human nature in books and art, so often lamented by strait-laced moralists, on balance even now does more for promoting a healthy and assured moral life than it does towards encouraging immoral tendencies; and if pruriency and taboo-fears were removed, the balance on the good side would be much greater.

With all this, however, prayer of the type I have described will always retain a vital and important function; for it is the product of the individual himself, a mode both of self-discipline and self-expression in relation to the problems which immediately beset him. Only actual creation in the field of art has this kind of value; and thoughtless people who contemn the average second-rate man or woman for painting or writing verse have simply neglected to think of the spiritual value, akin to that of the best type of prayer, which may be gained by the individual himself from his work.

*

One other very frequent psychological moment in religion is what may be called the desire to escape from self. The psychological basis of this would seem to be fairly easy to comprehend, although details will obviously differ at different levels of culture. On the one hand, the feeling of the self or ego builds itself up gradually out of the chaotic mind-life of the infant; and in the process some activities and thoughts are closely woven together into the texture of the 'I,' others remain outside or are repressed or but loosely connected, and when they irrupt and make connection with the ego, they are frequently felt as belonging to some external power or being. Meanwhile, of course, the 'I' is set off more and more sharply in thought against the 'not-I' of the outer world. But the outer world is bound to the individual soul through all sorts of ties, and these are strongest when, as in primitive thought, the emotional qualities, like sanctity in the case of religion, are felt as inhering in the outer objects, not projected into them from the mind; and the unorganised fringe of mind-life outside the boundaries of the ego is, of course, connected by all kinds of psychological channels with the central ego-core. The 'escape from self' on the primitive level generally has as its basis the desire to identify the self with the not-self, either with some aspect of the outer world, or with the god worshipped. In both cases, the objective outer world and the subjective un-self-organised parts of the mind are usually interwoven in what is felt as 'not-self.'

Anyone who has played a part in a play knows how the attempt to take on another's character does actually enlarge the mind, and how for the time being one's own individuality is in large part given up or blended with the imaginary personality; and the 'let's pretend' games of children show, on a simpler level, what satisfaction is achieved through the method of temporary identification of the self with some other person or object. At the cultural level of undeveloped religions, these universal motives are strengthened by belief in magic. Thus, masquerading as animals, when performed in special ways to the accompaniment of particular rites, may be believed in as a means of ensuring the increase of the animal, or of achieving success in its chase. Various methods are also in vogue of combining dramatic or symbolic ritual with the ideas of magic, in order to obtain communion with the deity. Sometimes the deity is supposed to be incarnate in a human being or an animal, and is then sacrificed, and communion with the divine spirit ensured by partaking of the flesh in a solemn or ritual way: this appears to have been the rule in the Orphic religion as well as many savage cults. Later, some object is often substituted, and communion ensured by partaking of this, as in

Christian ritual. Or the ritual meal may be omitted, and the sacrifice continued.

The rites of Thammuz or Adonis, in which the personified or symbolised god was each year sacrificed, to rise again as the expression of the next year's new-gained fertility, are fully analysed by Frazer (and see my *From an Antique Land*, 1954, Ch. 3). Miss Murray believes that a similar need for periodic sacrifice of a human being embodying divinity was one of the central tenets of the pre-Christian religion of Western Europe, which, driven underground by Christianity, came to be known as the witch-cult. Here the sacrifice had, it appears, to be voluntary, which would account for the numerous cases of voluntary confession, leading to inevitable death, by men and women 'witches' in the sixteenth and seventeenth centuries; and this voluntary sacrifice on the part of one of the adherents of the religion would give the sense of communion in the sacrifice to the whole congregation.[2]

D. H. Lawrence, in his *Mornings in Mexico*, has described the Deer dance of one of the Indian tribes. Lawrence was a novelist, not versed in anthropology; but he had a sensitive mind; and it is interesting to find how the sense of 'communion by identification' impressed him in watching the rite.

'Everything,' he says, 'is very soft, subtle, delicate. There is none of the hardness of representation. They are not representing anything, not even playing. It is a soft, subtle *being* something.

'Yet at the same time it is a game, and a very dramatic naïve spectacle. The old men trot softly alongside, showing all their wrinkles. But they are experiencing a delicate, wild inward delight, participating in the natural mysteries. . . . You have it all, the pantomime, the buffoonery, the human comicalness. But at the same time, quivering bright and wide-eyed in unchangeable delight of solemnity, you have the participating in a natural wonder.' As a reviewer of the book puts it, Lawrence finds the Indian 'merging all forces and himself in the mystery of creation, a drama that cannot be judged or rationalised because there is nobody to judge it from outside.'

The other root of the desire to escape from self is the desire to be rid of the burden of sin. I have not the space to embark on this formidable topic. But I can perhaps throw out a few

[2] In New Mexico, a heretical sect still carries out the secret and illegal practice of crucifying (now no longer by nails but by bonds) one of its members every Easter. Here too the sacrifice appears to be wholly voluntary.

hints towards its better consideration. Two important facts meet us at the outset—namely, that the sense of sin is often much more strongly developed in what the opinion of the world would class as quite virtuous people than in genuine criminals. Indeed, modern psychological study makes it clear that a considerable proportion of criminals become criminal because equipped by their development with a subnormal moral sense, an insufficient capacity for experiencing the sense of sin at all. In the second place, we often find that the sense of sin may be strongly aroused by infringing apparently neutral, stupid, or meaningless injunctions, much less than by the transgression of universally-recognized moral rules.

The first depends upon the psychological fact that there cannot be a sense of sin without a conflict. In general, the stronger the conflict, the stronger the sense of sin.[3] This is well illustrated by the records of those who have experienced sudden conversion; they almost invariably exaggerate, often to a ludicrous extent, the sinfulness of perfectly ordinary worldly activities, or of trivial moral lapses which occurred before their conversion. The second depends upon the power of taboos to acquire a formidable charge of sanctity.

The doctrine of original sin is a theological perversion of natural fact. It is a fact that all human beings begin life with an equipment of instincts, impulses, and desires, at war with one another and often out of harmony with the realities of the physical, social, and spiritual world. A child is like an animal or a bird in that one impulse at a time comes into full possession of its mental life, only to be replaced by another in a flash when the time comes. Rational self-restraint, altruism, and control, the uniting of the separate impulses into a unitary mental organism, and the moulding of this in adaptation to reality, can only come with the growth of reasoned reflection and emotional illumination.

Further, it is also a fact that, while the majority of human beings attain in their normal mental development to a reasonably balanced and adapted state, which may be called that of the reasonable natural man, yet a few here and there reach a further condition, sometimes called illumination, or grace, or faith, or salvation, in which they reach a devotion to an ideal and an inward certitude which is out of the ordinary.

---

[3] Infantile conflict appears to be the source of conscience, the Freudian super-ego, or a developed moral sense. See T. H. and J. S. Huxley, *Touchstone for Ethics*, Harper, New York, 1947.

But to assert the dogma that this latter fact is due to super-natural grace, and that man's normal state implies that we are all conceived in sin, born damned, by nature evil, is an unwarranted addition, the outcome of the theological necessity of linking up the story of the Fall with the supposed unique redemptive powers of Jesus, although the Fall had been believed in for centuries without *arrière pensée,* and precisely the same type of redemptive power had been ascribed to divinities, in Orphism, Mithraic worship and elsewhere, without involving the idea of original sin.

Sin and the sense of sin will always be with us, to torture and weigh down; but, as I have said elsewhere in this book, the religion of the future will try to prevent men's being afflicted with the sense of sin, rather than encourage it and then attempt to cure it.

The repression of experiences and impulses which are painful, and especially those which generate painful conflict, seems to be a necessary preliminary to conversion. On the other hand, there is the necessity, again and again during the process of organising the mind, not to take refuge in repression, but to bring the conflicting impulses into the open and face the pain involved in so doing, if it is desired to reach a higher level of mental adjustment; and this is the psychological basis for the stress laid upon suffering, especially moral suffering, as forwarding principle in religious development.

The chief psychological alternatives to repression, which seems invariably to be harmful, are suppression by conscious control, and sublimation. The word sublimation has been rather mishandled; but the essential point about it is that the growing mind, in its progressive self-organisation, can build instincts and impulses into its machinery in extremely various ways. The instincts and other more complex impulses are tendencies to action. Certain stimuli arouse particular emotions and give the motor machinery an impulse to action. In lower animals, both the type of stimulus which arouses a particular instinct, and the type of action in which the instinct, once aroused, will issue or attempt to issue, are relatively (though by no means absolutely) fixed and invariable. But in man, both the kind of stimulus and the kind of action may be altered within very wide limits. To take the end of action first, fear may be made to issue not in flight, but in greater alertness or prudence; the sex-instinct may be operative in the writing of a poem or the building of a business; or parental affection may be harnessed to work to pay the cost of education. On the other hand, by various processes, a different object from the normal may come to arouse the instinct or impulse—by association, as when a piece of the clothes worn by a holy man is believed to be sacred enough to work miracles, or by substitution, as when a childless woman lavishes her affection upon a pet. Finally, simple instincts can be built up into complex ones, and the instincts or innate dispositions to action can be combined with habit and the results of experience to produce the more elaborate dispositions to action which the professional psychologist, for lack of a better word, calls sentiments. The religious sentiment is one of these, and it is not inherited as such, although certain inherited capacities, like fear and reverence, enter into it.

The long and the short of it is that human dispositions to action are very plastic, and may be altered at either end, both where they are sensitive to the outer world and where they act upon it, and in the middle, which decides the kind of action. The sublimation of a repressed impulse implies the utilisation of the impulse for new ends of action; or its utilisation in conjunction with other impulses for a higher mode of action; or both.

*

So far, I have said little about what is often spoken of as the kernel of religion, namely, faith. This has been because faith can hardly be considered without some study of its psychological basis. As a start, I may quote from Thouless, who writes on religious psychology from the standpoint of a psychologist who is also a professing Christian. 'The method by which our beliefs are influenced by other people is not, on the whole, reasoned demonstration. The child does not have the existence of God proved to it in its religious lessons. It is still true in later life that the simple affirmation of religious doctrines by a person for whom we have respect, or the mere fact of the holding of such doctrines by the persons amongst whom we live, may have an authority over us compared with which the influence of the most convincing chain of reasoning is negligible. The method by which beliefs are transmitted to us otherwise than by reasoned demonstration is *suggestion*.'

McDougall, discussing the matter on purely scientific grounds, writes that suggestion is 'the imparting of a proposition in such a manner that it is accepted with conviction, independently of any logical grounds for such conviction.' Further, all authors are agreed that suggestion in the ordinary waking state differs only from suggestion in hypnotic trance in that the effects observed are not so extreme.

The precise methods by which suggestion is brought about need not concern us deeply. McDougall, in his *Abnormal Psychology,* summarises the psychological theories on the subject, while Pavlov, in his *Conditioned Reflexes,* brings us a little way towards the possibility of an explanation in terms of nerve-physiology.

In all cases, however, there comes in the feature, noted both by Thouless and McDougall alike, that an idea may obtain authority over our mind, and become accepted with a powerful sense of conviction, quite apart from its appeal to reason, logic, or experience. In some way or other, that is to say, the part of the mind concerned with the acceptance of the idea is more or less completely dissociated from, switched off from connection with, that part connected with the power of making rational judgments on the basis of past experience. In a good case of hypnotism, the dissociation is practically complete. A man may be persuaded that he is someone else; that he cannot unclasp his hands; that the back of a playing-card is a photograph of his father; that two out of five similar objects on the table under his eyes are not there at all; and so on;—and will act in full accordance with the induced belief. In ordinary suggestion, where the individual in his waking state accepts statements made by some authority without bothering about their logical implications, the dissociation is only partial. We may say that the control of experience and reason is weakened but not removed. The confidence trick and the gold brick swindle both depend upon successful suggestion. The procedure adopted in either case is hardly in accordance with common-sense or ordinary business experience; yet by suggestion the swindlers generate a belief which every year overrides the common-sense and business experience of dozens of 'hard-headed' fellows—and leaves them poorer in consequence. The Christian Scientist can believe that pain has no real existence: the fundamentalist can believe in Noah's ark or Jonah's whale: the be-propaganda'd patriot in the 1914 war could believe that all Germans were, not human beings, but fiends incarnate: the Mohammedan can believe and feel that it is shocking for a woman to show her face; while we can find it shocking for her to show her leg above the knee—at ordinary times, though we do not find it so on the bathing beach: those who are told that ghosts and witches exist experience no difficulty in finding evidence of them.

In most cases of waking suggestion, however, the fact suggested is either not too unlike ordinary experience to be impossible; or it has a basis of real truth; or the logical and rational reasons against its truth are unfamiliar or difficult of comprehension. The success of the confidence trick depends on the actuality of real confidence between friends; the belief of the Christian Scientist reposes upon the real fact that much pain can be made to disappear by not brooding over it; the suggestion that a particular garb or lack of garb is indecent depends upon the fact that indecency exists; the belief in witchcraft or in a flat or a central earth is possible because the chain of reasoning which excludes magic or demands a spherical circling globe is comparatively complex.

It might be thought, if suggestion always depended upon a partial disregard of our mental watch-dog, rational experience, that it must always be undesirable, and that it was very difficult to understand its origin on evolutionary principles. On the contrary, suggestibility can, on a little reflection, be seen to be a biological necessity, particularly in the early stages of man's evolution. If it is necessary for certain types of action to be performed in strict accord with the dictates of reason and experience, it is equally necessary for other actions to be performed unquestioningly at the behest of authority or of communal feeling. We all know that only one man can be captain aboard ship, and that what counts in war is victory. There must have been thousands of people on both sides in the World Wars who hated the idea of war, but who, once war was there, acquiesced as a necessity, though not without a feeling of nausea, in the unleashing of the forces of propaganda—in other words, of national suggestion—in order to enlist more of the will of the country.

But even apart from emergencies like war, suggestibility and acceptance are necessary for any community. To take the scientific sphere alone, it is probably quite impossible to-day for any one man, however brilliant and hard-working, to master the main evidence in all fields of scientific knowledge. How much more impossible, then, for the man with limited leisure to do so. This means, however, that many of the ideas of science must either be taken on trust by a great number of people, or else not accepted at all. In education, even the most ardent advocates of the child's finding things out for himself admit that, life being short and knowledge infinite, it is impossible to apply the principle radically, but that the child must be told some things and must believe them.

We may sum up by saying that on the one hand the concerted relation of leadership and subordination and also the diffusion of knowledge, would be impossible without some suggestibility.

On the other hand—and this is a vital point—suggestibility need not be abject, nor faith blind or misdirected. The educated man need not be able to follow all the evidence on which the modern theory of the atom or the hereditary constitution is based; but he can have a basis of scientific training and knowledge and an understanding of scientific method which makes his acceptance a reasonable one. The sailor need not understand the reasons for the order given by his superior officer; but he can understand why obedience on shipboard is necessary, and not merely obey like a dog.

We may put it from a slightly different angle. Suggestibility and its results, obedience or faith, irrespective of logical reasoning, are characters of the human species, mental properties which exist whether we like them or not; and they can be employed, like any other of the raw materials of the human mind, either well or ill.

The mind will employ them ill if it takes the bit between its teeth and allows the dissociation between suggested idea and rational experience to remain totally unbridged. It will employ them well if it does its best to test the irrational possibilities of suggestion against its store of reasoned knowledge. In this way it will acquire for its use the forcefulness of suggested convictions, but prevent them from leading the personality astray into actions not only non-rational but opposed to truth. Here, as everywhere else in the mental life, reason and experience, though they can do little to initiate, can do everything to guide and control.

Once it is properly appreciated that faith rests upon precisely the same basis as hypnotic suggestion, religiously-minded people should be the first to see that the faith which they have should not be purely arbitrary, the result of authority alone, but rational. The day has gone by when a saying such as Tertullian's 'Certum est quia impossibile est'—it is certain because it is impossible—could be regarded with approval. Nor will the saying, 'Faith is the evidence of things not seen,' meet the outlook of to-day. 'Faith is belief in the nobler hypothesis' is too reminiscent of such rhetoric as Disraeli's 'I am on the side of the angels' to be satisfying.

Is not faith rather the sum of our beliefs as they predispose us to thought and action, whether these beliefs are purely reasoned, or purely suggested, or based on suggestion tempered with reason; and ought it not to be a reproach instead of a boast that faith can be upheld in opposition to reason, and human nature, here again, divided against itself?

It will be objected that I have throughout been using the

term faith on its lower level of meaning, simply as belief in certain propositions or acquiescence in the commands of certain kinds of authority, and have neglected that higher (and, it is often claimed, specifically religious) kind of faith which has power to remove mountains, inspires steadfastness unto death, and is indeed a passion of the soul and not mere assent. Such faith is truly an amazing phenomenon of the mind. It is a complex state of the soul, in which complete conviction, such as is obtained by suggestion, is combined with the deepest and most powerful desires. It is not, however, true to say that it is solely a property of the religiously-minded. The choice of Regulus, or the behaviour of thousands in the world wars, shows that it may be generated in relation to patriotism; the fantastic exploits of true lovers (in which overpowering, but by no means necessarily rational or correct, belief that the loved one is of supreme value is combined with profoundest desire) show that it may be generated in relation to individual human beings. On the other hand, it will be found that its highest manifestations are those in which the sense of sacredness is involved, and where other religious motives too, in the shape of concern with general ideas of human destiny, also play their part. That faith at this highest pitch has a vital part to play in life, few would deny. But its passionate certitude carries with it the danger to the individual of self-delusion, the danger to others of intolerance and persecution. If the men whose business it is to think and to carry the burden of perplexity towards intellectual solution, the Marthas of the mind, can whole-heartedly admire the rare Mary whose spiritual passion of faith forces the soul into an inevitable rightness of growth and lovely flowering, they have also the right both to point out the all-too-numerous weeds which this same faith may generate when growth goes astray, and to demand from faith consideration and respect for their activities and the spiritual plants that grow from them.

The two are complementary; each has its sphere, its triumphs, and its failures; alone, both the one and the other tend easily to evolve into the incomplete or even the monstrous.

*

Ritual also deserves some consideration. This does not, so much as theology, become attached secondarily to the religious emotion, but rather grows directly out of it as its immediate expression. In some cases, even, non-moral actions (such as those performed in a state of exaltation) may be regarded as in themselves sacred, and here ritual, in the form of these actions, may make a primary contribution to religion. On the other hand, so soon as intellect and morality have been roped in to become part of the field of religion, conclusions can be drawn from them which demand fulfilment in ritual.

The simplest forms of ritual are those actions which are the natural accompaniments of a sense of awe or reverence: obeisance, kneeling, or prostration; exclamations; great care for the object of reverence, and a desire to adorn and beautify it. But there are certain actions and their accompanying feelings which are almost universally regarded as sacred by primitive man owing to the sense which accompanies them of being possessed by some fresh and external power—the various states of exaltation.

Exaltation may come in connection with epileptic fits; with intoxication; with the taking of various drugs; with dancing; with the communal frenzies, recorded even at many modern revivals, of 'shaking' and of 'speaking with tongues.' In so far as the sense of exaltation can at all be obtained by deliberate performance of certain actions, the ritual of these actions may be embodied as an integral part of a religion.

Some of the most curious feelings of exaltation are those associated with the taking of anæsthetics, like ether or 'laughing gas.' A number are mentioned by William James. The interesting thing is that just before becoming unconscious, the subject often has a thrilling sense of having solved the riddle of the universe, accompanied by both peace and exaltation. On waking, however, the 'revelation' turns out, apparently invariably, to be either meaningless or banal. Colonel Blood, for instance, one of James's correspondents, records having been vouchsafed an anæsthetic revelation which, in his remarkable style, he describes as consisting of 'nineteen centuries of brain-sweat crystallised in a jewel five words long.' The jewel, however, turned out to be merely the not very illuminating proposition: 'The Universe has no opposite.' Oliver Wendell Holmes, the writer and medical man, in his *Mechanism in Thought and Morals*, records a good example of the commonplace type, which he himself experienced after ether. 'The veil of eternity was lifted. . . . Henceforth all was clear; a few words had lifted my intelligence to the level of the cherubim. As my natural condition returned, . . . staggering to my desk, I wrote down the all-embracing truth still glimmering in my consciousness. The words were these (children may smile; the wise will ponder): "A strong smell of turpentine prevails throughout." ' As he rightly says, the wise will ponder.[4]

Eskimo and Indian priests (medicine-men) are often chosen on account of epileptic tendencies; certain dervishes produce a state of religious exaltation by violent dancing, as do various negro tribes; Rivers records how among the Todas of India divination may be accompanied by a species of hysterical 'possession'; the automatism known as 'speaking with tongues,' or in later psychological parlance as *glossolalia*, was highly prized by the early Christians as part of their religious life; the Bacchanals combined wine and the dance to produce a mystic frenzy; the modern sect of Shakers live up to their name; and extraordinary scenes of the sort are recorded of revivalist camp-meetings in America.

In such cases the ritual imposes itself directly as a part of the religious life. But when, for instance, belief in a powerful supernatural being prompts the adoption of rites of propitiation by sacrifice or offering, the ritual is added consequentially.

The highest forms of ritual are those in which the two aspects are united; ritual at its best is like a good work of art in that it both expresses and generates emotion and thought.

The difficulties which have grown up concerning ritual in the last few centuries are on the whole secondary difficulties, the necessary consequence of primary difficulties in the sphere of theology. Many of the Puritan and Protestant difficulties (like the difficulties of the great controversy about image-worship in the eighth century) about 'idols', visible images and pictures, the virtual worship of saints, and so forth, have a theological origin. If God is essentially a *purely* spiritual being, then it is logical to worship him by the aid of pure spirit alone, and any material representation is a degradation of this spirituality. But common sense has usually triumphed over this point, and allowed a reasonable symbolism.

Other difficulties are largely a matter of taste, such as that over vestments and elaborate ceremonial—though here, of course, the echoes of historical cleavages are still powerful, the Protestant often not judging such practices on their merits, but seeing in them the scarlet shadow of Rome.

---

[4] Mescalin and lysergic acid induce remarkable intensifications and modifications of consciousness, including often a sense of transcendence of self: see Aldous Huxley, *The Doors of Perception* and *Heaven and Hell*. Among some American Indians, the taking of mescalin forms part of religious ceremonies, as vividly described by Edna Ferber in *Cimarron*.

In general it may be said that for a common service, some form of ritual, however non-formal, is a necessity; but that the precise form of the ritual will inevitably depend partly on historical causes, partly on the taste and mental temper of the worshippers, the Quaker finding both Salvationist and Anglo-Catholic 'busied about vain things,' the ritualist finding the revivalist vulgar and the Quaker devoid of savour, and so forth. The chief psychological danger of ritual is that too much sanctity may become attached to its precise perform-ance, and so the means become an end. As a result, in the sphere of morals, rigid ritual taboos are substituted for true morality, as in later Jewish religion; while on the emotional or expressive side, reverence is swamped in what seems, to the outsider at least, a childish love of dressing up and of gorgeous mumbo-jumbo.

*

Another important point may perhaps be considered here: I am thinking of the satisfaction of religious feeling in ways which are outside the domain of religion as ordinarily under-stood and as organised in a church. Do not let us forget that in the Middle Ages the Church extended its sway over many more departments of life than it does to-day. The church building had not yet been cut off by the Puritan spirit as a bare House of God to the exclusion of all else. As a place for the exhibition of sacred and natural rarities, it served as a museum: it was usually the only approach to an art-gallery: as stage for the mystery plays it was a theatre, as place of plain-song and chanted mass a concert-room: the reading of the Bible stories in the lessons was half the average man's chance of literature.

The church porch is still used for many official notices: in old days it was much more both of a social and a business centre. In addition, before the rise of the universities, monas-teries were among the chief centres of scholarship and of medical knowledge as well as of various arts and crafts. That is all gone. There is now a division of function, and we have our museums, our art-galleries, our concert-halls, libraries, theatres, our secular universities; and the functions of the church, both as organisation and as edifice, are narrowed down.

From the point of view of the diffusion of thought and ideas, man has passed through four main stages and is now entering upon a fifth. He began with speech alone. He proceeded to the invention of writing, and so to the greater permanence and accuracy of his tradition. Then came printing, with the possibility of multiplication of the written word. With the industrial era there came the substitution of the machine-power for man-power, with consequent new multiplication of the multiplying capacity of the printing-press, and therefore the possibility of the dissemination of ideas literally to everybody, in every place, owing to the cheapness of mass-production.

Finally, in the last half-century or so, we have entered upon a new era, whose implications and whose possibilities we have hardly yet envisaged. This is the era of new modes of spreading human thought and human achievement. Even if we leave out photography and telegraphy, there remain the invention of the gramophone and sound-recorder, the cinema, the radio and television, and the perfection of cheap colour-printing. All these, in their several ways, are completely altering the whole problem of the diffusion of culture, and so of the growth of culture and civilisation itself. Not only is the spread of ideas and knowledge, already facilitated by writing and printing, now again facilitated and speeded up, but the achievements of the human spirit in music and painting can to-day be spread and enjoyed in ways previously impossible.

What, it may perhaps be asked, has this to do with religion? It has a good deal to do with it. Before the perfection of writing, religion could not but be mainly a social affair; its social ceremonials and shared beliefs were the chief way of expression for the religious spirit. With the introduction of writing, it was possible for those who could read and write to find an outlet in writing for the expression of their own personal ideas, and, in reading, to commune with the thoughts of other individuals, in addition to participating in the un-individual, socialised thought and feeling of organised religion. This process was accelerated by the introduction of printing, but so long as books were dear and education restricted— that is to say, even in the most civilised countries, until the middle of last century—organised religion was bound to remain socialised if it was to affect the bulk of the community.

But now industrialism, universal education, improved transport and communications, and the progress of invention are putting a different complexion on affairs. You remember what Milton once wrote: 'A good book is the precious life-blood of a master spirit, embalmed and treasured up on purpose to a life beyond life'. If the spiritual life-blood of the great masters of thought is available to everyone, why go to church and listen to familiar prayers and to a prosy sermon, when you could stay at home and receive new knowledge and deeper thoughts from a book? Goethe, Emerson, Wordsworth, Blake, Carlyle, Dante, Sir Thomas Browne, Shelley, and the rest of the assembly of immortal spirits—they jostle each other on your shelves, each waiting only to be picked up to introduce you to his own unique and intense experience of reality.

The *Origin of Species* is to-day a good deal more profitable as theology than the first chapter of Genesis, and William James' *Principles of Psychology* will be a better commentary on the Decalogue than any hortatory sermon. The poetry of Herbert or Donne or Vaughan, of Francis Thompson or Walt Whitman, will introduce you to new ways of mystic feeling; Trevelyan's *History of England* is likely to be a more salutary history lesson, because nearer home, than the historical books of the Old Testament; Whitehead's *Science and the Modern World* is more likely to help the perplexed mind of a twentieth-century Englishman than the apocalyptic visions of Revelations or the neo-Platonic philosophy of the Fourth Gospel; to sacrifice a score of Sundays to making acquaintance with the ideas of other great religions like Buddhism might be very much preferable, even from the purely religious point of view, to continuance in the familiar round and the familiar narrowness of one's own church.

And the same is true in other spheres. You may get much more spiritual exaltation and joy out of a Beethoven concert, or even out of Beethoven on the gramophone, than by listening to your local organist play Mendelssohn or the 'March of the Priests'. You may exercise your highest faculties by travel, now that travel is easy and cheap, or you may stay at home and discipline your mind with reproductions of what the great artists and sculptors and architects have imagined and expressed. If you are primarily in love with morality and character, you may obtain a fuller insight into them by reading the great novelists and playwrights, and the biographies of great men, than by confining yourself to the Bible and the saints.

What is more, there is no reason whatever why in all such activity you should not in your degree be participating in the religious life. All philosophy and science, all great art, all history, all lives of men—one and all may inspire to reverence or exaltation, or be made the subject of reflection which, being concerned with great problems of destiny in a grave and reverent way, is more truly religious than any pietism.

From the point of view of religious psychology it is important to remember that probably any intense emotion, whether fear, wonder, horror, disgust, sex-love, admiration, is capable of becoming the basis for religious sentiment, belief, and action; it is so capable because all really strong emotions come with such a feeling of externality, 'a sense of something given', as Wordsworth puts it, and are, in the literal sense of the word, so extraordinary, such mysterious visitations, that something of numinous quality hangs about them. It is through this fact that such curious objects can become objects of religious worship—the snake which inspires horror; the wild beasts which generate fear; the human sex-organs; and so forth.

What, in later development, remains within the bounds of organised religion depends largely upon the way reason has worked upon the original raw 'theoplasm', and upon social and historical accidents. But it should always be remembered that any particular religion will always be incomplete, and that many potential religion-arousing objects will not be utilised in it.

They may be forced into opposition, so to speak, and acquire negative sacredness, become taboo or sinful, as with sex in Christianity, in striking contradiction to many religions, like Hinduism, in which sex and its emblems are part of worship; or they may be simply left out, as with the sacredness of tribe or country in mediæval Christianity. As a result, with the growth of nationalism and the revival of this religious motive, patriotism has in reality become a subsidiary religion side by side with the other organised religious activities to which we usually restrict the term.

It might be said that if this is the case, there is no room left for organised worship. I do not think this is so. There will always remain the religious satisfaction of plunging the mind in a common social act, and always a satisfaction in familiar ritual hallowed by time and association. There is also to many people a satisfaction in symbolism; and to others in finding, in the combined privacy and publicity of the church service, a simultaneous release from the world and from the individual self.

On the other hand, it seems clear that the more opportunities there are for satisfying this or that aspect of the religious life outside a set service and a church building, the less important will service and building become.

As matters stand to-day, we have the cleavage between orthodox religion which has hitched its wagon—the sense of the sacred—not to a star, but to a traditional theology; and a large body of educated people who, rejecting the theology, are forced to stand outside religion too. And as one of the minor curious and unforeseen results of this state of affairs, we have the exaggerated deference and homage paid by a large section of the public to the artist and the imaginative writer. With them, the artist and the writer have taken the place of the prophet and the priest. Owing to their usual extreme individualism and lack of deep grounding in any common basis of knowledge, the artist and the writer on the whole very indifferently fulfil the rôle which has been thrust upon them. But the situation is more the churches' fault than theirs. It can only be remedied when the view of religion has come to be more limited in its ambition, but more catholic in its sweep; and great men and great art come into their due place in the religious outlook.

To be always religious, however, is as intolerable as to be always laughing, or always working, or always playing golf. For a man to have a religious disposition it is no more necessary for religious feeling to be always in possession of the mind than it is for a man of a humorous disposition to be incapable of sentiment or seriousness. The mere variety of human nature and human activity is its richness and its charm; and to give each faculty and each approach to reality its turn and its due place in life is to live not only fully but truly.

Variety is spiritual richness, and variety and indeed opposition are necessary for the highest achievements of individuals and of civilisations. We rightly admire the man of many-sided genius—Leonardo da Vinci, Goethe, Aristotle, Michelangelo. But that is not the only way of achievement; one-sidedness is as necessary for society as many-sidedness, and it can attain the highest heights and the deepest intensities. We do not demand that the cart-horse shall win races, nor that the hammer shall saw wood, nor the poet rule nations. A colour-blind man could give a new mathematical insight to the world; and Darwin's achievement was no more lessened by his inability, as he grew older, to take pleasure in art and literature, than was Newton's by his childish preoccupation with the esoteric interpretation of scriptural prophecy. St

Francis of Assisi was a living denial of nine-tenths of what to most men makes life worth living; and yet for most men he enriched life and its possibilities. William Blake had a hatred of all reason and organised knowledge; yet the most ardent believer in science and organisation may be enriched through reading him.

We need poets as we need artisans; we need visionaries as much as hard-headed business men; we need the man who devotes all his energy to invention; we need the artist and the man of science; we need the saint; we need achievement, and we need character.

If our religion is a true religion, a religion of fuller life, it must both tolerate and reverence variety. The efficient biologist or engineer who would deny all value to religious meditation and the religious life; the missionary who begins by suppressing all native activities of which he in the least disapproves; the scholastic theologians who denied independent value to natural science or humanist philosophy; the efficient administrator who would lock up as a vagrant everyone who is not constantly at work—all are limited in their outlook, and because limited therefore wrong. Even Plato, at the full flight of his imagination, desiring to banish poetry and art from his ideal republic, was subordinating reality to logic and had failed to gain a full vision of truth and virtue. But our tolerance must not be merely passive, a tired intellectual gesture; it must be active, springing from the belief and knowledge that truth is too large to be revealed in but one form, or one creed, or one way of life. We must accept the hard saying that out of diversity alone comes advance, and that any one human mind is too small to grasp more than a little truth, to live more than a little reality.

*

One of the most vital things is to have singleness of heart. If religion be an art, it must be unified, like a good work of art. The artist learns (or knows without learning, if he is a good artist) that it is not variety, or size, or quantity of objects represented which make a great picture, but its inherent quality—something which only comes through its being a whole, with a single vision, and uniting in the single expression all kinds of ideas, hints, formal beauties, reticences, conflicts. So it comes about that a single figure may contain far more, be much nearer infinity, than a vast scene—as indeed

is the case with Michelangelo's sybils in the Sistine Chapel
when compared with his Last Judgment there; or a picture of
a bedroom chair, like that by Van Gogh in the Tate Gallery,
may bring us nearer to something absolute than any corona-
tion scene by the most fashionable of court painters.

The same principle indeed works in other spheres. To love
one woman fully is to wish not to love any other woman fully.
If a philosopher existed who was both purely rational and
had also never fallen in love, this would doubtless seem to
him very absurd—how could one limited human female,
when so many and such diverse types exist, satisfy the mind's
craving for variety? The answer is that it is so; but also that
as a matter of fact this complete giving of the self in one way
to one person makes it possible—so is the mind constructed—
to give and to receive more freely, but in a different way, to
and from other beings; whereas the attempt to love many
completely is impossible in practice, and with no single one
does the love attain fullness.

In these and other cases, what counts, what brings us nearer
the absolute, is quality not quantity, unity overpowering diversity, not merely diversity itself. This, if in somewhat other
terms, was fully and finely stated by the great Spinoza; to
whose *Ethics* the reader is referred for much both true and
sublime on these hard subjects of freedom, eternity, and the
absolute.

So it is with religion. All religions which have passed the
primitive stage demand this singleness of approach; it may
be necessary for personal religion to achieve intensity at the
cost of limitation, in this again resembling artistic expression.

If this be so, then a difficult problem remains, as between
personal and organised religion, since, as we have repeatedly
seen, limitation of organised religion recoils on to life and
means that organised religion will sooner or later come into
conflict with expanding life on its road to progress.

The problem is how to organise religion so that the church's
creeds and ritual shall be comprehensive (and yet not colour-
less and general), while permitting freedom for the individual
worshipper to make his own religious life intense and personal
(and yet not bigoted or obscurantist). Luckily it is not for me
to suggest a solution.

One or two conclusions, as it seems to me, emerge clearly
enough from even a brief consideration of this difficult subject.

In the first place, all sorts of our strangest experiences are neither supernatural nor pathological, but are natural though uncommon possibilities of the human mind. Trances, visions, or locutions, whether hallucinatory or of the type known as interior; mental ecstasy; the reproduction of marks on the skin, such as St Francis' stigmata, by the power of suggestion; instantaneous cures of certain types of disease by faith; the imposing of one man's will on another through suggestion, whether in or out of hypnosis; the splitting of a personality into two; automatic writing; obsessions; impulses which act with compulsive force—all these are among the strange crops which may grow from the soil of human mind. Many of them may be pathological, but the majority are in themselves neutral, and whether they lead to disease or to fuller powers depends upon the objects towards which they are directed, and whether or no they are duly balanced and held in place in the system of checks and counterchecks which makes for sane mind and its good government. To be always seeing visions is often a sign of a disordered mind; and yet a vision may not only condense into concrete form the aspirations and ideas working within a personality, but may refresh and reinforce them with new vigour. In partially-dissociated personalities, automatic writing may reveal the existence of the subordinate personality and lead, under treatment, to a linking up of the two into one. Suggestion may be employed for good ends. The noblest faith, inspiring martyrs to die or saints to live, is an obsession, but an obsession with what is highest and strongest.

In the second place, to understand the machinery of this or that experience of the religious life is not to strip it of value. At first blush it may seem as if to accept the psychological account of inspiration, for instance, to believe that inspiration represents the inflow into consciousness of thoughts and feelings that had been fermenting in the subconscious, instead of believing that it was the authentic voice of God, is to disvalue it. On reflection, however, it is seen that the sense of disappointment is due only to the intellectual views which you may have previously held about theology. If you interpret reality in the dualist terms of, on the one side, a supernatural being who is power and love and truth, and, on the other, poor mortals who are of no account without divine assistance and grace, these views will have so coloured your thoughts that you cannot quickly adjust them to a new scheme of ideas; but if you believe that the desire and capacity for love and truth and beauty and right action do reside in the human mind, and that inspiration is a name for one of the ways in which these desires and capacities become manifested and actualised, it does not, even under strictest psychological analysis, lose one jot or tittle of its true value, though it may be stripped of false trimmings. Not only that, but the psychological interpretation has one great advantage over the theological—it does not puff up men or churches with a false assurance of certitude.

The feeling of forgiveness and grace to a soul struggling with the sense of sin; the poignant experience of the value of others' atonement or of one's own suffering; the sense of communion with and peace in the realities that are around us—not only do these remain facts of psychological experience whatever interpretation or explanation of them be offered, but their value is not in the interpretation, but in themselves.

It is, of course, true that a false interpretation may give a fictitious value to this or that fact or experience, as when the false interpretation which we call magic gives fictitious value to various incantations or rites; or a false belief in the literal inspiration of the oracle at Delphi led to the attachment of a fictitious value to the oracle's deliveries; or a false theology gives fictitious value to scriptures supposed to be literally inspired, and so leads to irreconcilable disputes and even to wars. What I am concerned to show is rather that there are many experiences belonging to the religious life which are of value in and for themselves, and that neither does their supernatural interpretation add to them anything essential, nor the naturalistic interpretation strip them of anything vital; and my last point is that a patient study of psychology is essential if we want to have a religion which will do more good than harm. Without that study we shall always be prone to accept at too high a value the dogmatic assurances of those who believe themselves inspired; we shall continue to be misled by the blind certitudes of feeling; we shall fail to call the sense of sanctity to heel within our own souls, but shall allow it to enwrap powers and creeds and books and customs and ethics until they become idols immune from criticism, and healthy progress is made difficult; we shall help to perpetuate the dualism which means one set of ideas for Sunday, another for the rest of the week, and also, by making religion supernatural, keeps it remote from ordinary life.

Perhaps most important of all from the religious point of view are strange facts concerning self-delusion and unacknowledged compulsion. It is perfectly easy for a reasonably healthy mind to feel entirely confident of being in the right, and yet to be in the wrong; buried instincts and repressed tendencies, which are not only unacknowledged by but actually unknown to the conscious part of the mind, may yet dictate to action and even make the conscious self find what it considers the best of reasons for the actions. Desire and suggestion between them will override reason and experience every time they come into conflict unless the power of conscious reflection and deliberation is kept very wide awake. Psychology will help us in the comprehension of others, and even in the comprehension of ourselves.

The mind is capable of the most unlikely performances, the grossest errors. We are not likely to be able to set it right, to adjust it when it goes wrong, to keep it tuned up to its highest spiritual and intellectual efficiency, unless we take the trouble to know more about its machinery. We should not expect a motor mechanic to be able to repair our car unless he knew how the engine worked, nor, still more, a motor designer to design or make a more efficient car without not merely the empirical knowledge of how the engine works, but also a good deal of the general scientific principles, mechanical, electrical, and thermodynamic, which underlie its working. The human mind is a far more complex and intricate bit of machinery than a motor-car; and yet religion is for the most part not concerned to know how it works before it sets out to repair it, nor to get a grasp of the physiological and psychological principles underlying that working before it seeks to raise it to new levels of efficiency and well-being.

'Know thyself' has always been a valued injunction to the individual. It is still more important for an organisation like a religious body, whose views and decisions reverberate down the centuries. Through comparative religion and psychology, religion can come to know herself, her limitations, and her capacities.

The consciousness that something in life is sacred, worth living and dying for, is one of humanity's moral indispensables, and religion is the fruitful mother of it.—Rev. H. E. FOSDICK.

> . . . Such fear and awe
> As fall upon us when we look
> Into our Minds.
> —WILLIAM WORDSWORTH.

It is very strange; want itself is a treasure in Heaven; and so great a one that without it there could be no treasure. . . . You must like a God that you may be satisfied like a God.
. . . .
Love is deeper than at first it can be thought. It never ceases but in endless things.—THOMAS TRAHERNE, *Centuries of Meditations.*

The decay of Christianity and Buddhism, as determinative influences in modern thought, is partly due to the fact that each religion has unduly sheltered itself from the other. The self-sufficient pedantry of learning and the confidence of ignorant zealots have combined to shut up each religion in its own forms of thought . . .
Both have suffered from the rise of the third tradition, which is science, because neither of them had retained the requisite flexibility of adaptation. Thus the real, practical problems of religion have never been adequately studied in the only way in which such problems *can* be studied, namely, in the school of experience.—A. N. WHITEHEAD, *Religion in the Making* (1927).

As I stood behind the coffin of my little son the other day, with my mind bent on anything but disputation, the officiating minister read, as a part of his duty, the words, 'If the dead rise not again, let us eat and drink, for to-morrow we die.' I cannot tell you how inexpressibly they shocked me. Paul had neither wife nor child, or he must have known that his alternative involved a blasphemy against all that was best and noblest in human nature. I could have laughed with scorn. What! because I am face to face with irreparable loss, . . . I am to renounce my manhood, and, howling, grovel in bestiality. Why, the very apes know better, and if you shoot their young the poor brutes grieve their grief out and do not immediately seek distraction in a gorge.
—T. H. HUXLEY, *Life and Letters.*

I cannot but say that I believe that some day our conception of God will have become independent of nearly all that has come into it from the primitive Jewish tribal and other pagan conceptions of God which have passed into Christianity, and that our conception will be constantly renewed and growing from all human knowledge and experience, from all science, philosophy, and psychology.—Canon J. M. WILSON, in *The Modern Churchman* (1924).

> Serene will be our days and bright,
> And happy will our nature be,
> When Love is an unerring light,
> And Joy its own security.
> —WILLIAM WORDSWORTH.

8

Developed Religion

The future remains. What is it to bring forth? Religion, if it is to be vital not only to the individual but also to the community, makes three demands. It must be a deeply-felt personal way of life—'what a man does with his solitariness', is how Whitehead puts it: I should prefer to think of it more specifically, as a shared way of life based on a particular emotional and spiritual approach, certain beliefs, certain preferences in the realm of values, and certain attitudes towards human destiny.

In so far as definite religious communities or churches exist, these must have some sort of organisation of their own. Organisation is as necessary to any body important enough to merit the name of a church as is a skeleton to one of the larger animals; and the organisation will be as necessary on the intellectual and moral sides as on the purely material and social side.

But finally—and this has been much lost sight of in the past, owing to the unfortunate dualism underlying most religious thought and popular philosophy—the religious communities and the lives of individual religious people must have some organic relation with the community as a whole, their thought with its thought, their morals with its morals, their feelings with its feelings. We are apt to forget that the world is really growing up. Man as organism is still a young species, and civilisation, if we date it from the twin discoveries of metalworking and agriculture, is a mere day in the biological centuries. But so rapid, during that negligible period of less than 10,000 years, has been the evolutionary advance made possible by speech and tradition and the other new properties of the human organism, that it is now justifiable to say that civilised man is in his adolescence, and has the chance of attaining maturity. I say 'has the chance', for a species or a society is not pinned down like an individual among the higher animals to an inevitable development; it is plastic, and, like some of the lower organisms, may reverse its differentiation, grow backwards, and revert to a simpler stage.

Whether, as in the Dark Ages, the civilised world is going to undergo such a process of dedifferentiation, it is impossible to say. It can be asserted, however, that it has at least the chance of maturity. As H. G. Wells pointed out in the *Outline of History*, every civilised community in the present age knows more about the general conditions of the human race in any and every previous age, than did any single individual or community at the time. As for our perspective of knowledge in time, our continuity of historical outlook, it has never been even remotely approached. What could a historical outlook achieve to which 4004 B.C. was the date of the world's creation, or one to which classical Greece was the remotest horizon of antiquity, or human and animal evolution were a sealed book, undreamt-of?

The same is true for our knowledge of nature. It was impossible, before the later nineteenth century, to have any properly-grounded idea of the unity of the natural world. Such ideas had been indulged in, but were rightly treated as hazardous speculations: now, they are forced upon our minds by the irresistible body of tested knowledge. In the same way, there is the sense of solidity given by the mere detailed knowledge and comprehension of the facts of nature—how the wind blows and the clouds arise; how valleys and mountains obtain their forms and gradually change; how the sun shines and the earth and moon circle round it; why earthquakes and volcanic eruptions take place; the how of chemical combination and the knowledge of the composition and properties of familiar substances; the way in which we and animals breathe, digest, move, feel, reproduce; how diseases are caused by bacteria, parasites, definite poisons or lack of definite food-substances—in all these and a hundred other ways civilisation has an assured sense of acquaintance, a foundation of knowledge built in the world of external nature, which was impossible to any previous age.

Equanimity and foresight used to move on a much thinner crust over the abyss of fear and mystery, acquiescence or despair. The solid Romans themselves directed their campaigns by augury from the flight of birds and the entrails of animals. The Plague of London must have acquired an enormous addition of horror from the complete ignorance of the cause of the disease or any methods by which it could be combated. How could even the highest religious outlook expect any full achievement when, as in the Middle Ages, it found itself in an atmosphere of widespread superstition, belief in miracles and in frankly magical ceremonies, when the most enlightened and influential rulers regulated their actions according to astrological calculations? How could morals, even the sternest, not become immoral when, as in the seventeenth century, knowledge had not banished belief in witchcraft and the irrational fears and hates that naturally arose therefrom?

The same, *mutatis mutandis,* is true for our control of nature. For a society founded on tradition, where discoveries were made only by accident, alteration was gradual and unconscious, stability seemed natural and man's main concern to make the best of what was inevitably given. The application of scientific knowledge has produced a very different outlook. Civilised man is beginning to realise that he can, if he so wishes, in large measure model the world in accordance with his desires. He has for some time realised this pretty thoroughly with regard to inorganic nature, and has now reached the same point in his outlook on organic nature other than himself—noxious insects and parasites, tropical diseases, afforestation, agriculture, fisheries. He is beginning to see its full implications in regard to social development—witness the outburst of activity in promoting town-planning, nature reserves, and the conservation of wild life, in preserving beautiful buildings from destruction, in saving the countryside from vandalism, in national education, in the concerted appeal for playing-fields for poor children, and in a hundred other ways. Finally, there is the extension of the same outlook to his own nature. That has hardly as yet got a foothold; but it is coming. This will bring profound changes of practice. Psychology and education between them are revealing what can be done in helping the individual to control himself; the study of heredity and population-growth, and the knowledge of eugenics and of birth-control are pointing the way to wholly new aims—to a conscious control by man of his own nature and racial destiny. Medicine is ousting the idea, common to all primitive societies, and accepted by all early religions, that disease is due to supernatural causes, whether magic or the will of a god, and pointing the way to man's achievement of health. How can the twentieth century, grounded in this outlook, which is not only actually but inevitably new, be content with the same religious outlook which satisfied it when the natural world was uncomprehended, appeared chaotic as much as orderly, and the ideas of control and conscious change had not yet been born?

Bearing this in mind, we may feel it natural and even desirable that a religion such as Christianity, for instance, should at its origin have set itself up as definitely hostile to the whole outlook of the world into which it was born; that when science was almost non-existent, morals chaotic, cruelty rampant, force the one great arbiter, and religions of every complexion, including those of barbaric crudity and beastliness, were jostling each other, all tolerated, in the imperial city, Christianity should have proclaimed itself not merely as a way of salvation, but as the only way.

But to-day humanity is facing the possibility of attaining its maturity. We cannot really think it tolerable that it should be faced with perpetual conflict at the central heart of its being. If its maturity is to be stable or fully fruitful, it will be necessary for any religion of the future to be an aspect of its unitary and interconnected thought and life, not one of two opposing tendencies.

I feel that any such religion of the future must have as its basis the consciousness of sanctity in existence—in common things, in events of human life, in the gradually-comprehended interlocking whole revealed to the human desire for knowledge, in the benedictions of beauty and love, in the catharsis, the sacred purging, of the moral drama in which character is pitted against fate and even deepest tragedy may uplift the mind.

Nor must it be narrow-minded, but it must admit that this same high sense of sacredness and transcendent value may be vouchsafed in many ways and in many objects. Some may find it in poetry. Shelley was an avowed atheist and a hater of Christianity, but he was obviously of religious temperament. This could hardly be claimed of Keats, but to him beauty was certainly a sacrament. It may come through art or music; it may be vouchsafed through love. It may be found in the pursuit of pure truth—think of Lucretius, Galileo, Pasteur, Thomas Huxley. It may be found in the practice of a life devoted to the service of humanity's suffering, as with Father Damien, or Mrs Elizabeth Fry, or Dr Schweitzer. Still others, like Richard Jefferies or Wordsworth or Thoreau, may find it in the solitudes of nature; or, again, like born patriots, in a sanctification of their country.

Let me give a couple of quotations to illustrate my assertions. Sir Henry Newbolt speaks of poetry as 'a transfiguration of life, heightened by the home-sickness of the spirit for a perfect world'. That well describes the sacramental effect of great poetry. John Donne, one of those rare souls in which poetical, intellectual, sensual, and religious ardours were blended, in *The Ecstasy*, describes the state of two lovers:

> *Our hands were firmly cémented*
> *By a fast balm, which thence did spring;*
> *Our eye-beams twisted, and did thread*
> *Our eyes upon one double string.*
>
> *. . . As, 'twixt two equal armies, Fate*
> *Suspends uncertain victory,*
> *Our souls—which to advance their state,*
> *Were gone out—hung 'twixt her and me.*
>
> *And whilst our souls negotiate there,*
> *We like sepulchral statues lay,*
> *All day the same our postures were,*
> *And we said nothing, all the day.*

The state, only with its objects altered, is just that which is found in religious mystics at a certain stage of their mystical development.

Religion properly so-called differs only from these in relating the objects of its feeling of sanctity to the individual's desire for salvation or righteousness, and to a definite set of beliefs or scheme of thought about the mystery of the universe and man's destiny therein. But if its brand of sanctity excludes that of the thrill of poetry, or denies the absolute value of intellectual discovery, or is hostile to the feeling of sanctity enveloping and spending itself upon purely humanitarian ends, then so much the worse for it. All it has a right to ask is that those who pursue other approaches shall try to see whether their ideas are not narrow, whether they cannot be related to a wider sweep of reality.

It is all very well for Browning to say 'we live by admiration, hope, and love.' Even had he struck a rather deeper note by substituting *veneration* for *admiration*, and introduced a plea for pure knowledge, this would have been but a partial view. What we live by must be organised: the different ideas and aspirations, the goals and springs of conduct, must be brought into relation with each other and with a full experience of outer reality, in the widest possible way. This is where *organised* religious thought makes its contribution to civilisation.

In any such intellectual organisation of religious thought

there appear to me to be three main categories to be considered. The first is constituted by the powers of nature; the
second by the ideal goals of the human mind; the third by
actual living beings, human and other, in so far as they
embody such ideals.

As we have already seen, the personification and glorification of these would give us an approximation to the theological doctrine of the Trinity, though in various details, especially
as regards the first person, there would still remain considerable differences.

These three categories of fact are closely related. Abstract
ideas and pure ideals are properties of living human organisms; human organisms are continuously linked with all other
organisms, plant and animal, by the evolutionary process; and
this existing stream of organic life must itself have evolved
by continuity from non-living matter.

All three are merely different aspects of one reality; and,
in so far as our human destiny is concerned, the historical
processes at work have been such as to make the spiritual and
mental sides of this one reality emerge from insignificance
into greater and greater importance until they come largely
to dominate and control the material aspects.[1]

A recognition of these relationships and this unity is
equally essential with the recognition of the three separate
sets of facts.

Thomas Hardy, throughout his writings, has stressed the
arbitrary and capricious power, indifferent to human life and
human thought, as which it seems to me external nature
must be perceived by anyone not blinded by theological
preconceptions or his own desires. Where I would suggest he
has gone astray is in setting this up as the one essential reality,
and in neglecting to notice its relationship to the other
realities I have been discussing.

The three categories themselves, and their relationship,
are not the same thing as the sum of the isolated brute facts
which go to compose them. They are the facts as apprehended by the powers of the mind—they are reality embodied in experience, and so becoming organised and unified
into an ordered and more vital reality.

Had the word God not come, almost universally, to have

[1] Malthus was expressing the same general idea in terms of a
different system of thought when, in his celebrated *Essay* (1st ed.,
p. 294), he wrote: 'The impressions and excitements of this world
are the instruments with which the Supreme Being forms matter
into mind.'

the connotation of supernatural personality, it could be properly employed to denote this unity. For if my reasoning has been correct, what has been called God by men has been precisely this reality, or various aspects of it, but obscured by symbolic vestures. Perhaps the day will come when men will recognise this, and throw away the veils. Until that time, it is best to use some other word or phrase. In any case, this reality, as a proper object for the religious sentiment, is something unitary and deserves a name. For the moment I shall call it the Sacred Reality. The precise term, however, does not matter. What does matter is the recognition that the experience of the universe as affecting human life and therefore as invested with sanctity is a reality, and is the proper object of religion.[2]

As regards the relationship of this reality to human life, one further comment is in place. The category of natural power transcends human life on the material side, as matter. It is external, and what is given in it is alien and unfamiliar. Humanity is one combination of the elements of reality; but there are an infinity of others, some exceedingly diverse. Humanity, however, consists of a number of bits of living matter, and is thus rooted in what transcends it.

The category of pure spirit also transcends humanity, but on the spiritual side, and in a different way. It transcends any and every particular by being general, exceeds anything and everything actual by being ideal, and yet the capacity for thinking in these general and ideal terms is a capacity of particular and actual human beings. Humanity is much more intimately entangled with this aspect of reality, and transcendence and immanence are there more intricately interwoven.

The only Absolute that man can know is the absolute of general idea—truth, beauty, goodness, holiness, unity. He can never reach absolute completeness in any field, nor absolute perfection. But he can attain satisfaction, a satisfaction embracing and profound. The satisfaction may be one of achievement, happiness, or rapture; or it may be one, paradoxical and yet very profound, of realising his own littleness, dependence, and sinfulness over against the awful completeness and sanctity of the ideal. In such satisfaction it can properly be said that man touches the absolute and has a momentary perfection. He may attain as much completion, be in contact with

[2] Cf. George Santayana (Introduction to *The Ethics of Spinoza*):
'The spirit of God, accordingly, means simply the genius of men, the ground of which lies indeed beyond them, in the universal context and influence of nature; but the conscious expression and fruition of it first arises in them severally, as occasion warrants.'

as much of the absolute, as is possible for him at that moment. But it is inevitable that each of his experiences and states is temporary, and that always further possibilities lie ahead, in which the old can be swallowed up.

There is an absolute of truth; and though no one can grasp all truth or, what comes to the same thing, all the implications of a single truth, yet we may solve the particular problem we have held before us, we may see in a flash our solution, its truth, and its relation to many of our other ideas.

In just the same way we can touch the absolute of beauty and, through our spirit, perceive it investing common things and common vision; we can touch the absolute of goodness and realise something of the good in a single course of action. There is an absolute of harmony and unity; we can experience in ourselves a moment of that harmony when we succeed in adjusting the diverse and conflicting elements of our life, as they happen to exist at the time, all in a single unity. It is but momentary; we must continue to grow, and new equilibria will come to be necessary; but in that moment we shall have tasted a knowledge which is absolute, and embodied something of ideal harmony in our actual temporal being. There is an absolute of righteousness; that, too, we can touch by moments; and this grace is most intensely felt when it rescues us from the opposite extreme, of a sense of sin or unrighteousness. But it is simply not a fact that it is the exclusive privilege of Christian believers. There is a grace of holiness which can be attained in love; without it ungratified desire is pain, desire gratified is merely transitory release from tension or brings satiety and revulsion—but with it super-added, ungratified desire is itself desirable, prayer and beauty are one, gratified desire a sacramental transcendence of the boundaries of the self, a consummation on which, as Blake says, 'the soul expands her wing.'

In all these and many other ways we may touch the absolute, sacramentally transcend ourselves. It is in this sphere that virtue is its own reward; this is the true coin in which human nature receives its best gifts, most valued because not deserved or simply earned as a right, but (I repeat) a present, a gift distilling out of the inner nature of things.

On the other hand, the spirit must labour for wages too, and earn them. I believe that to live solely or mainly for these moments of transcendence, whether in religion, or love, or beauty of art or nature, or intellect, is mere selfishness. Like other selfishness, it brings its own penalties, which may be no less severe in spite of never being realised. The world demands work. Work is needed for the mere maintenance of life; more work is needed for the maintenance of a particular level of civilisation; still more work is needed if we look to the future and aim at giving later generations better chances of fuller life.

When we come down to more detail, there are many facts which need to be taken into account to get a proper picture of reality. We must accept, for instance, the fact that men are not fundamentally equal, but unequal in being endowed by the natural processes of reproduction with chemically different outfits of hereditary units. Development, both of body and mind, achievements and character, is a gradual realisation of some of the potentialities inherent in these outfits. Development is a true *epigenesis*, to use the technical term, a bringing into existence of actually new and more complex organisation. It is brought about by interaction of the hereditary outfit with the outer environment. Factors in hereditary constitution or in environment may limit, very definitely, the possibilities of development both on the physical and the mental side. If, for instance, one particular gene or hereditary unit be different from normal in a particular way, the human organism is incapable, always and inevitably, of distinguishing red and green colours: or if one particular chemical substance be absent from the child's diet, it will inevitably grow up stunted and deformed, a sufferer from rickets.

Though the conditions in respect of higher intellectual and spiritual characters are, clearly, much more complex, the same, undoubtedly, holds good for them as well. The automatic working of mendelian law may, to take an extreme example, produce a congenital imbecile, who is no more capable of any comprehension of what a Christian means by God than he is of lecturing on advanced physics; and the converse is seen in those whose hereditary outfit equips them from the start with more than usual talent, in music, say, or mathematics, or spiritual sensitiveness. But, *per contra*, those same talents can only unfold into actuality when developing in a suitable environment; a wolf-child could not become a mathematician, nor could a paleolithic man, in the absence of musical tradition and musical instruments, have become a great musician.

Fate is the limiting force of heredity and environment; and freedom is human plasticity—the variety of possible development opening before a man endowed with a definite heredity.

One salient way in which man differs from other animals is in the much greater range of potentiality given to him. There is very little difference between two healthy jelly-fish; a little more, but still not much, between two monkeys; but the difference between two normal men may easily exceed the difference between a jelly-fish and a monkey. This difference is, of course, mainly in the mind; but the mind is the most important part of man.

From another aspect, it is equally clear that had circumstances been but a little different, a human mind might have developed into a mental organism quite different from its actual state; and equally that even the best-developed minds fail to realise more than a fraction of the possibilities open to them, while the average man allows his mind to remain a baby instead of encouraging it to grow up, lives all his life like a chrysalis in a cocoon without realising that he might, if he wished, emerge winged.

Out of this raw material of possibilities, man builds his personality. Sometimes he does not realise what lies waiting to his hand; at others, he concentrates on some parts only of the mental dispositions, and (consciously or unconsciously) suppresses or represses the rest. These neglected or repressed realities of being have a way of taking their revenge and suddenly flooding up into consciousness, so that the personality which had thought itself secure, in the privacy of its smug self-imposed limitations, suddenly finds itself in the presence of tremendous forces, not personal, and yet part of its own flesh and blood, vital realities which it had thought to escape, now confronting it and threatening, unless both welcomed and disciplined, to strike it down from off its pedestal of equilibrium.

One of the most insidious enemies of true freedom is this unreasoned repression of certain instincts and all things connected with them. They continue to work in the subterranean part of the mind, and will influence the process of thought going on above, so that consciousness is all the time finding reasons for acting in this or that way, rather than using reason.

Thus a false organisation of the self, with its failure to unify the raw materials of spiritual gifts and its unresolved conflicts of desires or values, is a powerful source of instability and incompleteness, and must distort or cramp the religious outlook. On the other hand, the most potent force for ensuring that the personality shall be stably organised is a proper scale of values. The ethical history of man has been the gradual enlarging of his scale of values and the relegation of certain values from high to low position and vice versa. The greatest change wrought by Christianity, for instance, was the dethronement of many such primitive values and their replacement by love, mercy, sacrifice, and humility. The scale of values is like the architect's plan which determines how the piles of timber and brick and stone shall be built into a building.

Primitive man receives most of his scale of values ready-made; he imbibes them like the air he breathes; they are hard set in the tribal customs and standards whose foundations he does not even think about, much less question.

The educated modern, however, must contribute something of his own effort to his scale of values. If he be not a spiritual and intellectual cipher, he will, however much he may have unconsciously absorbed during childhood, be faced with the need for readjusting his ideas as experience is forced upon him. Once he is made to look into the matter, he will find that vast stores of experience, gathered by others, are available to him in books and in the minds of living men, and he is driven on, if he is worth his salt, until he has explored the main lines of knowledge, however cursorily, for himself, and found out what kinds of fact there are which bear upon his personal problems. This is one of the main ways in which a developed differs from a primitive civilisation; the one is locked up, away from expansion and change, in its little world of tight traditions, while the other is set in an open land whose boundaries of knowledge recede over the horizon. If the religious believe that the spirit of truth be a gift from or a part of the third person of the Trinity, then to continue to shut oneself up in the swaddling-clothes of primitive doctrine when the limbs of the spirit might be freed for action is a sin against the Holy Ghost.

Developed religion from this point of view may be thought of as confronting the external world with an inner scale of values, and attempting to harmonise the two in life. If to this it be added that the specifically religious feeling of sacredness and reverence must play its part in the ceaseless encounter between outer and inner, the result is a good working definition. It may also be added that, from the standpoint of the individual, development and change must enter into the process. The child's mind cannot but be unorganised, must lack experience, must work on the childish plane, with crude association instead of sharpened reason, with undisciplined wish and phantasy instead of tempered desire and purpose. The passage from a childish to a mature way of thinking and feeling, from the infantile to the adult mental plane, is necessary. In the process, experience alters the scale of values, and they in their turn alter the way of dealing with experience.

The various ways in which the individual spirit may succeed or fail, partly or wholly, in this traject from infancy to true manhood, are the province of the psychologist. It may, however, be safely asserted that for the majority of human beings, though by no means all, a scale of values which includes elements of a religious nature is needed if the development is to be at all complete or satisfactory.

We men are from one point of view mere trivial microbes, but from another the crown of creation: both views are true, and we must hold them together, interpenetrating, in our thought. From the point of view of the stellar universe, whose size and meaningless spaces baffle comprehension and belief, man may appear a mere nothing, and all his efforts destined to disappear like the web of a spider brushed down from the corner of a little room in the basement of a palace; but meanwhile he is engaged upon a task which is the most valuable of any known, the most valuable which by him can be imagined, the task of imposing mind and spirit upon matter and outer force. This he does by confronting the chaos of outer happenings with his intellect, and generating ordered knowledge; with his æsthetic sense, and generating beauty; with his purpose, and generating control of nature; with his ethical sense and his sense of humour, and generating character; with his reverence, and generating religion.

I would accordingly like to supplement my more comprehensive but static definitions, which I intended to apply to primitive as well as to developed religion, by something more specifically the concern of modern civilisation, applying only to developed religion in which general ideas of morality and reason have asserted their right to attach themselves to the primitive concept of sacredness and to modify and extend the domain of religion and its expression.

A developed religion, then, must satisfy the following requirements. It will not merely be confined to man's more or less immediate reaction to the mysterious or sacred; it will not be content with a system (often incomplete or self-contradictory) of mythology or of primitive rationalisation as its theology; nor only with traditional ritual or formalism as its code of action. On the contrary, it will always extend its conception of what is sacred and a proper object of religious feeling to include man's destiny and his relation with the rest of the world; it will apply the pure force of intellect to its ideas, and attempt a theology or intellectual basis which shall be both logical and comprehensive, accurate and coherent; it will also inevitably perceive that ethics and morality are keystones of human destiny, and link up its sacred beliefs with a pure ethic and a reasoned morality. It will, in a word, not be content to leave its religious life chaotic and unordered, with loose ends unconnected with the rest of reality, but will come more and more consciously to aim at an organised and unified scheme of religion, which further shall be connected with all other parts of the mental life; and it will attempt to achieve this by putting forward a scheme of belief and a scale of values around and over which man's aspirations to sacredness in emotion, thought, and action may most securely grow.

Thus a developed religion should definitely be a relation of the personality as a whole to the rest of the universe, one into which reverence enters, and one in which the search for the ultimate satisfactions of discovering and knowing truth, experiencing and expressing beauty, and ensuing the good in righteous action, all have the freest possible play.

No one who will turn his eyes upon himself and his own being and contemplate the spectacle in a spirit of detachment from practical details of every-day, so far as possible *sub specie æternitatis,* but will come to feel something of reverence at what we may call the miracle of the mere existence of such an organisation of material and mental qualities. If he has had some scientific training, his sense of wonder will be increased. This *man is* a small block of the general substance of which the whole universe is formed, just as is a stone or a stream or a piece of bread. Not only, however, does it share with all other portions of substance which we call alive the power of maintaining its form and character in the midst of continual change, continually building into itself new raw material of substance in less organised forms, and utilising as the source of its own vital energy the breaking-down of other substance which it then discards; not only does it possess in common with them the power of reproduction, based on the amazing architecture of self-reproducing units which genetics has recently discovered in the chromosomes; but it has come to possess, as the result of many millions of generations of natural evolution, as the result of automatic forces working to preserve what from the point of utility is best worth having in the struggle for existence, the most surprising qualities. This piece of world-stuff possesses not only form and movement, but the capacity for knowing about other parts of the world, even stars a thousand light-years off, events ten million years ago. It possesses the capacity for will, and with will and knowledge working together has learnt to control in notable degree both outer nature and its own nature. In some ways most extraordinary of all, it possesses the capacity for feeling, and for feeling in such a way that before some emotions all practical considerations fall away as unimportant; through feeling, this sentient portion of the world-continuum may be exalted to states which have value higher than anything else in the same world-continuum, and are often regarded as having absolute value.

Here is a mass of a few kilograms, of substance that is indivisibly one (both its matter and spirit), by nature and by origin, with the rest of the universe, which can weigh the sun and measure light's speed, which can harness the tides and organise the electric forces of matter to its profit, which is not content with huts or shelters, but must build Chartres or the Parthenon; which can transform sexual desire into the love of a Dante for his Beatrice; which can not only be raised to ineffable heights at the sight of natural beauty or find 'thoughts too deep for tears' in a common flower, but can create new realms and even heavens of its own, through music, poetry, and art, to which it may be translated, albeit temporarily, from this practical world; which is never content with the actual, and lives not by bread alone; which is always not only surmounting what it thought were the limitations of its nature, but, in individual and social development alike, transcending its own nature and emerging in newness of achievement.

*

Any conflict which prevents the personality from attaining wholeness is a hindrance: all taboos against considering any part of the universe in relation to man and his destiny are hindrances: so, too, are all restrictions upon the free use of reason, or the free appeal to conscience.

In other words, any religion which is not an affirmation of the ultimate value of truth and knowledge, beauty and its expression, and goodness and moral action, which ever sets itself up against these, is in that respect a false, low, and incomplete religion.

So far from Salomon Reinach's definition of religion as 'a sum of scruples impeding the free use of human faculty' being a true one, it is the opposite of the truth for a properly developed religion. It is, unfortunately, the fact that it applies well enough to many primitive and moderately-developed religions; but its applicability may be taken as an excellent touchstone for the degree of development which a religion has attained.

Religious ideas and practices may be, as in many primitive peoples, closely adapted to the general life of society: when civilisation is rapidly changing, however, they are often either ahead of or behind the general thought of the time. The ethics and spiritual insight of Jesus and of Buddha, for instance, were far ahead of their times, as was the theological insight of Abelard, or the moral zeal of some of the Hebrew prophets, or the love of learning by the better of the monks in the Dark and early Middle Ages. More often, however, the unfortunate tendency of the sacred to become the untouchable, and therefore for religion to become an unduly conservative force, has often led to religious thought and practice being below the general level of its times. The anti-evolution agitation in this country a hundred years ago, and in the United States in the present century, is an instance in the intellectual sphere; the refusal of the Roman Catholic and other churches to discuss such subjects as divorce or birth-control in any reasonable spirit is an example in the moral sphere; the excessive formalism of orthodox Jewish religion in the time of Jesus is an example in the field of ritual; the intolerance by many missionary societies of native custom and belief, as compared with the views of anthropological science and of enlightened administrators, will serve in the field of social ethics.

What must never be forgotten is the fact that all sides of a religion must be considered. All will remember Nurse Cavell's remarkable words on the eve of her death: 'Patriotism is not enough.' The idea can be taken and applied to religion and its place in human life. Belief is not enough; and the sincerest religious feeling is not enough. In the long run the most devout religious spirit will do more harm than good if it is coupled with false or incomplete intellectual views, or with a rigid code of morals based on authority instead of reasoned value, or with intolerance. In the long run falsity or fixity, timidity, incompleteness, or sloth, in whatever department of the religious field, will take their revenge.

Just because religion is so powerful and universal, just because it can embrace all human faculties and actions and all aspects of the world about us, therefore it can be a potent and violent force for evil as much as for good.

Once this two-edged nature of religion is recognised, its potentialities for harm faced by the religious, its potentialities for good acknowledged by the rationalist, there will be more chance of progress from low, fixed, undeveloped or underdeveloped religion which clogs the wheels of progress, to higher, forward-moving, developed or developing religion which helps to lead the way.

An undeveloped religion is one which does impede human faculty. A developed religion is one which is so organised that it helps to unify the diverse human faculties, and to give each of them the fullest play in a common task.

All parts a way for the progress of souls;
All religion, all solid things, arts, governments—all that was or is ap-
     parent upon this globe or any globe, falls into niches and corners
     before the procession of souls along the grand roads of the uni-
     verse.
Of the progress of the souls of men and women along the grand roads
     of the universe, all other progress is the needed emblem and sus-
     tenance.—WALT WHITMAN, *The Song of the Open Road.*

> I that saw where ye trod
>   The dim paths of the night,
> Set the shadow called God
>   In your skies to give light;
> But the morning of manhood is risen, and the
>   shadowless soul is in sight.
>
> The tree many-rooted
>   That swells to the sky,
> With frondage red-fruited
>   The life-tree am I;
> In the buds of your lives is the sap of my leaves; ye
>   shall live and not die.
>
> But the Gods of your fashion
>   That take and that give,
> In their pity and passion
>   That scourge and forgive,
> They are worms that are bred in the bark that falls off;
>   they shall die and not live.
>   —ALGERNON CHARLES SWINBURNE, *Hertha.*
>
> To see a World in a grain of sand,
>   And a Heaven in a wild flower,
> Hold Infinity in the palm of your hand,
>   And Eternity in an hour.
>   —WILLIAM BLAKE, *Auguries of Innocence.*

Through love, through hope, through faith's transcendent dower,
We feel that we are greater than we know.
                    —WILLIAM WORDSWORTH.

> Your creeds are dead, your rites are dead,
>   Your social order too.
> Where tarries he, the Power who said:
>   See, I make all things new.
>   —MATTHEW ARNOLD, *Obermann.*

9

Evolutionary Humanism as a Developed Religion

The position as it appears to-day may be summarised in the following brief argument.

Man is always concerned about his destiny—that is to say, his position and rôle in the universe, and how he is to maintain that position and fulfil that rôle. All societies of men develop some sort of organs for coping with this problem— organs for orientating their ideas and emotions and for constructing attitudes of mind and patterns of belief and behaviour in relation to their conception of their destiny. All these social organs concerned with destiny can, I think, properly be included under the head of religions. Even if some of them are exceedingly primitive and consist of little but magic rituals, while others are highly developed and claim to be entirely rational, they are all, from Haitian voodoo to Roman Catholicism, from neolithic fertility religions to Marxist Communism, concerned with this same general function. In the same sort of way, the tube-feet of a starfish, the legs of a horse, the pseudopods of an amoeba, and the wings of a bird, though profoundly different organs from each other, are all animal organs concerned with the same general function of locomotion.

*

Homo sapiens—man, for short—is a unique organism, whose maintenance and transformations depend primarily on psychosocial mechanisms, in which mental activities play a dominant rôle; while those of all other organisms depend primarily on the biological mechanisms of genetics, mutation, and natural selection.

181

Although the terms *mind* and *mental* have been bedevilled by differences in common usage, I shall employ them, *faute de mieux,* in the widest possible sense, to describe all activities involving awareness, from cognitive to emotional awareness, from purely intellectual to spiritual and aesthetic, from intensely conscious activities to those that are subconscious or even, in Freudian terminology, unconscious. It would be convenient to have some new term, uncontaminated by earlier modes of thought, to characterise all psycho-social mechanisms in which communicable mental activities play a predominant rôle. If so, I suggest the term *noetic;* and I shall sometimes employ it with this connotation.

Religions are thus noetic organs of evolving man. Their special function concerns his position and rôle in the universe, his relations to the rest of the cosmos, and in particular, his attitude to the powers or forces operating in it, including those of his own nature: or in the fewest possible words, with his attitude towards his destiny. Furthermore, this attitude always involves the sense of sacred power in some form or other—a feeling of reverence, or mystery, or wonder, or transcendent power or beauty. To perform this function, a religion requires some interpretative beliefs, notably about the spiritual powers in the universe; some picture of the cosmos in which man's destiny is cast, some mobilisation of the emotional and spiritual forces at work within man himself; some form of ritual, in the widest sense of the term, to express and maintain this religious attitude; and some relation to the practical problems of existence, both individual and social.

The beliefs may be mere assumptions lacking precise definition, as in those underlying the magic rituals of many primitive peoples; or they may be elaborate systems involving precise intellectual formulation, like the creeds of Christian theology; or they may be *post-hoc* rationalisations, quite subsidiary to the ritual elements of the religion, as in Chinese ancestor-worship.[1]

The inner psychological forces may be given violent expression as part of a sacred ritual, as in orgiastic cults like that of Dionysos or in some aspects of Haitian voodoo; or they may be sternly disciplined, or even largely repudiated, as in some Protestant sects or in the different forms of asceticism; or they may be cultivated and developed so as to provide new fulfil-

[1] See A. R. Radcliffe-Brown, *Structure and Function in Primitive Society,* London, 1952, pp. 153f.

ments, as in the various systems of mysticism. The ritual may be magical, or dramatic, or symbolic; it may consist in formalistic observances, in prayers, in orgiastic releases, in mass celebrations, like those of the Holy Year or the rallies and parades of Nazism and Communism, in pilgrimages, or in sacrifices.

And the relation to practical existence may be one of escape, as in asceticism or pure Buddhism; or of full participation, as in classical Greece or the city-states of ancient Mesopotamia; or of rendering unto Caesar the things that are Caesar's, as in usual Christian practice.

The form of the beliefs about the spiritual forces at work in the universe colours and affects the rest of the religious system. The three chief hypotheses on which past religious belief-systems have in fact been erected are the magic hypothesis, the spirit hypothesis, and the daimonic or god hypothesis.[2]

Both the magic hypothesis and the god hypothesis appear to be based on the well-known psychological tendency to projection. Putting the matter rather crudely, man has experiences of sacred power. On the magic hypothesis, he projects the sacred power *into* phenomena, into some external object or event, including rituals and forms of words. On the god hypothesis, he projects the sacred power *behind* phenomena, and clothes it in the garb of a personality.

The magic hypothesis leads man to ascribe practical efficacy and importance to dramatic rituals like rain-making ceremonies, to witchcraft with its spells and curses, and to omens and auguries.

The god hypothesis, with its central idea of personal spiritual powers behind phenomena, leads naturally and almost universally to the idea that misfortunes like earthquakes and pestilences are divine punishments for sin,[3] to the belief that gods need propitiation by sacrifices and offerings and glorification by worship, and that they can be influenced by petitionary prayers.

[2] *Daimonic* is a useful term to cover all classes of superhuman spiritual beings, whether good or evil or ethically neutral, including both gods and devils of various kinds and various degrees of importance, angels, local spirits, tutelary deities, etc. See R. Turner, *The Great Cultural Traditions*, Vol. I (McGraw-Hill, New York, 1941), p. 92 on 'the Concept of the Daimonic Universe'. For my present purpose, however, the term *god hypothesis* will serve.

[3] See T. D. Kendrick, *The Lisbon Earthquake* (Methuen, London, 1956).

The combination of magic and god hypotheses may produce singular results, such as the development of prayer-wheels worked by wind- or water-power in Tibet.

The bases of the spirit hypothesis appear to be more complex; but its effects on practice are equally obvious. When sacred power is supposed to reside in the spirits of the dead, we may find special rituals of burial designed to keep the dead from plaguing the living, or the cult may develop into an elaborate system of ancestor-worship.[4]

And of course when religious beliefs are largely concerned with survival in a supernatural world, the practical effects may be enormous. We need only think of the pyramids, and the economic importance of the mortuary priesthood of ancient Egypt; or of the rôle of Indulgences in helping to bring about the Reformation.

Many religions utilise all these belief-hypotheses. Thus in Roman Catholicism, while the god hypothesis is central and basic, the spirit hypothesis plays a not inconsiderable part, for instance in assigning an important rôle to the spirits of dead saints; and certainly for most Protestants as well as for rationalists, Catholic beliefs about the efficacy of relics and pilgrimages and various ritual observances involve the magic hypothesis. Furthermore, the three hypotheses often combine to exert a joint effect on religious attitude and practice.

The belief in spirits, and still more markedly the belief in gods, involves another basic hypothesis—the hypothesis of dualism. In general, theistic religions are based on the assumption of a dualism between the natural and the supernatural; and this is often equated with a dualism between the material and the non-material or spiritual.[5] For brevity's sake, I shall use the term supernaturalism to include the combination of the god hypothesis and the spirit hypothesis which characterises most higher religious systems.

An almost universal and perhaps inevitable consequence of the god hypothesis in its developed forms is the assumption of absolute truth. A monotheistic religion almost invariably claims to be in possession of the absolute truth about human destiny: the fact that rival religions make similar claims is

[4] For some horrifying practical results of accepting a daimonic-spirit hypothesis, Aldous Huxley's *The Devils of Loudun* should be consulted.

[5] For the historical development of the dualism between matter and spirit, see V. G. Childe, *Society and Knowledge* (1956).

usually disposed of by affirming that they are 'false', while only one's own religion is 'true'.[6]

Furthermore, theistic religions usually adopt the hypothesis of revelation: they assert that the truth has been revealed in a set of god-given commandments, or a holy book, or divinely-inspired ordinances. The beliefs of theistic religions thus tend inevitably to be authoritarian, and also to be rigid and resistant to change. When change does occur, as is sometimes inevitable in our changing human world, it often involves merely the substitution of one authoritarianism for another, as when the Protestant reformers set up the authority of the Bible in place of that of the Church or the Pope.

Hypotheses are valuable and necessary instruments of the human mind for its dual task of adding to and organising its knowledge. But they become dangerous when they are erected into absolute affirmations or dogmas, and pernicious when they claim immunity from constant testing against fact.

The magic hypothesis in its straightforward form can no longer be seriously entertained, even though elements of it continue to colour theistic religious practice, and though it survives in many forms among the illiterate, and has given birth to new versions of old superstitions among the half-educated.

The supernatural hypothesis, taken as involving both the god hypothesis and the spirit hypothesis and the various consequences drawn from them, appears to have reached the limits of its usefulness as an interpretation of the universe and of human destiny, and as a satisfactory basis for religion. It is no longer adequate to deal with the phenomena, as disclosed by the advance of knowledge and discovery.

This is the crux of the so-called conflict between science and religion, which should more properly be described as a conflict between the progress of established knowledge and a particular type of religious hypothesis.[7]

It would be interesting to discuss the history of this conflict, and to show how, for instance, the advance of knowledge, both

[6] Arnold Toynbee, in his recent book *An Historian's Approach to Religion,* though his general conclusions differ largely from mine, equally condemns fixed dogma, final revelation, and in general the 'idolisation' of sacred books, holy places and ecclesiastical and theological systems.

[7] For a critical discussion of modern theology in terms of philosophy, see R. W. Hepburn, *Christianity and Paradox* (Watts & Co., London, 1957).

in the natural and the human sciences, has led to modifications in the god hypothesis—how the Newtonian and the Darwinian revolutions combined to push the deity ever further into the background, until his only rôle in cosmic affairs appears as that of initial creator of a self-running machine; how, with our increasing knowledge of the orderly working of nature, the idea of miraculous intervention has grown progressively less and less tenable, until it has now become repugnant and indeed intellectually immoral to a growing body of those educated in the scientific tradition; how theistically minded astronomers and philosophers have been reduced to presenting god in the unsatisfying rôle of a cosmic mathematician, or the nebulous guise of an absolute principle.

But I have no space for this, and can merely state the plain fact that the advance of knowledge is making supernaturalism in general, and the god hypothesis in particular, untenable for an increasing number of people.

The vital question is this: Can we find any other basic hypothesis about the spiritual forces at work in the cosmos on which to build our beliefs? Such a hypothesis must square with the facts of established knowledge, and must be religious in the broad sense, in being relevant to the problem of human destiny.

Marxist Communism has adopted the hypothesis of materialism, which denies any real importance to spiritual forces. For Marxism, mental or psychological activities in general are essentially epiphenomena, always the resultant and never the cause of 'objective' material events.

I am, of course, aware that, through a complicated process of fine-spun dialectic, Marxist philosophers manage to rescue a good many psychological phenomena from this wholesale jettisoning and keep them safely aboard the communist ship; and that in practice a great deal of attention is paid to activities like art and philosophy and science, which to most of us would appear to involve a major mental or noetic component. But the underlying hypothesis is explicitly materialist; and this fact has all kinds of important consequences, not least among which will be its ultimate consequences for the religious efficacy of Communism, as a system of beliefs and attitudes concerning human destiny.

Again it would be interesting to pursue the subject; but again I have no space. I would only say that the materialist hypothesis, in denying the importance of mental and spiritual factors in the cosmos, is to me as erroneous as, though more sophisticated than, the naive notions of the magic hypothesis, which projects spiritual force into material events. It is still, perhaps unconsciously, dualist, and, through failing to take account of a large body of fact, is as untenable as the supernaturalist hypothesis. But it has provided the basis for the first important non-theistic religion of modern times, and its existence makes the task of finding an adequate alternative even more urgent.

I submit that the discoveries of physiology, general biology, and psychology not only make possible, but necessitate, a naturalistic hypothesis, in which there is no room for the supernatural, and the spiritual forces at work in the cosmos are seen as a part of nature just as much as the material forces. What is more, these spiritual forces are one particular product of mental activity in the broad sense, and mental activities in general are seen to have increased in intensity and importance during the course of cosmic time. Our basic hypothesis is thus not merely naturalistic as opposed to supernaturalist, but monistic as opposed to dualistic, and evolutionary as opposed to static.

Another postulate of modern thought is that truth is not revealed once and for all, but has to be progressively discovered. This is itself a scientific discovery, and one of the first magnitude. It is also an inevitable consequence of our basic hypothesis of evolutionary naturalism; and the fact that modern science has resulted in the progressive discovery of new and more truth is a confirmation of that hypothesis.

It may well be that future discoveries, in parapsychology for instance, will alter our views on the nature of the relation between material and mental or spiritual events and activities; but meanwhile the monistic evolutionary hypothesis best meets the known facts, and its implications need to be followed out and tested in detail, in full confidence that they will be fruitful.

In the light of such a view, religions, like sciences or philosophies, are creations of man, and gods are products of the human mind just as much as scientific 'laws of nature'.

The comparison is illuminating. Both gods and scientific generalisations must be derived from experience and must have some basis in reality. The question is how much of a basis: how far do they correspond with reality, how accurately do they embody experience? The laws of nature did not exist as such before men began scientific investigation: what existed was the welter of natural events, and the laws of nature are constructions of human thought which attempt to give a comprehensible general formulation of how those events operate. Similarly gods did not exist as such before men built up theistic religious systems: what existed was the clash of natural forces, physical and spiritual, including those of the human mind, and the gods are attempts to give a comprehensible formulations to these forces of destiny.

The difference—but an important one—is that, in the history of religion, gods appear to correspond to men's pre-scientific constructions in the investigation of natural phenomena—productos of imaginative speculation like the four 'Elements', or the principle of Humours, or the idea of spontaneous generation.

*

With evolutionary naturalism as our basic hypothesis, we can begin exploring the new religious situation of our twentieth century, without spending more time in the unprofitable task of discussing the theoretical or practical inadequacies of earlier religious systems.

Twentieth-century man, it is clear, needs a new organ for dealing with destiny, a new system of religious beliefs and attitudes adapted to the new situation in which his societies now have to exist. The radically new feature of the present situation may perhaps be stated thus: Earlier religions and belief-systems were largely adaptations to cope with man's ignorance and fears, with the result that they came to concern themselves primarily with stability of attitude. But the need to-day is for a belief-system adapted to cope with his knowledge and his creative possibilities; and this implies the capacity to meet, inspire and guide change.

In other words, the primary function of earlier systems was of necessity to maintain social and spiritual morale in face of the unknown: and this they accomplished with a considerable measure of success. But the primary function of any system to-day must be to utilise all available knowledge in giving guidance and encouragement for the continuing adventure of human development.

I am here treating of religious systems as social organs whose function it is to adjust man to his destiny. No previous systems could perform this function with full adequacy, for the simple reason that no previous age had sufficient knowledge to construct an adequate picture of the drama of destiny or of its protagonist, man. The present epoch is the first in which such a picture could begin to take shape.

This is due to the fact that scientific investigation has now for the first time begun to cover the entire range of phenomena involved in human destiny. Beginning with the physical phenomena and proceeding to the biological, it has now invaded the social, psychological and historical fields, and is at last being forced to deal with the phenomena of values. Immense tracts of ignorance are still to be explored, and await annexation to the growing empire of knowledge; but we can already affirm that the cosmos is unitary, that it is a process of transformation in time, and that values and other products of mental and spiritual activity play an important operative rôle in that sector of the process with which we are involved.

More specifically, the present is the first period in the long history of the earth in which the evolutionary process, through the instrumentality of man, has taken the first step towards self-consciousness. In becoming aware of his own destiny, man has become aware of that of the entire evolutionary process on this planet: the two are interlocked. This is at once an inspiring and a sobering conception, to which I shall return.

The present age also differs from all earlier ages in the increased importance of science, and its universal extension. There should no longer be any talk of conflict between science and religion. Between scientific knowledge and certain religious systems, yes: but between science as increasing knowledge of nature and religion as a social organ concerned with destiny, no. On the contrary, religion must now ally itself wholeheartedly with science. Science in the broad sense is indispensable as the chief instrument for increasing our store of organised knowledge and understanding. Through evolutionary biology, it has already indicated the nature of human destiny. Scientific study is needed to give religion a fuller understanding of destiny, and to help in devising better methods for its detailed realisation.

Meanwhile, science must not allow any ancient prejudices against certain aspects of previously established religions to hold it back from giving its aid when called upon.

Industry and agriculture, after a good deal of resistance on the part of so-called practical men, have already discovered the indispensability of science, both pure and applied. It now remains for religion, together with other social activities, to make the same discovery. For without the fullest aid from science, we will assuredly not be able to bring into being a religion adequate to our needs, any more than we could have brought into being an aeroplane capable of flying or antibiotics capable of killing disease-germs.

Once it is realised that religions are the product of man's creative mind, working on the data provided by personal or collective experience, the need for enlisting science in the religious task becomes apparent. In any event, the march of knowledge and events has made it imperative to reach a new formulation of human destiny and a new attitude towards it. This is a task for the human species as a whole, to which all can bring their contribution. The co-operation of the religiously-minded and the scientifically-trained is essential for its adequate performance.

The contribution which science can make is two-fold. It can contribute an enormous body of hard-won, tested, organised knowledge; and also a spirit of disinterested devotion to truth, and a willingness to apply this spirit to any problem, irrespective of prejudices or possible consequences.

An immense co-operative effort of creative discussion is needed. In what follows I submit the thesis which I am calling evolutionary humanism to that discussion, fully conscious that, though based on the accumulated results of unnumbered others, it is only the personal contribution of one biologist.

In the first place, evolutionary biology has given us a new view, impossible of attainment in any earlier age, of our human destiny. That destiny is to be the agent of the evolutionary process on this planet, the instrument for realising new possibilities for its future.

The picture of the universe provided by modern science is of a single process of self-transformation, during which new possibilities can be realised. There has been a creation of new actualities during cosmic time: it has been progressive, and it has been a self-creation.

The entire cosmos, in all its appalling vastness, consists of the same world-stuff. Following William James, I use this awkward term deliberately in place of *matter*, because 'matter' is commonly opposed to 'mind', whereas it is now apparent that the world-stuff is not restricted to material properties.[8] When organised in certain ways—as, for instance, in the form of human bodies and brains—it is capable of mental as well as

[8] Physics has revealed the inseparability and indeed interchangeability of matter and energy. For simplicity's sake I am using *matter* as equivalent to matter-and-energy, and *material* as denoting physically measurable properties.

material activities. Furthermore, the study of animals shows that there is no sharp line to be drawn between human and animal behaviour, except in the essential human capacity for the cumulative transmission of experience, knowledge, and ideas; and it is now clear that minds, in the sense of all activities with an obvious mental component, have evolved just as much as have material bodies: mental activities of every kind, from awareness and knowledge to emotion, memory and will, have become increasingly intense and efficient, and mental organisation has reached ever higher levels. Through sense-organs and brains, the mind-like potentialities of the world-stuff have been progressively intensified and actualised, in the same sort of way as its electrical properties have been intensified in the electric organs of the torpedo-fish or through the agency of human constructions like dynamos.

Since natural selection is the sole or main method of biological evolution, and since it can only operate to produce results of biological utility, it is clear that the mental properties of organisms are not mere useless by-products, but must be of value to their possessors. Furthermore, they can and do play an operative rôle in the evolutionary process: thus the awareness of colour and pattern found in some higher animals has led to the further evolution of colour-patterns of various sorts, and has assisted in the birth of that evolutionary novelty we call beauty.

If the self-creation of novelty is the basic wonder of the universe, this eliciting of mind from the potentialities of the world-stuff, and its intensification and increasing importance during evolution, is the basic wonder of life.

During evolution, the onward-flowing stream of life breaks up into a vast number of branches or trends, each resulting in improvement of one sort or another.

The great majority of these become so specialised that life in them finds itself in a blind alley, incapable of further improvement or of transformation for another way of existence. After this, they either remain essentially unchanged for tens or even hundreds of millions of years, or else wholly die out, becoming extinguished in the sands of time. We need only recall the extinction of the dinosaurs and other strange reptiles of the Mesozoic, or the lack of essential change shown by such successful groups as the birds for over twenty million years, or the ants for over fifty.

But through this radiating fan of restricted improvements and blind-alley specialisations there runs a trend towards major advance; and this current of biological advance has continued through the two thousand million years of life's existence. It is marked by increase of over-all biological efficiency and by improvement in general plan of working. During its course, there has been an enormous rise in level of harmonious organisation—think of a bird or a mammal as against a flatworm or a jellyfish; in flexibility and the capacity for self-regulation; in physiological efficiency, as shown in muscular contraction or rate of nervous conduction, or manifested in sheer strength or speed; in the range of awareness, as seen in the evolution of sense-organs—think of an eagle's eyes or an antelope's ears as against the complete blindness and deafness of a polyp or an amoeba; and in the intensity and complexity of mental processes such as knowing and perceiving, feeling and willing, learning and remembering—think of a dog or a monkey as against a sea-anemone or a snail.

When we look at the actual course of the evolutionary process, we find that general biological advance has been achieved in a series of steps, through the emergence of a series of dominant types. Each new dominant type possesses some improvement in general organisation, which enables it to spread and multiply at the expense of the previously dominant group from among whose less specialised members it has evolved. This progressive replacement of dominant types and groups is most clearly shown in the later history of vertebrates. The reptiles replaced the moist-skinned amphibians as a dominant type of land animal, and were in turn replaced by the warm-blooded mammals and birds.

It is thus perfectly proper to use terms like *higher* and *lower* to describe different types of organism, and *progress* for certain types of trend. A higher organism is one which has realised more of the inherent possibilities of living substance, and biological progress denotes those trends which do not restrict the further realisation of those possibilities.

The next fact of importance is that during evolutionary time the avenues of possible progress have become progressively restricted, until today only one remains open.

Let me amplify this point. Well before the end of the Cenozoic Era, the limits of physiological efficiency seem to have been reached by life. The largest size possible to efficient land animals was attained by the dinosaurs over sixty million years ago; the temperature-regulating mechanism of higher mammals reached the profitable limit of accuracy perhaps half-way through the Cenozoic; it appears to be physically impossible to evolve an acuity of vision or a speed of flight greater than that of a falcon.

The only avenue of major advance left open was through the improvement of brain and mind. This was the line taken by our own ancestors, and it was this advance which enabled man to become the latest dominant type in evolution. His rise to dominance is very recent—an affair of less than a million years—but its later course, in the short period since the waning of the last phase of glaciation, has been spectacularly rapid, and it has been accompanied by marked decline and widespread extinction of the previously dominant mammals, as well as by a radical transformation of the environment by man.

Furthermore, it is clear that man is only at the beginning of his period of evolutionary dominance, and that vast and still undreamt-of possibilities of further advance still lie before him.

Biology, I repeat, has thus revealed man's place in nature. He is the highest form of life produced by the evolutionary process on this planet, the latest dominant type, and the only organism capable of further major advance or progress. Whether he knows it or not, whether he wishes it or not, he is now the main agency for the further evolution of the earth and its inhabitants. In other words, his destiny is to realise new possibilities for the whole terrestrial sector of the cosmic process, to be the instrument of further evolutionary progress on this planet.

The past history of biological evolution gives us a certain further guidance. We can justifiably extrapolate some of the main trends of progress into the future, and conclude that man should aim at a continued increase of those qualities which have spelt progress in the biological past—efficiency and control of environment, self-regulation and independence of outer changes, individuation and level of organisation, wholeness or harmony of working, extent of awareness and knowledge, storage of experience, degree of mental organisation. In particular, man is likely to fulfil his destiny more successfully if he exploits to the full those improvements which have given him his position as latest dominant type, notably his properties of reason, imagination and conceptual thought, and his unique capacities of accumulating, organising, and applying experience through a transmissible culture and set of ideas.

These include the capacity to construct religions in the broad sense—systems of attitude, in which knowledge can be combined with ideals and imaginatively fused with our deep spiritual emotions to form a stable framework of sentiments and beliefs, which in turn will influence behaviour and help to determine moral and practical action.

From this point of view, the religion indicated by our new view of our position in the cosmos must clearly be one centred on the idea of fulfilment. Man's most sacred duty, and at the same time his most glorious opportunity, is to promote the maximum fulfilment of the evolutionary process on this earth; and this includes the fullest realisation of his own inherent possibilities.

Let us follow up some of the implications of this important general conclusion. Evolutionary biology makes it clear that the developed human individual personality is, in a strictly scientific sense, the highest product of the cosmic process of which we have any knowledge; accordingly, we can formulate the ultimate aim of the human species as the realisation of more possibilities by more, and more fully developed, individuals.

On the other hand, human individuals cannot realise their possibilities except as members of social groups, and through means which only organised societies can provide. Furthermore, organisation on the human level can not be reproduced, still less improved, except through the social agency of cultural transmission. Thus the paramountcy of the individual is not absolute: it is limited by the need of maintaining and improving social organisation.

Man inhabits a world of ideas which he has created, and of social institutions and achievements which those ideas have generated. In this psycho-social world he lives and moves and has his being. It is in a certain sense an artificial environment which he makes for himself, but can better be regarded as an essential part of the radically new type of evolving organisation represented by the human species—the internal environment of psycho-social man.

There is inevitably some conflict between the interests of individuals and those of society. But the conflict is in large measure transcended in this conception of man as an evolving psycho-social organism. This dictates certain conclusions. In the longest-term point of view, our aim must be to develop a type of society and culture capable of ever-fresh evolution, one which continually opens the way to new and fuller realisations; in the medium-term point of view, we must secure the reproduction and improvement of the psycho-social organism, the maintenance of the frameworks of society and culture and their transmission in time; and in the immediate point of view we must aim at maximum individual fulfilment.

What needs stressing, however, is that, from the angle of evolutionary humanism, the flowering of the individual is seen as having intrinsic value, as being an end in itself. In the satisfying exercise of our faculties, in the pure enjoyment of our experience, the cosmic process of evolution is bringing some of its possibilities to fruition. In individual acts of comprehension or love, in the enjoyment of beauty, in the inner experiences of peace and assurance, in the satisfactions of creative achievement, however humble, we are helping to realise human destiny.

Above all, the individual should aim at fullness and wholeness of development. Every human being is confronted with the task of growing up, of building a personality out of the raw materials of his infant self. A rich and full personality, in moral and spiritual harmony with itself and with its destiny, one whose talents are not buried in a napkin, and whose wholeness transcends its conflicts, is the highest creation of which we have knowledge, and in its attainment the individual possibilities of the evolutionary process are brought to supreme fruition.

But if the individual has duties towards his own potentialities, he owes them also to those of others, singly and collectively. He has the duty to aid other individuals towards fuller development, and to contribute his mite to the maintenance and improvement of the continuing social process, and so to the march of evolution as a whole.

However, to realise the practical importance of such general conclusions, we need to amplify and illuminate them by following out their implications. To do this satisfactorily in any detail is beyond the possibilities of a single essay, or indeed of a single individual. But I must at least make some attempts at annotation, in the hope that they will serve to stimulate further exploration by others.

The basic postulate of evolutionary humanism is that mental and spiritual forces—using the term *force* in a loose and general sense—do have operative effect, and are indeed of decisive importance in the highly practical business of working out human destiny; and that they are not supernatural, not outside man but within him. Regarded as an evolutionary agency, the human species is a psycho-social mechanism which must operate by utilising those forces. What is the nature of those forces; where, within the psycho-social mechanism, do they reside; and where are their points of application?

In the first place, there is evil in man as well as good. This obvious ethical fact has found theological expression in elaborate doctrines like that of original sin, and has been projected into hypotheses of supernatural powers of good and evil, like God and the Devil, Ormuzd and Ahriman. But the crude distinction in terms of ethical absolutes like 'good' and 'evil' requires reformulation in the light of psychology and history. We then see that the important distinction to make is between positive and negative, between constructive and destructive or purely restrictive. On the one side we have such forces as hate, envy, despair, fear, destructive rage and aggressiveness, restrictive selfishness in all its forms, from greed to lust for power, and negations of effectiveness such as internal disharmony, frustration, and unresolved conflict; on the other we have comprehension, love in the broadest sense, including love of beauty and desire for truth, the urge to creation and fuller expression, the desire to participate and to feel useful in contributing to some larger enterprise or purpose, pure enjoyment and the cultivation of intrinsic talents and capacities, and that constructive disposition of forces that we may call inner harmony.

These forces operate not only within individual minds, but through the social framework. A society may be so organised that it generates large amounts of hate or envy or despair; or creates vast tracts of ugliness; or imposes subnormal health or inadequate mental development on large sections of its population. Or its organisation may serve to encourage and facilitate constructive enthusiasm, to create beauty, and to promote full and healthy individual development.

This is so obvious that we are sometimes in danger of disregarding it. The fact remains that social organisation does canalise and concentrate the psychological forces of human nature in different ways, so that society can act either as an organ of frustration or an organ of fulfilment. Once we have grasped that fact, it is up to us to make the attempt to improve its design.

Evolutionary humanism has the further implication that man is at one and the same time the only agent for realising life's further progress, and also the main obstacle in the path of its realisation. The hostile outer world was his first obvious adversary; but the only opponent ultimately worthy of his steel is himself. Man has learnt in large measure to understand, control and utilise the forces of external nature: he must learn to understand, control and utilise the forces of his own nature.

This applies as much to the blind urge to reproduction as to personal greed or desire for power, as much to arrogance and fanaticism, whether nationalist or religious, as to straightforward sadism or self-indulgence.

Let me pursue one example in a little more detail. Most individual human beings feel themselves saddled with some burden of guilt or uncleanness or unrighteousness, and desire a positive assurance of righteousness or cleansing or worth. The exact nature of the sentiment varies from culture to culture, and also as between different individuals, but they always involve feelings of rightness and wrongness.

The simplest and most primitive method of coping with this dual problem is to increase one's assurance of rightness by projecting one's own guilt or wrongness outwards onto events or, if possible, onto a human or humanly personified enemy.

The process may be wholly unconscious, or merely rationalised; but this does not render it any less wrong or any less dangerous. It prevents the proper development of the individual personality by standing in the way of its wholeness and harmony or organisation; and it obstructs the development both of society and of the species as a whole by magnifying or even creating conflicts and by converting potential partners into actual enemies. The text-books of psychology illustrate in detail the workings of this subconscious tendency to justification by projection. In any case it is clearly an opponent of progress, standing in the way both of individual and evolutionary fulfilment, and it needs to be understood, faced, and overcome, if man is to advance.

The business of individual development thus poses a triple problem. The individual has to come to terms with the battery of powerful and often conflicting impulses with which he has been equipped willy-nilly by heredity; with the forces of his immediate social environment—family, class, and nation; and with what I may call transcendent forces—all those which transcend that immediate environment—including the impact of nature's enduring framework, the concept of the human race as a whole and its welfare, the driving force of man's own ideals and aspirations.

Freud has shown how the infantile and often unconscious struggle between love and hate colours all early development, and can become transformed into a conflict between the sympathetic impulses making for interdependent co-operation and the aggressive and power-greedy impulses making for hostility and violence.[9] And we all experience consciously the shock of the powerful emergence of the sex-impulse in adolescence, and the difficulty of harnessing it satisfactorily to our vital chariot.

The immediate social forces will influence the way in which the individual's impulses are adjusted: for instance, social approval and disapproval largely determine the form in which conscience develops. As modern anthropological research has served to emphasise, the personality-moulding forces of the social environment vary from society to society, so that the commonest types of individual psychological organisation found in South Africa, for instance, will differ from those in Bali or in Soviet Russia.

The transcendent forces have tended to be neglected by social scientists, perhaps partly in reaction against their over-emphasis by religious thinking, and partly because the very phrase *social science* tends to focus scientific attention on actual immediate social organisations. But they are of great importance. When Wordsworth wrote of

> *High instincts before which our mortal nature*
> *Doth tremble like a guilty thing surprised*

he may not have provided a scientific formulation, but he gave convincing expression to a potent element in human life.

In any case, man's capacity for generalisation and abstract thought inevitably generates what we call ideals, and ideals inevitably affect behaviour and the personal development of psychological organisation. Furthermore, the basic human sense of dependence and need for maximum assurance makes it inevitable that men will seek for the enduring elements in or behind the disconcerting flux of experience, and will attempt to express them in psychologically effective form.

Here, as elsewhere, the problem is to ensure that the resultant formulations shall be not only effective but true, in

[9] In fact from this primal conflict there is engendered the rudiment of conscience—the Freudians' super-ego, or as I prefer to call it, the protoethical mechanism. See T. H. and J. S. Huxley, *Evolution and Ethics*, Harper, New York, 1947.

the sense of corresponding with reality to the greatest possible extent. From our evolutionary humanist point of view, they need to be related to the optimum future development of humanity.

Individual mental and spiritual development thus always and inevitably involve the adjustment or reconciliation of conflicts of various sorts—between different impulses, between the demands of the individual and those of society, and between the immediate and the transcendent or enduring. This last conflict can today be more precisely formulated as the conflict between the demands of the existing society into which the individual happens to be born, and those of the evolving human species as a whole.

It is easy to say that evolutionary humanism establishes the duty of the individual as the optimum realisation of his possibilities: but this is too general. The fact that he must reconcile his individual demands with the needs of society and the claims of further evolutionary progress defines the problem rather more closely, but still leaves it vague in many important details. I have space only for a few brief comments. In the first place, it is clear that there are different degrees of fruition, different levels to be attained by the developing personality. In religious phraseology (which can readily be translated into the more cumbersome terms of scientific psychology), the organisation of the soul can reach different grades of perfection. It is always possible to know and understand more, to feel and to sympathise more comprehensively, to achieve a fuller internal harmony. The right kind of individual development is thus one which leaves the way permanently open for fresh possibilities of growth (just as evolutionary progress was only achieved through trends of improvement which did not bar the way to further improvement). The developing self has the possibility of transcending itself in further development;[10] but in practice, different selves stop at different levels. There is thus in some sense a scale of development among personalities, more or less corresponding to the scale of higher and lower among non-human organisms.

In the second place three main contrasted ideals of personal development are possible. One is specialisation: the fullest exploitation of some particular capacity, as seen in many successful professional men. The second we may call allroundness by summation: the cultivation of every kind of

[10] See Charles Morris, *The Open Self*, Prentice-Hall, New York.

fulfilment separately. This was, broadly, the ideal of the ancient Athenians and of our own Elizabethans. The third is difficult to characterise in a word: we may perhaps call it comprehensive wholeness: the cultivation of inner harmony and peace, the development of a unitary and comprehensive pattern of intellectual and spiritual organisation. This has been the aim of the saints, the mystics, and the philosophic sages.

The first is in some degree necessary for personal success in life: but pushed to extremes it is as dangerous as biological specialisation, and stands in the way of the higher levels of personal development. The second does justice to the variety of apparently conflicting fulfilments possible to man. The Greeks gave it a religious sanction by divinising various separate human activities or modes of fulfilment. The coexistence of Aphrodite and Artemis, of Ares and Athena in the Greek Pantheon implies that, to the same individual at different times, both physical love and chastity can be sacred, that a man can find high fulfilment both in war and in peaceful learning.

The organisation of personality round a number of separate and apparently disparate modes of fulfilment corresponds roughly on the human plane to the organisation of behaviour round a number of separate and mutually exclusive instincts in an insect, or impulses or drives in a bird or a mammal. It is an important method of utilising apparently conflicting or contradictory capacities to achieve a high sum-total of fulfilment. But it does so by the avoidance of conflicts, not by their reconciliation. It thus, if pushed to its logical extreme, stands in the way of achieving the third ideal: wholeness, the unity and continuity of the highest types of personality, just as the mammals' separate emotional drives and their series of isolated experiences had to be brought together in consciousness before the continuity of man's mental life could be realised.

Some kind of wholeness is thus indispensable for the higher levels of human fulfilment. But here again restriction or over-specialisation can have unfortunate results. The dangerous over-specialisation here is emphasis on unity and harmony to the neglect or exclusion of comprehensiveness, richness and variety. A holy life may be strongly unified, but may be sadly restricted in scope. Its pattern may be a whole in the sense of having a well-marked unity; but it may fall far short of possible wholeness in failing to utilise many of the potentialities of human development.

Wholeness, however, if properly understood, remains the key to the higher reaches of personal development and fulfilment. The personality is a spiritual and mental construction, a work of art like other human constructions. Wholeness is to this construction what design is to a building, conferring a new beauty and significance on what would otherwise be a mere assemblage of separate parts. This applies whether the building be a cottage or a cathedral, whether the personality be that of a simple labourer or a great archbishop.

It is all too obvious that, in the great majority of human beings, the great majority of their possibilities, whether physical or spiritual, intellectual or aesthetic, remains unrealised; while our rather meagre knowledge of mysticism and Yoga makes it clear that some regions of human potentiality remain virtually unexplored, or at least unavailable to mankind as a whole. I would venture to prophesy that one of the next important steps in human progress will be the development of a science of human possibilities—their nature, their limits, and the communicable techniques for their fuller realisation.

*

Evolutionary humanism, with its naturalism and its twin goals of present fulfilment for the individual and of long-term progressive realisation of possibilities for man and the planet he inhabits, imposes a transvaluation of values. For one thing, it helps to restore our unity with nature. It brings back the objects of our adoration and the goals of our spiritual longings out of supernatural remoteness and sites them nearer home, in the immediacy of experience. As an example, let us consider the beauty and richness of nature. Rare Christian mystics like Traherne have found in it a religious fulfilment, and great poets like Wordsworth, in spite of the theological preconceptions of their time, have succeeded in expressing its transcendent value. The gospel of evolutionary humanism generalises that value. The enjoyment of the beauty and varied wonder of the natural world—an experience engendered jointly by nature and the capacities of man's mind—is seen as one of the indispensable modes of human fulfilment, not to be neglected without peril, involving something essentially religious or holy even though we may not burden it with any such heavy designation.

As a corollary, we have the collective duty of preserving wild nature—partly for its own sake, but mainly as one of the necessary means for man's fulfilment. To exterminate a living species, be it lion or lammergeier, to wipe out wild flowers or birds over great tracts of country, is to diminish the wonder and the interest of the universe.

The same, *mutatis mutandis,* is true of the beauty of art and architecture. For evolutionary humanism, one of the ultimate aims of man appears as the creation of more and fuller beauty. Failure to create beauty is a dereliction of duty, and the creation of ugliness and meanness is immoral. Judged by humanist values, the cities and other parts of the artificial environment man has created for himself, stand in large measure condemned.

The conservation and proper exploitation of natural resources is another of the essentially sacred duties imposed by a humanist ideology—because they provide the indispensable material basis for higher fulfilment.

We perceive the same need for compromise or adjustment between social values as appeared for modes of individual fulfilment. We obviously should not preserve all wild life everywhere, nor leave all nature untamed for the enjoyment of nature-lovers. But neither should we allow economic exploitation to become universally dominant. Though much can rightly be accomplished in the way of reconciling diverse interests in a single pattern, it is often impossible to do so completely. Then we must be content with all-roundness by summation, and allot areas in which separate interests are paramount—wild life in one area, natural beauty in another, exploitation of resources in a third.

The most important of all the major trends that we find in evolution concerns the *awareness* of organisms, in the broadest possible sense—the organs of experience, by which they become aware of happenings in the external environment and in themselves, of the world and of their situation in it. Eventually, the improvement of awareness led to the emergence of man as dominant type, and in so doing opened up new opportunities of evolution beyond those possible through purely physiological improvement.

I cannot embark on a detailed discussion of this improvement of biological awareness. It must suffice to remind my readers that there has been a great increase in the range and acuity of sense-organs; that the awareness of pain has been specialised so as to help animals to profit by experience; that the higher animals are aware of a wide range of emotional states, often intense, and closely linked with adaptive instinctive actions; that there has been a trend towards the integration of different elements of awareness into increasingly complex patterns, as illustrated by the evolution of pattern-vision, or later by the combination of sight and touch and muscular sense to provide perceptual awareness of solid and coloured objects in three-dimensional space; that the capacity to organise awareness in transmissible and cumulative form is the distinctive property which has permitted the evolutionary rise of man; and finally, that man's future progress depends very largely on how he continues this trend towards the greater extension and better organisation of his awareness.

Before going further, let me remind you that the organisations of awareness that play a part in our mental life are all our own creations—of course in partnership with external fact, but none the less human productions. This is true even of our perceptions, as is illustrated by such work as that of Ames and Cantril and by the study of how blind people learn to see after recovering their power of vision.[11] We do not merely receive direct impressions or representations of some external reality. We have to learn, albeit for the most part quite unconsciously, to organise the chaos of coloured patterns, which is all we receive in sensation, into coherent perceptions on the basis of repeated experience. Perceptions, in other words, always involve some degree of assumption and interpretation.

An obvious example is the night sky: the 'natural' interpretation of this was to perceive the sky as a hemisphere studded with equidistant stars; now, with the aid of telescopes and astronomers' brains, we see it as a fathomless depth of space. Even when, as with the night sky, such interpretative assumptions are largely dependent on conscious intellectual processes, they modify the way in which our raw awareness is perceptually organised.

This is still more obviously true of the concepts and verbal symbols which are the chief vehicles for communication. Human societies have to create them: individuals have to learn them: each of us has to build up his own organisation of significance round verbal concepts like *horse* or *mathematics*. And so it continues, up to the most complex levels of

[11] See J. Z. Young, *Doubt and Certainty in Science,* Oxford University Press, New York, 1952; D. O. Hebb, *The Organization of Behavior* (Wiley, New York, 1949); H. Cantril, *The 'Why' of Man's Experience* (Macmillan, New York, 1950); and my *Evolution in Action* (Harper, New York, 1953).

organisation to the construction of laws of nature to subsume vast quantities of observations and experiments on the welter of events, of works of art to bring together many diverse ideas and emotional experiences in a single unified whole, of gods to unify the chaos and the conflicts of spiritual and religious experience.

Collective awareness is thus the distinctive and most important organ of the human species. It can be improved both quantitatively, by adding to knowledge and extending the range of experience, and qualitatively, by improving its organisation. Scientific hypotheses and laws are better organisations for coping with our experience of physical phenomena than are trial-and-error methods, or traditional precepts, or pseudo-explanations in terms of metaphysical principles. Monotheism provides a better organisation for certain important aspects of religious experience than does polydaimonism.

But meanwhile the total volume of knowledge available to man for the business of living and evolving has increased to a prodigious and spectacular extent, and this very increase in extent demands constant modification of the organisations of knowledge, including sometimes the creation of quite new types of organisation and the scrapping of old ones.

On this last point, the conclusions dictated by evolutionary humanism can be briefly summed up as follows. First, man finds one of his ultimate fulfilments in comprehension. Fuller comprehension is one of the basic duties (and privileges) of the individual. Secondly, accumulated and organised knowledge and experience are necessary instruments or organs for human advance. Thus scientific research in all fields is essential, and its encouragement is one of the most important tasks of a civilised society.

Then it is clear that the common pools of accumulated and organised knowledge on which civilisation and human advance depend, will perform their psycho-social functions more adequately as they are more fully available to and more fully utilised by all the members of a community, and as they merge more fully into a single universal pool for the whole human species. Education is extending the possibilities of participation in knowledge and ideas, while natural science is already international, and has laid the foundations for a comprehensive global system of knowledge.

Science has also contributed a discovery of the first magnitude—the discovery of the principle of limited but increasing certitude as the best method of extending and organising knowledge. The principle of limited certitude not only includes scientific method in the restricted sense—the method of dispassionate observation and, where possible, experiment, of framing hypotheses, and of their testing and modification in the light of further observation and experiment. But it comprises more than this: it involves a general attitude to experience. It implies a fundamental humanity, in acknowledging at the outset our enormous ignorance, the vast extent of what we do not know. But it also implies a legitimate pride and assurance—pride in the extent of the areas already annexed to the domain of knowledge from the wastes of ignorance, assurance in the tested validity of the accumulated facts and in the efficacy of the scientific method; and an assurance also that the scientific method of accumulating and organising knowledge can be profitably extended to the entire psychosocial field, to the workings of society and of human nature, in such a way that knowledge can become in a full sense the basis of wisdom.

The scientific spirit and the scientific method have proved the most effective agents for the comprehension and control of physical nature. It remains for man to apply them to the comprehension and control of human destiny. For this to happen, science must understand that a religion of some kind is a necessary organ for coping with the problems of destiny; and religion must not only accept and utilise the findings of science, but must be willing to admit the central principle of limited certitude, with its implication of progressive but always incomplete achievement of a better religious construction.

There are a few other points on which I would like to touch. The importance of the population problem for human destiny is looming larger every year. The implications of evolutionary humanism here are clear. If the full development of human individuals and the fulfilment of human possibilities are the over-riding aims of our evolution, then any over-population which brings malnutrition and misery, or which erodes the world's material resources or its resources of beauty or intellectual satisfaction, is evil. Among the world's major and immediate tasks is the working out of an effective and acceptable population policy.

In the ultimate light of humanist values, the deliberate encouragement of over-population for military or political ends, as in pre-war Italy and Japan, the intellectual dishonesty of the Russian Communists in asserting that over-population is an invention of the 'Morganist-Weismannist hirelings of

American monopolists',[12] designed to justify American imperialist expansion, and the theological dogmatism of the Roman Catholics which denounces birth-control and prevents the scientific discussion of population problems even in international bodies like the World Health Organisation—all are seen as immoral and indeed wicked.

Evolutionary humanism has eugenic implications also. These are, for the moment, largely theoretical, but in due time will become intensely practical. Within a century we should have amassed adequate knowledge of what could be done negatively to lighten the burden of inherited deficiency of mind or body which presses so cruelly on so many individual human beings and hangs so heavily on evolving humanity as a whole, and positively to raise the general level of innate human possibilities and capacities. When this has happened, the working out of an effective and acceptable eugenic policy will be seen as not only an urgent but an inspiring task, and its political or theological obstruction as immoral.

Before concluding, I must say a word about the arts. Art, science and religion are the three main fields of man's creative activity: all are indispensable for his fulfilment and the greater realisation of his possibilities. In its recent manifestations, Western civilisation has tended to exalt science and its technological applications at the expense of the arts. But we can grasp how important and indispensable they really are by imagining a world without them. Think of a world without music or poetry, without its churches and noble houses, without ballets, plays, novels, and films, without pictures and sculptures: such a world would be intolerable, and life in it unlivable.

The practice of various arts—painting and modelling, music and acting—can play an important rôle in the development of individual personality in education; this is especially true of children in whom intellectual interests are not naturally strong, but in any case intellectual interests alone will favour a one-sided distortion of development. And throughout life the arts can provide individual fulfilments unattainable by any other means.

But for my present purpose it is the social relations of the artist and the social functions of the arts that are more relevant, as well as being in more need of clarification.

Two extreme positions are possible. Art may be regarded merely as self-expression, and the individual artist may ac-

[12] Quoted from the New York *Herald Tribune's* summary, April 5th, 1948, of an article by Professor Gluschenko in *Pravda*.

knowledge no responsibility to the society in which he happens to live, but only to himself and to whatever ideas of art he may happen to hold. Or it may be regarded merely as an instrument of the State, and the artist be required to subordinate his own ideas entirely to the task of expressing the aims and interests of official policy. At the moment, both these extreme positions are actually held—the former by many among the more rebellious artists in Western countries,[13] the latter by the U.S.S.R. with its officially enforced doctrine of Socialist Realism. Neither extreme is really tenable by itself, but the partial truths embodied in them may be reconciled. In the light of evolutionary humanism art appears not as an instrument of the State, but as an organ of the evolving human species; and though it agrees that the variety of individual genius and the duty of experimenting with new possibilities of vision and expression must be admitted, it insists that the artist, like all other men, has some responsibilities to the community of which he is a member, as well as to the gifts with which, by no merit of his own, he may have been endowed.

Viewed in this light, the duty of the artist comprises not only the duty of cultivating his personal talents and expressing his own individuality and ideas, but also the duty of understanding something of the universe in which he lives, of the social process of which he is a part, and of his own relations with and possible rôle in it.

In the light of evolutionary humanism, the essential function of the arts is seen as one of bearing witness to the wonder and variety of the world and of human experience. In more precise but more forbidding phraseology, it is to create vehicles for the effective expression and communication of complex emotionally charged experiences, which are of value in the process of human fulfilment. Both science and art are instruments for comprehending the world, and for communicating that comprehension. They employ different methods, and are important in different ways: but the two are complementary, and both are indispensable.

Indeed, in every sphere, evolutionary humanism appears as one which both necessitates and makes possible the reconciliation of extreme positions and the adjustment of conflicting interests. Conflicts may be transcended in the process of becoming.

[13] It is curious to note how in some cases, for instance Picasso, extreme individualism in practice may be combined with a theoretical Communism.

The central concept, of a process of becoming, a self-transformation of humanity with a desirable direction and rate, provides a framework of synthesis in which many conflicts can be transcended, many antithetic opposites can be reconciled—continuity and change; doubt and certainty; the immediate and the enduring; rivalry and co-operation; the actual and the possible; individualism and collectivism, at all levels from isolated individuals through family, local group, class or nation, to humanity and indeed to life as a whole.

In the actual process of individual development, the stress is seen falling on the reconciliation of conflicting impulses in a harmonious personal unity, in that of social development on the adjustment of conflicting interests in a pattern of maximum fruitfulness.

Above all, its central concept of greater fulfilment through the realisation of possibilities brings ideals and ultimate values into relation with actual imperfections and present efforts, and links them as participants in the common task of better achieving human destiny.

This brings me back to where I started—the idea of religion as an organ of destiny. It is clear, as I suggested earlier, that twentieth-century man needs a new organ for dealing with destiny, a new system of beliefs and attitudes adapted to the situation in which he and his societies now have to exist and thus an organ for the better orientation of the human species as a whole—in other words, a new religion.

Like all other new religions, and indeed all other new movements of ideas, it will at the outset be expressed and spread by a small minority: but it will in due course of time tend to become universal, not only potentially and in theory, but actually and in practice. The properties of man's psychosocial nature make this inevitable. Man cannot avoid the process of convergence which makes for the integration of divergent or hostile human groups in a single organic world society and culture.[14] And an integrated world society cannot operate effectively without an integrated common pool of thought and body of ideas. Thought and practice interact; but in the modern world thought is likely to move the faster so that a universalist system of ideas, if firmly based in reality, can be expected to play an important part in effecting the process of practical and institutional integration.

Science, as a system of discovering, organising and apply-

[14] See Père Teilhard de Chardin's remarkable book *Le Phenomène Humain* (Paris, 1955; shortly to appear in an English translation).

ing mutual knowledge, is already unified and universal in principle, though its efficiency as an organ of the human species could still be much increased. It remains for man to unify and universalise his religion.

How that religion will take form—what rituals or celebrations it might practise, whether it will equip itself with any sort of professional body or priesthood, what buildings it will erect, what symbols it will adopt—that is something which no one can prophesy. Certainly it is not a field on which the natural scientist should venture. What the scientist can do is to draw attention to the relevant facts revealed by scientific discovery, and to their implications and those of the scientific method. He can aid in the building up of a fuller and more accurate picture of reality in general and of human destiny in particular, secure in the knowledge that in so doing he is contributing to humanity's advance, and helping to make possible the emergence of a more universal and more adequate religion.

The most significant contribution of science in this vital field is the discovery of man's position and rôle in evolution. Let me restate this, as follows. Man is that part of reality in which and through which the cosmic process has become conscious and has begun to comprehend itself. His supreme task is to increase that conscious comprehension and to apply it as fully as possible to guide the course of events. In other words, his rôle is to discover his destiny as agent of the evolutionary process, in order to fulfil it more adequately. This is a practical task, to which science can and must contribute. If we want to achieve any adequate understanding and control of the electrical forces operating in nature, or the processes of plant growth and heredity, we must call on science to help. The same is true if we want to acquire any adequate understanding and control of our destiny.

Sixty-four years ago my grandfather T. H. Huxley, in his Romanes Lecture on *Evolution and Ethics,* summed up his lifelong preoccupation with the central problem of human destiny in a celebrated exhortation: 'Let us understand, once and for all, that the ethical progress of society consists not in imitating the cosmic process, still less in running away from it, but in combating it.' To-day, we must say that the ethical progress of society, and indeed human progress in all its aspects, consists not in combating the cosmic process but in wrestling with it (as Jacob wrestled with the angel), and in finding out what we can do to direct it. And this depends on our understanding of it, and on our learning how to discharge our rôle of leadership in it. If T. H. Huxley were alive to-day, I believe that he would agree with this formulation (though I am sure that he would have phrased it better), and that he would accept the general way of thinking about man's destiny which I have called Evolutionary Humanism.

In exposing my thesis, I have had to range discursively into many fields. In concluding, perhaps I may be permitted to bring them together in a personal focus. I can, at any rate, testify to the fact that the concept of evolutionary humanism has been of value to myself. It has enabled me to resolve many of the dilemmas and conflicts with which any enquiring and aspiring mind is inevitably beset. It has enabled me to see this strange universe into which we are born as a proper object both of awe and wondering love and of intellectual curiosity. More, it has made me realise that both my wonder and my curiosity (like those of any other human being) can be of significance and value in that universe. It has enabled me to relate my experiences of the world's delights and satisfactions, and those of its horrors and its miseries, to the idea of fulfilment, positive or negative. In the concept of increased realisation of possibilities, it has provided a common measuring rod for all kinds of directional processes, from the development of personal ethics to large-scale evolution, and given solid ground for maintaining an affirmative attitude and faith, as against that insidious enemy, Goethe's *Geist der stets verneint*, the spirit of negation and despair. It affirms the positive significance of effort and creative activity and enjoyment. In some ways most important of all, it has brought back intellectual speculation and spiritual aspiration out of the abstract and isolated spheres they once seemed to me to inhabit, to a meaningful place in concrete reality; and so, in a word, it has restored my sense of unity with nature.

Ever since my boyhood, I have been deeply impressed by Wordsworth's lines in *Tintern Abbey*:

> *I have felt*
> *A presence that disturbs me with the joy*
> *Of elevated thoughts; a sense sublime*
> *Of something far more deeply interfused,*
> *Whose dwelling is the light of setting suns,*
> *And the round ocean and the living air,*
> *And the blue sky, and in the mind of man.*

Yet I was unable to see how experiences of this kind, though I could personally testify to their value, could be linked up with the framework of ideas that I was attempting to build up on the basis of my scientific education. In the light of evolutionary humanism, however, the connection is clear, though the intellectual formulation given to it by Wordsworth was inadequate. The reality behind his thought is that man's mind is a partner with nature: it participates with the external world in the process of generating awareness and creating values.

The importance of this idea of participation, of co-operative partnership in a joint enterprise, had been brought home to me in various separate contexts. I had met with it as a keystone of our colonial policy in Africa; as a necessary basis for the work of Unesco; as the concept inspiring the Colombo Plan and the United Nations' programme of technical assistance. I read Bertrand de Jouvenel's illuminating definition of politics as action directed towards inducing men to co-operate in a common enterprise; and evolutionary biology shows us the destiny of man on earth as a partnership between man and nature, with man in the leading position—a common enterprise involving the participation of the entire human species for its most fruitful execution.

It has inevitably been a source of satisfaction that my almost life-long interest in evolution has led me to a better understanding of the relations between human life and the apparently hostile universe in which it exists. Man, both as individual and as species, turns out to be profoundly significant in the cosmic process.

When Hamlet pronounced man 'the paragon of animals', 'the quintessence of dust', he anticipated Darwin and all the implications of Darwin's work for our ideas about man's origin and destiny. But, he also said, 'man delights me not, no, nor woman either', thereby voicing some of the disillusion and horror which we all sometimes feel at human frustration, stupidity and cruelty. That disillusion and horror have been sharpened for us moderns by the events of the last few decades—though, if we had been willing to cast our eyes backward into history, we should have found abundance of stupidities and cruelties to rival those of our own times.

However, in the light of our newer knowledge of psychology and history, the moral of those failures and horrors is not that human nature is unchangeable, or incurably evil. Human nature always contains the possibilities of evil, waste and frustration; but it also contains those of good, of achievement and of fruition. The lesson of evolution is that we must think in the limited but positive terms of fulfilment—

the degree to which we, individually and collectively, manage to realise our inherent possibilities.

Finally, the concept of evolutionary humanism has helped me to see how, in principle at least, science and religion can be reconciled. It has shown me outlets for ideas and sentiments which I think can legitimately be called religious, but which otherwise would have remained frustrated or untapped. And it has indicated how vital a contribution science can make to religious progress.

My grandfather, in the famous essay in which he defined agnosticism, stated as self-evident that 'every man should be able to give a reason for the faith that is in him'. My faith is in the possibilities of man: I hope that I have here succeeded in stating some of my reasons for that faith.

Bibliography

*A short list of important, useful or representative works
in the vast and diverse literature of the subject*

GENERAL:

CASSIRER, ERNST: *An Essay on Man*, New Haven, Yale University Press, 1944.

MACBEATH, A.: *Experiments in Living*, New York, St. Martins, 1952.

MICKLEM, NATHANIEL: *Religion*, New York, Oxford University Press, 1948.

SANTAYANA, GEORGE: *Reason in Religion*, New York, Charles Scribner's Sons, 1936 (2nd ed.); abridged and revised in *The Life of Reason*, New York, Scribner's, 1955.

WESTERMARCK, E. A.: *The Origin and Development of the Moral Ideas* (2nd ed., 2 vols.), New York, Macmillan, 1912.

EARLY RELIGION:

CORNFORD, F. M.: *From Religion to Philosophy*, New York, Harper Torchbooks, 1957.

FRANKFORT, HENRI, and others: *The Intellectual Adventure of Ancient Man*, Chicago, University of Chicago Press, 1950.

FRAZER, J. G.: *Folk-Lore in the Old Testament* (abridged ed.), New York, Macmillan, 1923.

FRAZER, J. G.: *The Golden Bough* (abridged ed.), New York, Macmillan, 1922.

MARETT, R. R.: *The Threshold of Religion* (2nd ed.), New York, Macmillan, 1914.

MURRAY, GILBERT: *Five Stages of Greek Religion*, Boston, Beacon Press, 1952.

NILSSON, MARTIN P.: *Greek Piety* (trans. H. J. Rose), New York, Oxford University Press, 1948.

HISTORICAL RELIGIONS:

BOUQUET, A. C.: *Comparative Religion, A Short Outline* (5th ed.), Harmondsworth, Penguin Books, 1956.

BOUQUET, A. C.: *Sacred Books of the World*, Harmondsworth, Penguin Books, 1956.

REINACH, SALOMON: *Orpheus: A History of Religions*, New York, Liveright, 1930; revised and partly rewritten, trans. Florence Simmonds.

MYSTICISM:

GOLLANCZ, VICTOR: *From Darkness to Light*, New York, Harper, 1956.

HUXLEY, ALDOUS: *The Perennial Philosophy*, New York, Harper, 1945.

LEUBA, J. H.: *The Psychology of Religious Mysticism*, New York, Harcourt Brace, 1925.

MARTIN, P. W.: *Experiment in Depth: A Study of the Work of Jung, Eliot, and Toynbee*, New York, Pantheon, 1955.

NICHOLSON, D. H. S., and A. H. E. LEE, eds.: *The Oxford Book of English Mystical Verse*, Oxford, Clarendon Press, 1932.

UNDERHILL, EVELYN: *Mysticism*, New York, E. P. Dutton, 1926.

PSYCHOLOGY AND PHILOSOPHY OF RELIGION:

D'ARCY, M. C.: *The Nature of Belief*, London, Sheed and Ward, 1937.

GRENSTED, L. W.: *The Psychology of Religion*, New York, Oxford University Press, 1952.

JAMES, WILLIAM: *The Varieties of Religious Experience*, London and New York, Longmans, Green, 1902.

MACMURRAY, JOHN: *The Structure of Religious Experience*, New Haven, Yale University Press, 1936.

OTTO, RUDOLF: *The Idea of the Holy* (2nd ed.), New York, Oxford University Press, 1952, trans. J. W. Harvey.

STRATTON, G. M.: *Psychology of the Religious Life*, London, Allen and Unwin, 1911.

TENNANT, F. R.: *The Nature of Belief*, London, G. Bles, 1943.

THOULESS, R. H.: *An Introduction to the Psychology of Religion*, New York, Macmillan, 1923.

SCIENCE, RELIGION AND PHILOSOPHY:

BOUTROUX, EMILE: *Science and Religion in Contemporary Philosophy*, New York, Macmillan, 1911, trans. Jonathan Nield.

BURY, J. B.: *A History of Freedom of Thought* (2nd ed.), New York, Oxford University Press, 1952.

CHILDE, V. GORDON: *Society and Knowledge*, New York, Harper, 1956.

HUXLEY, JULIAN: *Evolution in Action*, New York, Harper, 1953.

LANGE, F. A.: *The History of Materialism* (3rd ed., trans. E. C. Thomas, with an introduction by Bertrand Russell), New York, Harcourt Brace, 1925.

MASCALL, E. L.: *Christian Theology and Natural Science: some questions on their relations,* London and New York, Longmans, Green, 1956.

NEEDHAM, JOSEPH, ed.: *Science, Religion and Reality,* New York, Macmillan, 1925.

RUSSELL, BERTRAND: *Religion and Science,* New York, Henry Holt, 1935.

STACE, W. T.: *Religion and the Modern Mind,* New York, Lippincott, 1952.

WHITEHEAD, A. N.: *Religion in the Making,* New York, Macmillan, 1926.

WHITEHEAD, A. N.: *Science and the Modern World,* New York, Macmillan, 1925.

MODERN CHRISTIANITY AND ITS CRITICS:

BRAITHWAITE, R. B.: *An Empiricist's View of the Nature of Religious Belief,* New York, Cambridge University Press, 1956.

FLEW, ANTONY, and ALASDAIR MACINTYRE, eds.: *New Essays in Philosophical Theology,* New York, Macmillan, 1955.

HEPBURN, R. W.: *Christianity and Paradox,* London, Watts, 1957.

MARITAIN, JACQUES: *True Humanism,* New York, Scribner's, 1938, trans. M. R. Adamson.

TILLICH, PAUL: *The Protestant Era,* Chicago, University of Chicago Press, 1948.

RELIGION WITHOUT REVELATION:

DEWEY, JOHN: *A Common Faith,* New Haven, Yale University Press, 1934.

DURKHEIM, EMILE: *Sociology and Philosophy,* trans. D. F. Pocock, with an introduction by J. G. Peristiany, Chicago, Free Press, 1953.

PHENIX, PHILIP HENRY: *Intelligible Religion,* New York, Harper, 1954.

SPINOZA, BENEDICT DE: *Ethics,* New York, E. P. Dutton, 1910.

WODEHOUSE, HELEN M.: *One Kind of Religion,* New York, Macmillan, 1944.

Index

Absolute, 31, 32, 50, 172

Absolute in morals, interpretation of, 84

Adolescence, impressions of social inequality in, 74; moral problems in, 74

Aesthetic truth, perception of, 39

Agnosticism, when justifiable, 17

Anger, type of situation tending to arouse, 21

Animatism and early animism, 126

Apartheid, religious justification of, 60

Arnold, Matthew, definition of religion, 96; intellectual qualities of, 67

Arnold, Thomas, 66-7

Art and religion, points of resemblance between, 104-5

Association, principle of, 108

Authority, force of, 107

Awareness, improvement and organisation of, 202-3; collective, 230

Awe, feeling of, 104, 118

Aztecs, human sacrifices of, 106

'Begging letter' type of prayer, 33

Belief, most important role of, 16-7; need for naturalistic type of, 62

Belief hypotheses, 183-4

Beliefs, methods by which transmitted, 147; satisfactory foundations for, 15

Bergson, adaptivity of reason, 134

Bible, quality of inspiration in, 26

Birth control, 167

Blake, allegorical mysticism of, 43-4

Blanshard, Paul, on authoritarianism and religious dogma, 59

Booth, General, unsatisfactory definition of religion by, 40

Brain, relaxation of higher centres of, 138

Buddhism, advantage of Christianity over, 44-5; disbelief in supernatural being, 20; morality of, 20; no mention of God in original form of, 94; transition in, 128

Burma, prohibition of headhunting in, 124

Carpenter, Estlin, on exterior definition of religion, 98-9

Cassirer, Ernst, on mythical thought, 53

Catastrophes, ascribed to supernatural beings, 94-5

Categorical Imperative, 84

Catherine, Saint, of Genoa, 140

Certitude, limited but increasing, 204

Chesterfield, Lord, definition of religion by, 98

Childbirth, Moroccan taboos, 121

Childhood, taboo-feeling attached to sex matters in, 71

Christian Science, 148

Christianity, advantage over Mohammedanism and Buddhism, 44; rescued by Saint Paul from narrow nationalism, 127; early claims of, 168; conversion of Polynesians to, 119; and Doctrine of

216

THE MENTOR PHILOSOPHERS

The entire range of Western speculative thinking from the Middle Ages to modern times is presented in this series of six volumes. Each book contains the basic writings of the leading philosophers of each age, with introductions and interpretive commentary by noted authorities.

"A very important and interesting series."—*Gilbert Highet*

75 cents each

The Age of Belief: The Medieval Philosophers *edited by Anne Fremantle.* (#MT463)

"Highly commendable . . . provides an excellent beginning volume." —*The Classical Bulletin*

The Age of Adventure: The Renaissance Philosophers *edited by Giorgio de Santillana.* (#MT437)

"The most exciting and varied in the series." —*New York Times*

The Age of Reason: The 17th Century Philosophers *edited by Stuart Hampshire.* (#MT367)

"His (Hampshire's) book is a most satisfactory addition to an excellent series." —*Saturday Review*

The Age of Enlightenment: The 18th Century Philosophers *edited by Sir Isaiah Berlin.* (#MT473)

"(Sir Isaiah) has one of the liveliest and most stimulating minds among contemporary philosophers." —*N. Y. Herald Tribune*

The Age of Ideology: The 19th Century Philosophers *edited by Henry D. Aiken.* (#MT421)

". . . perhaps the most distinct intellectual contribution made in the series." —*New York Times*

The Age of Analysis: 20th Century Philosophers *edited by Morton White.* (#MT353)

"No other book remotely rivals this as the best available introduction to 20th century philosophy." —*N. Y. Herald Tribune*

CATHOLIC THEOLOGICAL UNION
BL51.H891957 C001
RELIGION WITHOUT REVELATION NEW AND REV

3 0311 00006 2062

gious Classics

...led and arranged by James Reeves.
...New Testaments, a continuous
...King James text.

(#MD116—50¢)

The Meaning of the Glorious Koran: An Explanatory Translation *by Mohammed Marmaduke Pickthall.* The complete sacred book of Mohammedanism.

(#MT462—75¢)

The Teachings of the Compassionate Buddha *edited with commentary by E. A. Burtt.* The best translations of the writings of the great Oriental religion of Buddhism.

(#MP380—60¢)

The Song of God: Bhagavad-Gita *translated by Swami Prabhavananda and Christopher Isherwood.* The timeless epic of Hindu faith. Introduction by Aldous Huxley.

(#MP466—60¢)

The Upanishads: Breath of the Eternal *translated by Swami Prabhavananda and Frederick Manchester.* Ancient Hindu scriptures concerned with the knowledge of God and the highest aspects of religious truth. (#MP386—60¢)

The Way of Life: Tao Te Ching *by Lao Tzu.* A masterpiece of ancient Chinese wisdom, translated by R. B. Blakney, presenting the philosophy of Taoism. (#MP416—60¢)

The Sayings of Confucius *translated by James R. Ware.* The sayings of the greatest wise man of ancient China, teaching the ageless virtues of civilized men. (#MP497—60¢)

The Living Talmud: The Wisdom of the Fathers and Its Classical Commentaries, *selected and translated by Judah Goldin.* A new translation, with an illuminating essay on the Talmud in Jewish life and religion. (#MT286—75¢)

To Our Readers: If your dealer does not have the Signet and Mentor books you want, you may order them by mail, enclosing the list price plus 5¢ a copy to cover mailing. If you would like our free catalog, please request it by postcard. The New American Library of World Literature, Inc., P. O. Box 2310, Grand Central Station, New York, N. Y., 10017.